Ethics, Security, and The War-Machine

Ned Dobos is Senior Lecturer in International and Political Studies at The University of New South Wales at the Australian Defence Force Academy. He is the author of *Insurrection and Intervention: The Two Faces of Sovereignty* (Cambridge, 2012) and co-editor of *Challenges for Humanitarian Intervention: Ethical Demand and Political Reality* (Oxford, 2018).

'If the best works of philosophy challenge our commonly held ideas, then this book is one of the best of its kind. Eloquently written, powerfully argued, and original in its approach, Ned Dobos masterfully and systematically dismantles our unquestioned acceptance of the need for societies to have military establishments...A wonderful book which should be read by everyone interested in politics and international relations.'

Richard Jackson, University of Otago

'Ned Dobos has written an extraordinarily comprehensive, deeply insightful, and highly readable book on the true costs of our military arrangements...I cannot think of a better book to provoke people to reflect on the ways in which war impacts our lives—some not always evident.'

Cheyney Ryan, University of Oxford

'Dobos's argument is characteristically lucid and engaging, and the book is not only excellent and highly welcome, but it is also a necessary addition to the current philosophical literature surrounding the ethics of war. Moreover, its profound practical, social, and political implications mean that the argument presented does not only deserve the attention of philosophers, politicians, or the military, but indeed of the average citizen.'

Uwe Steinhoff, University of Hong Kong

Ethics, Security, and The War-Machine

The True Cost of the Military

NED DOBOS

OXFORD
UNIVERSITY PRESS

Great Clarendon Street, Oxford, OX2 6DP,
United Kingdom

Oxford University Press is a department of the University of Oxford.
It furthers the University's objective of excellence in research, scholarship,
and education by publishing worldwide. Oxford is a registered trade mark of
Oxford University Press in the UK and in certain other countries

First published 2020
First published in paperback 2022

Published in the United States of America by Oxford University Press
198 Madison Avenue, New York, NY 10016, United States of America

British Library Cataloguing in Publication Data
Data available

Library of Congress Cataloging in Publication Data
Data available

ISBN 978-0-19-886051-8 (Hbk.)
ISBN 978-0-19-288784-9 (Pbk.)

Contents

Acknowledgements

Chapters of this book have been presented to academic audiences in Australia, Japan, the US, and Europe, and I have had the opportunity to discuss the material informally with many thoughtful people over the last few years. I am grateful to everybody that listened and offered comments and criticisms along the way, including: Andrew Alexandra, Peter Balint, Ed Barrett, Tony Coady, Toni Erskine, Christopher Finlay, Tom Frame, Luke Glanville, Marcus Hedahl, Adam Henschke, Roger Herbert, Joshua Kassner, Brent Kyle, Judith Lichtenberg, David Luban, Joseph MacKay, Josiah Ober, Umut Ozguc, Igor Primoratz, Neil Ramsey, David Stahel, and Scott Sagan. Most of all I am indebted to Cheyney Ryan for his detailed and erudite written feedback on an earlier draft. All of the usual disclaimers apply.

I owe thanks also to the McCoy Center for Ethics in Society at Stanford University, for hosting me as a visiting fellow while I finalised the manuscript in 2019, and to Peter Momtchiloff of Oxford University Press for his continued support and patience. Parts of Chapter 1 appeared previously in a special issue of *Philosophical Forum* (vol. 46, 2015), under the title "Punishing Non-Conscientious Disobedience: Is the Military a Rogue Employer?". I thank the publisher of the journal for granting permission to reuse this material.

Thanks, finally, to my wife Kelly, for her care and endurance.

Introduction

Jus Ante Bellum: Justifying the War-Machine

Ethicists dealing with war and armed conflict have invested most of their energies in two questions. First, under what circumstances is it morally permissible for a state to resort to military force? This is the question of *jus ad bellum*—the justice *of* war. Second, once hostilities are underway, how should combatants conduct themselves? This is the question of *jus in bello*—justice *in* war. In recent years the inquiry has been extended to cover justice *after* war (*jus post bellum*). Here the emphasis is on post-war relations, reconstruction, reparations, and so on.[1]

This is certainly a positive development, but we ought to be extending the inquiry in the opposite direction as well, to address questions of *jus ante bellum,* or justice *before* war. In particular this one: Under what circumstances is it justifiable for a polity to *prepare* for war by militarizing? When (if ever) and why (if at all) is it morally permissible to create and maintain the potential to wage war? This is not about whether war-*making* is justified, but about whether war-*building* is justified.[2] It is not about how we should use the military resources we amass; it is about whether we should be amassing those resources in the first place. Just as the *ad bellum* question asks of particular wars whether they are (or were)

---

[1] See for instance Brian Orend, 'Justice After War', *Ethics and International Affairs*, vol. 16, no. 1, March 2002, pp. 43–56. The decision to bring an ongoing war to an end—the *transition* from war to post-war—has also received some philosophical attention of late. David Rodin discusses it under the heading *jus terminatio*. Darrel Moellendorf prefers *jus ex bello*. David Rodin, 'The War Trap: Dilemmas of Jus Terminatio', *Ethics*, vol. 125, no. 3, 2015, pp. 674–95; Darrel Mollendorf, 'Jus Ex Bello', *The Journal of Political Philosophy*, vol. 16, no. 2, June 2008, pp. 123–36.

[2] I owe this distinction to Cheyney Ryan. See his essay 'Pacifism', in Seth Lazar and Helen Frowe (eds.), *The Oxford Handbook of Ethics of War*, Oxford: Oxford University Press, 2016, and his article 'Pacifism, Just War, and Self-Defense', *Philosophia*, vol. 41, no. 4, 2013, pp. 977–1005.

Ethics, Security, and The War-Machine: The True Cost of the Military. Ned Dobos, Oxford University Press (2020).
© Ned Dobos.
DOI: 10.1093/oso/9780198860518.001.0001

justified, the *ante bellum* question is best understood as asking of particular war-making *institutions* whether they are justified in existing.

If it is never morally permissible for a state to wage war, as pacifists think, then it probably goes without saying that states ought not to build and maintain military institutions.[3] After all, if war-making is always wrong, then creating an institution whose *raison d'être* is war-making does nothing but enable us—and perhaps even tempt us—to do things we should never do. What this suggests is that war must be justifiable sometimes in order for militaries to stand any chance of being justified. The former is necessary for the latter. But it would be a mistake to assume that the justifiability of war is also *sufficient* to justify the existence of any given military establishment.

If pressed, I suspect that most of my compatriots would admit that there are conceivable circumstances under which torture is justified—in ticking time bomb-type scenarios, for example. But almost nobody would say that we should therefore create a Department of Torture, taxpayer-funded torture facilities, and academies where people are trained in torture techniques.[4] If pressed, most of my compatriots would also accept that armed rebellion against our government would be justified if it ever became sufficiently oppressive. But again almost nobody would say that it is therefore permissible for us right now to form a militia and acquire the high-powered weaponry that would be necessary for successful rebellion should the need ever arise.[5] Clearly, the fact

---

[3] By 'pacifism' I mean the view that waging war is always morally impermissible. This is not the only way that the term has been used, admittedly. For a comprehensive overview see Andrew Fiala, 'Pacifism', in Edward N. Zalta (ed.), *Stanford Encyclopedia of Philosophy*, Fall 2018, available at: https://plato.stanford.edu/archives/fall2018/entries/pacifism/, and Andrew Fiala, *Tranformative Pacifism: Critical Theory and Practice*, London: Bloomsbury, 2018.

[4] As Seumas Miller rightly points out, 'it is perfectly consistent to concede that torture might be morally justifiable in certain one-off emergency situations, and yet oppose any legalization or institutionalization of torture'. Seumas Miller, 'Torture', *Stanford Encyclopedia of Philosophy*, Summer 2017 Edition, Edward N. Zalta (ed.), available at: plato.stanford.edu/archives/sum2017/entries/torture/.

[5] In the 1700s Immanuel Kant argued that 'there is no right of sedition, and still less of rebellion, belonging to the people … It is the duty of the people to bear a*ny abuse of the supreme power*' (emphasis added). Immanuel Kant, *The Science of Right*, 1790, Second Part, '*Public Right*'. Full text available online at: https://www.marxists.org/reference/subject/ethics/kant/morals/ch04.htm. Nobody believes this anymore. Today it is widely accepted that, if a government becomes tyrannical and begins violating the basic rights of its citizens, those citizens have a right to fight back and even to overthrow their oppressors if they can. See Ned Dobos, *Insurrection and Intervention: The Two Faces of Sovereignty*, Cambridge: Cambridge University Press, 2012, chapter 1. Even so, few of us think it is acceptable for individuals to possess automatic rifles and explosives and missile launchers simply because there are conceivable circumstances under which it would be acceptable for citizens to use such weapons against

that a particular action is sometimes permissible does not entail that an institution devoted to it ought to be created and maintained.[6]

This is because social institutions, even if they do some good, can also introduce serious costs and dangers into our lives, and there are going to be cases where these costs are simply not worth bearing. Even if some criminals deserve to die, and executing them does help to deter others, the courts will invariably reach a faulty verdict from time to time, leading to the execution of an innocent person. We might reasonably think this too high a price to pay for the sake of having an institution that administers 'just executions'.[7] Hence many people are of the view that capital punishment (the institution) should be abolished even if capital punishment (the act) is not always wrongful. There is nothing contradictory or wrongheaded about this.

By the same token, there may be cases where the costs and risks generated by a military establishment are too great for its existence to be justified, and this is *even if* we think that some wars are necessary and consistent with the demands of morality. It is a mistake to suppose that pacifism and anti-militarism stand or fall together, as if rejecting the former must also take the latter off the table philosophically. On the contrary, one can be an anti-militarist, or a military abolitionist, without being a pacifist—this is a perfectly coherent intellectual position. A few historical examples should help to illustrate this point.

Non-Pacifistic Anti-Militarism

In 1948, after a short but bloody civil war in Costa Rica, a revolutionary junta was established under the headship José Figueres Ferrer,

the state. Ted Cruz is a notable exception. He wrote in an email to supporters that the Second Amendment right to bear arms was 'the ultimate check against government tyranny'. Greg Sargent, 'Ted Cruz, Slayer of Tyrants', *The Washington Post*, 15 October 2015.

[6] The same might be said for the use of terrorism. 'As morally reprehensible as terrorism is, there might be, on very rare occasions, circumstances in which it is permissible or even obligatory to commit an act of terrorism. But this does not mean that we should have a Department of Terrorism, or government-funded and trained terrorists standing by to commit acts of terrorism'. Saba Bazargan-Forward, 'Varieties of Contingent Pacifism in War', in Helen Frowe and Gerald Lang (eds.), *How We Fight*, Oxford: Oxford University Press, 2014, pp. 2–3.

[7] Igor Primoratz interrogates this argument in chapter 8 of his book *Justifying Legal Punishment*, Amherst, NY: Humanity Books, 1989.

affectionately known as Don Pepe. Figueres disbanded the vanquished forces, as one would expect, but he then did something unheard of. He disbanded his own armed forces, the very same that had brought his regime to power. In a public event, Don Pepe took a sledgehammer to the outer wall of the country's Cuartel Bellavista army base, to 'symbolize the elimination of the remnants of the Military Spirit of Costa Rica'.[8] To this day, on 1 December each year, the Costa Ricans celebrate Día de la Abolición del Ejército: their 'military abolition day'.[9] Article 12 of the country's constitution declares that 'the Army as a permanent institution is proscribed'. The Cuartel Bellavista was turned into a museum and the defence budget was repurposed for education, healthcare, and environmental protection.

By most accounts Costa Rica has fared rather well since demilitarization. Its territory has not been annexed by a foreign power, despite being surrounded by some hostile regimes. It leads Latin America and the Caribbean in primary education, has one of the region's lowest infant mortality rates, one of its highest literacy rates, the best healthcare system in Central America, and its citizens are ranked the happiest in the world, according to the Happy Planet Index.[10] Needless to say, each of these achievements must be due to a combination of factors, but the decision to demilitarize is—rightly or wrongly—thought to have made it all possible. In 1987, president Oscar Arias boasted before US Congress: 'I belong to a small country that was not afraid to abolish its army in order to increase its strength.' He went on to explicitly connect the low rates of poverty and unemployment in Costa Rica to the absence of warships and artillery pieces.[11]

When asked by reporters to explain his decision to abolish the military, Don Pepe allegedly replied: 'Why not? Most nations need an army

---

[8] Jose Gerardo Suarez Monge, 'Costa Rican Army Abolished', *Howler Magazine*, 31 July 2018, available at: https://howlermag.com/Costa-rican-army-abolishd-history-in-photos, last accessed November 2018.

[9] Gilbert Barrera, 'The Hammer Blow that Changed Costa Rica', *The Costa Rica News*, 1 December 2017.

[10] Amanda Trejos, 'Why Getting Rid of Costa Rica's Army 70 Years Ago Has Been Such A Success', *USA Today*, 5 January 2018, available at: https://www.usatoday.com/story/news/world/2018/01/05/costa-rica-celebrate-70-years-no-army/977107001/, last accessed November 2018.

[11] David P. Barash, 'Costa Rica's Peace Dividend: How Abolishing the Military Paid Off', *Los Angeles Times*, 15 December 2013.

like they need a hole in the head.'[12] It's not that Figueres was oblivious to the utility of armed forces—he did not deny that they could be, and sometimes were, used for good. It's just that Figueres was acutely aware of the trade-offs that having such forces at the ready involved. There were the obvious budgetary pressures; Figueres and those around him were sensitive to the economic opportunity costs of military expenditures. But Figueres was also cognizant that militaries in the region had developed a bad habit of turning against the states they were supposed to protect; several neighbouring Latin American countries had experienced coup events during this period.[13] Costa Rica's 'traditional position of having more teachers than soldiers' also featured in Figueres' reasoning.[14] He and his advisors felt that a permanent military establishment was inconsistent with—and indeed corrosive of—their country's culture and character. Whatever the benefit of having a professional army, the Costa Rican leadership evidently judged that the cons outweighed the pros.

Japan is another country whose constitution outlaws a permanent military establishment, or at least it appears to. Article 9 reads: 'The Japanese people forever renounce war as a sovereign right of the nation and the threat or use of force as means of settling international disputes.' It goes on to promise that 'to accomplish the aim of the preceding paragraph, land, sea, and air forces, as well as other war potential, will never be maintained'. The way that the constitution has been interpreted by the courts, however, has effectively allowed Japan to gradually re-militarize since the armed forces were dismantled at the end of the Second World War, to the point that the country now has one of the largest defence budgets in the world.[15] This has caused considerable disquiet among segments of the general population. Like the architects

---

[12] Quoted in the award-winning documentary *A Bold Peace* (2016), directed by Matthew Eddy and Michael Dreiling.

[13] See Tord Høivik and Solveig Aas, 'Demilitarization in Costa Rica: A Farewell to Arms?', *Journal of Peace Research*, vol. XVIII, no. 4, 1981, pp. 341–3.

[14] Mario Kamenetzky, *The Invisible Player: Consciousness as the Soul of Economic, Social, and Political Life*, Rochester: Park Stress Press, 1999, p. 262.

[15] Mark A. Chinen, 'Article Nine of Japan's Constitution: From Renunciation of Armed Forces "Forever" to the Third Largest Defense Budget in the World', *Michigan Journal of International Law*, vol. 27, 2005, p. 60.

of Costa Rica's de-militarization, the opponents of Japan's re-militarization have not denied the possibility that armed force might one day be needed to fend off a foreign threat. They simply think the premiums on this insurance coverage are too expensive, so to speak. The risks and costs of having a military are thought to be greater than the risks and costs of going without one.

There are several concerns in play here. One is that if Japan is allowed to re-militarize, the country might again become embroiled in unnecessary and immoral wars, as has happened in the past.[16] This fear is based partly on the historically accumulated mistrust that many Japanese still feel towards soldiers. After all, these people were seen as the main propagators of the poisonous nationalism that had led the country astray in the first half of the twentieth century.[17] Hence after the end of the Second World War many Japanese blamed the military, and saw themselves as its victims, rather than its authors or enablers.[18] The resulting suspicion of the armed forces endures to the present day, so much so that even routine military planning activities by the JSDF (Japan Self-Defense Force) can arouse public controversy.[19] Besides this, there is also a fear of 'entrapment'. Japan and the United States remain the closest of allies. Some Japanese worry that the commitments generated by this alliance will rope their country into one or more of the military misadventures that the US is perceived as having a penchant for. The thought is that if the US calls for military support from its allies, Japan will be among the foremost expected to respond to the call, given the relationship between the two. Hence Japan might find itself politically compelled to participate in unjust wars. The only way to avoid this, according to some of Japan's

---

[16] Yasuhiro Izumikawa, 'Explaining Japanese Antimilitarism: Normative and Realist Constraints on Japan's Security Policy', *International Security*, vol. 35, no. 2, Fall 2010, pp. 123–60. For discussion of the idea that militarization weakens democratic norms, which is another concern among Japanese anti-militarists, see Andrew Alexandra, 'Pacifism: Designing a Moral Defence Force', in Jeroen van den Hoven, Seumas Miller, and Thomas Pogge (eds.), *Designing In Ethics*, Cambridge: Cambridge University Press, 2017.

[17] See Thomas U. Berger, 'From Sword to Chrysanthemum: Japan's Culture of Anti-militarism', *International Security*, vol. 17, no. 4, Spring 1993, p. 134.

[18] According to Berger, the chief lesson that the Japanese took away from the war is that 'the military is a dangerous institution'. Berger, 'From Sword to Chrysanthemum', p. 120.

[19] Berger, 'From Sword to Chrysanthemum', p. 136. During the Gulf crisis JSDF personnel were even prohibited from reporting directly to Japanese cabinet, for fear that the influence of military thinking would distort government decision-making. Berger, 'From Sword to Chrysanthemum', p. 146.

anti-militarists, is to ensure that the country remains permanently devoid of all war-making capabilities.[20]

To be sure, there are anti-militarists in Japan who express a deeper, principled objection to the use of violence as a means of foreign policy; they are pacifists as well as being anti-militarists. But others are of the view that even though some conceivable wars may be necessary and just, the existence of a war-machine in their country is nevertheless not justified, on account of the potential for its misuse.

The United States constitution does not proscribe a permanent military establishment, but some people desperately wanted it to. Under the pseudonym 'Publius', three of the founding fathers—Hamilton, Madison, and John Jay—published a collection of essays supporting the ratification of the constitution of 1787. These came to be known as the Federalist Papers. Lesser known are the so-called Anti-Federalist papers, written by various authors who were critical of the draft constitution for one reason or another. The most influential of these were published in the *New York Journal* between October 1787 and April 1788, under the pseudonym 'Brutus' (generally believed to be Robert Yates, a New York judge). Several of the essays vehemently opposed the proposal for a standing army.[21]

Brutus was worried that a permanent military would be mishandled by the government: 'the rulers may employ them [soldiers] for the purpose of promoting their own ambitious views'.[22] He implored his compatriots to 'let the monarchs, in Europe, share among them the glory of depopulating countries, and butchering thousands of their innocent citizens, to revenge private quarrels, or to punish an insult offered to a wife, a

[20] Izumikawa, 'Explaining Japanese Antimilitarism', pp. 131–4.
[21] See Laurence M. Vance, 'Brutus on the Evils of Standing Armies', 7 February 2004, LewRockwell.com, available at: https://www.lewrockwell.com/2004/02/laurence-m-vance/the-evil-of-standing-armies-2/, last accessed November 2018.
[22] Brutus #10, 24 January 1788, available at: http://www.constitution.org/afp/brutus10.htm, last accessed December 2018. This is the chief concern of modern-day 'diversionists'. They worry that national leaders are prone to start wars for the pettiest reasons, like improving their political standing at home or distracting their constituents from domestic issues. See Jack S. Levy, 'The Diversionary Theory of War: A Critique', in Manus I. Midlarsky (ed.), *Handbook of War Studies*, Boston, MA: Unwin Hyman, 1989, pp. 259–88. Some commentators memorably offered a diversionist explanation for the Clinton administration's bombing of a pharmaceutical factory in Sudan in the late 90s, claiming that its ulterior purpose was to divert attention away from the Monica Lewinsky scandal. The affair drew comparisons with the comedy *Wag the Dog*, in which a Hollywood film producer is hired to construct a phony war with Albania in order to shift the public's attention away from a sex scandal involving the US president.

mistress, or a favorite'.[23] More than this, though, Brutus was concerned about the risk of a military coup against the state. In one essay he approvingly reproduced the following passage from a speech delivered in the British parliament:

> If an army be so numerous as to have it in their power to overawe the parliament, they will be submissive as long as the parliament does nothing to disoblige their favourite general; but when that case happens, I am afraid, that in place of the parliament's dismissing the army, the army will dismiss the parliament.[24]

For Brutus, this made a standing army 'in the highest degree dangerous to the liberty and happiness of the community'.[25] It is worth noting that, though they may not have agreed with all of his conclusions, Hamilton, Madison, and some of the other founding fathers thought Brutus had a point. Madison admitted that in many places 'armies kept up under the pretext of defending, have enslaved the people'. Thomas Jefferson recognized that standing armies often become an 'engine of oppression'. Hamilton was concerned enough to propose that Congress should vote every two years 'upon the propriety of keeping a military force on foot'.[26]

For his part, Brutus's proposal was to allow the government to raise a citizen's militia in times of war, rather than building war-potential during peacetime. Importantly, then, Brutus did believe that the use of armed force for national defence might one day be necessary and justified. And he even seemed to appreciate the argument that a standing army would be better prepared to prosecute such wars, and therefore more likely to win them. Nevertheless, he insisted that this was not reason enough to justify the existence of such a dangerous organization. Brutus was what we might call a *non-pacifistic anti-militarist*. Despite his openness to the prospect of legitimate political violence, he was opposed

---

[23] Vance, 'Brutus on the Evils of Standing Armies'.
[24] Vance, 'Brutus on the Evils of Standing Armies'.
[25] Vance, 'Brutus on the Evils of Standing Armies'.
[26] Phil Klay, 'The Citizen-Soldier: Moral Risk and the Modern Military', *The Brookings Institution*, 24 May 2016, available at: http://csweb.brookings.edu/content/research/essays/2016/the-citizen-soldier.html, last accessed July 2018.

to the idea of having an establishment dedicated to it. The same label could be affixed to the military abolitionists of Costa Rica and Japan.

The upshot is simply this: If we want to answer the *ante bellum* question of whether it is permissible to build and maintain a permanent military establishment, we do need to ask the *ad bellum* question of whether war can ever be justified. But that is not the *only* thing we need to ask. We also need to consider the various costs and risks associated with having some such establishment, and to assess whether they are worth bearing, all things considered. Our answer to the *ad bellum* question is relevant to, but it does not settle, the *ante bellum* one.

Unfortunately, while a great deal continues to be written about the costs of war-making, little philosophical attention is paid to the costs of war-building. As Cheyney Ryan puts it, 'the great shortcoming of received thinking is to focus on the first to the exclusion of the second'.[27] To its credit, the UN has tried to remedy this neglect. A key recommendation arising out of its First Special Session on Disarmament in 1978 was that all governments should 'prepare assessments of the nature and magnitude of the short- and long-term economic and social costs attributable to their military preparations, so that the general public can be informed of them'.[28] No serious attempts at this have been made, at least not in relation to the social costs. That is where this book comes in.

The True Cost of the Military: Outline of the Book

In 2017, global military spending topped 1.73 trillion dollars annually. The growth has been driven largely by increases in the defence budgets of Asian and Middle Eastern countries, especially China and India, rather than by expenditures in the Euro–Atlantic region.[29] This trend might be short-lived, however. At the 2018 NATO Summit, US President Donald Trump admonished European leaders for failing to devote 2 per cent of their GDP to military spending, as per NATO guidelines. He then urged

---

[27] Ryan, 'Pacifism', p. 278.
[28] Quoted in Alex C. Michalos, 'Militarism and the Quality of Life', *Annals of the New York Academy of Sciences*, vol. 577, no. 1, December 1989, p. 216.
[29] Daniel Brown, 'The 15 Countries with the Highest Military Budgets in 2017', *Business Insider*, 3 May 2018.

member states to double their commitment, to 4 per cent of GDP. Were
this to happen, military spending within the NATO organization alone
would climb to 1.5 trillion dollars annually.[30]

In a speech to the American Society of Newspaper Editors, former US
President and army general Dwight Eisenhower memorably called attention to the significant opportunity costs of such expenditures—the goods
that a society forgoes by directing its scarce resources into war preparation. 'Every gun that is made, every warship launched, every rocket
fired', Eisenhower said,

> signifies, in the final sense, a theft from those who hunger and are not
> fed, those who are cold and are not clothed ... The cost of one modern
> heavy bomber is this: a modern brick school in more than 30 cities. It is
> two electric power plants, each serving a town of 60,000 population. It
> is two fine, fully equipped hospitals. It is some fifty miles of concrete
> pavement. We pay for a single fighter plane with a half million bushels
> of wheat. We pay for a single destroyer with new homes that could
> have housed more than 8,000 people.[31]

Clearly there are large amounts of money at stake, but this is only part of
the story. The full cost of a military cannot be adequately captured in
economic terms alone. The purpose of this book is to begin cataloguing
some of the less appreciated cultural and moral costs, and the security
sacrifices associated with creating and maintaining a permanent military
establishment. Rather than trying to provide an exhaustive list, I will
focus instead on the costs and dangers that I take to be the most
generalizable; the ones that are borne to some degree by most militarized
polities, not just those with particular histories, internal political dynamics, or international entanglements.

Wherever there is a military establishment, men and women must be
recruited into it and conditioned to be effective war-fighters. Whether or

[30] Lindsay Koshgarian, 'Trump's NATO Military Spending Request Would add $600 billion
to World Military Spending', *National Priorities Project*, 13 July 2018, available at: https://www.
nationalpriorities.org/blog/2018/07/13/trumps-nato-military-spending-request-would-add-600-
billion-world-military-spending/, last accessed January 2019.
[31] Dwight Eisenhower, *Address to the American Society of Newspaper Editors*, 16 April 1953,
Slater Hotel, Washington, DC, transcript available at: http://www.edchange.org/multicultural/
speeches/ike_chance_for_peace.html, last accessed September 2018.

not they are ever deployed, there is a respect in which this conditioning is morally damaging to those involved. Or so I will argue in Chapter 1.

Wherever there is a military establishment, there is a prospect of it turning against the political community that it is meant to protect. In other words, there is a risk of a 'domestic political intervention' or a coup. This is the focus of Chapter 2.

Wherever there is a military establishment, there is a possibility that it will provoke the very thing that it is meant to deter. A foreign enemy might be driven to attack us not *despite* our armed forces, but *because of* them. This is the focus of Chapter 3.

Wherever there is a military establishment, there is a risk that its use will not be confined to the prosecution of 'just wars' and interventions. In other words, there is a risk of the armed forces being *overused* or misused by the state. This is the focus of Chapter 4.

Wherever there is a military establishment, there must be a cultural infrastructure that supports and sustains it. Certain values and ideals must be cultivated in, and celebrated by, the organization, in order for it to effectively deploy organized violence on behalf of the state. When these values penetrate into civilian society—as they almost invariably do—there can be pernicious results. Chapter 5 elaborates on this point.

These are not the costs of war, but the costs of the war-machine, generated by the presence of a military establishment even when it is running idle, so to say. And they are not limited to states with corrupt or predatory militaries. As David Keen illustrates in *Useful Enemies*, some national armies behave more like protection rackets than security guards.[32] These rogue institutions will certainly generate many of the costs and risks discussed in the pages that follow, and others besides. But that is hardly surprising or interesting. What is interesting is that even professional, well-intentioned, and well-regulated military forces will produce these costs to some extent.

I am hardly the first to notice this. Immanuel Kant appreciated the fact that militaries can unintentionally provoke instead of deterring attacks. This is why he thought that, in order for perpetual peace to be achieved, standing armies would eventually need to be abolished. 'For they

---

[32] David Keen, *Useful Enemies: When Waging Wars is More Important than Winning Them*, New Haven, CT: Yale University Press, 2012.

incessantly menace other states by their readiness to appear at all times prepared for war; they incite them to compete with each other in the number of armed men, and there is no limit to this.'[33] In *The Art of War* Machiavelli addresses the risk of a coup at length. He sees this as a danger that arises when some citizens are allowed to make military service their livelihood (i.e. to become professional soldiers). 'For no infantry can be so dangerous as that which is composed of men who make war their only calling, because a prince either must keep them continually engaged in war, or must constantly keep them paid in peacetime, or must run the risk of their stripping him of his kingdom.'[34] Since the first two options are only for corrupt and/or incompetent governments according to Machiavelli, a prince worthy of the title that insists on keeping a standing army 'must run no small risk of losing his kingdom' to it.[35]

Are the costs of a military worth bearing? That will obviously depend on the circumstances; there can be no universally correct answer here. Each of the costs discussed in this book is a consideration pulling in favour of military abolition; each identifies *a respect in which* a political community is better off without a military. (And it is worth emphasizing at the outset that each identifies a respect in which a political community is better off without a military *even if other states remain militarized.* In other words, these are considerations in favour of even unilateral military abolition.) But, of course, there are bound to be considerations pulling in the opposite direction as well, and there is no reason to assume that the downsides of militarization will always or necessarily outweigh the benefits. But there is no reason to assume that the opposite is true either, and that is the point.

The purpose of this book is not to convince the reader that military abolition is the morally and/or prudentially appropriate course of action for every state today, or indeed for any state. Its purpose is to shine a light on the significant costs that a society bears simply by keeping a permanent military establishment, regardless of how often it is used to wage war. At the very least this should persuade the reader that whether a military

---

[33] Immanuel Kant, *Perpetual Peace: A Philosophical Proposal*, Helen O'Brien (trans.), London: Sweet and Maxwell, 1927, p. 21.

[34] Niccolo Machiavelli, *The Art of War*, Ellis Farneworth (trans.), Indianapolis, IN: Bobbs-Merrill, 1965, p. 20.

[35] Machiavelli, *The Art of War*.

is worth having ought always to be treated as an open question. Currently it isn't. In most societies the only things up for discussion are how much to invest in the armed forces, and what to use them for, not whether their continued existence is justified to begin with.

The true cost of the military ought to be taken into account by statespersons whenever revisiting their commitments to, and investments in, their armed forces. But besides policymakers and public servants, I hope the book will find its way into the hands of military personnel, both currently serving and prospective, such as the ones that I teach at the Australian Defence Force Academy. Society increasingly expects the decisions of these people to be ethically informed, but current scholarship provides inadequate guidance in this connection. That scholarship may help soldiers judge the ethics of particular wars, and guide their conduct once hostilities are underway. But it does not help them evaluate the very existence of the institution to which they will devote their lives and, sometimes, for which they will give their lives. That is what this book aspires to do.

Whether or not the costs of a military establishment are worth bearing will depend on, among other things, the availability of alternative arrangements for national defence. A full analysis of non-military defence options is beyond the scope of this monograph, but in the epilogue I will briefly present and interrogate the late Gene Sharp's proposal for a 'post-military' civilian-based defence system. While this alternative arrangement for national defence would have limitations and problems of its own, no doubt, it would not be nearly as dangerous, nor as morally and socially damaging, as professional militaries all too often are.

1

Military Conditioning and Moral Damage

Introduction

Most of us would agree that it is perfectly appropriate for a war criminal to experience emotional anguish. These feelings indicate that the culpable individual recognizes his/her moral failing. But what about soldiers who conduct themselves ethically? If a combatant is participating in a just war and only killing legitimate military targets, would it still be appropriate for him/her to experience emotional distress?[1] St. Augustine answers in the affirmative. In *City of God* he writes:

> … everyone who reflects with sorrow on such grievous evils [as seen in war], in all their horror and cruelty, must acknowledge the misery of them. And yet a man who experiences such evils, or even thinks about them, without heartfelt grief, is assuredly in far more pitiable condition, if he thinks himself happy, simply because he has lost all human feeling.[2]

In a similar vein Oliver O'Donovan argues that, whether a soldier's use of lethal violence is morally justified or not, 'we would expect at least a frisson of horror at the thought that one had killed a man. To have taken a human life, so sacred and serious a thing before God, should make even a spirit feel appalled, and that irrespective of his views on ethics

---

[1] This question is taken up at length by Christopher J. Eberle, *Justice and the Just War Tradition: Human Worth, Moral Formation, and Armed Conflict*, New York and London: Routledge, 2016, chapter 7.

[2] St. Augustine, *City of God*, Henry Benson (trans.), New York: Penguin, 1972, p. 862. Quoted in Eberle, *Justice and the Just War Tradition*, p. 141.

Ethics, Security, and The War-Machine: The True Cost of the Military. Ned Dobos, Oxford University Press (2020). © Ned Dobos.
DOI: 10.1093/oso/9780198860518.001.0001

and war.'³ Grady Davis concurs: 'To imagine yourself a killer without feeling the enormity of the act is a sure sign of corruption...The more decent the soldier, the more horrified at the prospect of killing.'⁴ Daniel Bell makes the same point with these words: 'If the enemy is killed, the appropriate posture is not revelry but regret...A just warrior is, in a sense, a sad warrior.'⁵

It's not that a soldier owes enemy combatants an obligation to feel sorrow over their deaths, or that he commits some injustice against them when he fails to sorrow. The claim, rather, is that failing to experience any emotional distress in these circumstances is a sign of morally defective character. It reveals the absence of a particular virtue, what R.C. Roberts calls the 'virtue of proper affect'. This is simply the disposition to be emotionally moved in a way that is fitting to the moral gravity of what one does and encounters. A soldier that is able to kill and maim people without feeling anything is lacking in this connection. This does not necessarily mean that he is a 'bad person' all things considered; it just means that there is a respect in which he is morally deficient.⁶

Admittedly, even this weaker claim may seem bizarre. If a soldier is not doing anything wrong—if we think that all of his actions are permissible or even obligatory—then why is it virtuous, or a sign of moral decency, that those actions cause him emotional hardship?

The curiousness of this view subsides, however, once we notice that we make such seemingly paradoxical judgements all the time. Take a fairly trivial example. In the movie *Old Yeller* a young boy (Travis) is forced to put down his beloved pet dog after it contracts rabies. There is no denying that this is the right thing to do, both for the dog and for those that it might endanger. In fact, we might say that it would be wrong for Travis *not* to euthanize the animal. In the movie, Travis

---

³ Oliver O'Donovan, *In Pursuit of a Christian View of War*, Bramcote Notts: Grove Books, 1977, p. 4.
⁴ Grady Scott Davis, *Warcraft and the Frugality of Virtue*, Moscow, ID: University of Idaho Press, 1992, p. 28.
⁵ Daniel Bell, *Just War as Christian Discipleship*, Grand Rapids, MI: Brazos Press, 2009, pp. 163–4.
⁶ Robert C. Roberts, 'Aristotle on Virtues and Emotions', *Philosophical Studies*, vol. 56, 1989, pp. 293–306.

hardens himself and does his duty with great emotional torment, but suppose it did not play out this way. Imagine that Travis found it easy, or even found some pleasure in the act of killing the dog. In this case we might think that there is something *wrong with him*, morally, even though there is nothing wrong with what he has done. Sometimes, a good person will find it difficult to behave correctly. To the extent that he does not find it difficult, we are justified in revising our belief that he is good.[7] The authors quoted above are simply extending this sentiment to soldiers in battle. Experiencing emotional anguish at killing enemy combatants, even if they are 'liable' to it, is being characterized as a marker of moral virtue. This does not strike me as particularly controversial. It does, however, carry some potentially controversial implications.

Combat training is geared towards making recruits more comfortable with killing, so that they can do it repeatedly and efficiently, without thinking too much or feeling too deeply. One of its aims is to enable recruits to use lethal violence without suffering emotional distress. But we have just said that a morally decent person *would* experience distress in these circumstances. The upshot seems to be that military conditioning is (or tries to be) morally damaging, or corrosive of virtue.[8] The first half of the chapter elaborates on this point. The second half introduces and responds to counterarguments. One of them says that even if military conditioning can cause moral damage, it need not. On this view it is possible for militaries to function effectively without inflicting moral damage on recruits; all it would take are some fairly modest reforms. The second counter says that, while there may be a respect in which military conditioning is morally damaging, there are other respects in which it is actually morally *enhancing*, or virtue-promoting. Both of these responses are found wanting.

---

[7] C.D. Myers uses the same example, but reaches the opposite conclusion, in 'The Virtue of Cold Heartedness', *Philosophical Studies*, vol. 138, 2008, pp. 233–44.

[8] Joshua Goldstein gestures towards the idea that military preparation can be injurious when he writes that 'the omnipresent potential for war causes cultures to transform males, deliberately and systematically, by damaging their emotional capabilities'. Joshua S. Goldstein, *War and Gender: How Gender Shapes the War System and Vice Versa*, Cambridge: Cambridge University Press, 2001, p. 283.

Making Killers

S.L.A. Marshall once described war as 'the business of killing'.[9] And yet many war-fighters throughout history have gone out of their way to avoid it. Marshall himself estimated (though some say he exaggerated, or even fabricated) that only 15–25 per cent of infantry soldiers in the First World War fired their weapons in any given battle.[10] The rest were so-called 'non-firers'; they had the opportunity to shoot at enemy soldiers but failed to do so. Marshall added that even those who did shoot often deliberately missed their target—they were so-called 'mis-firers'. These 'passive combat personnel', as they are sometimes called, have long been a thorn in the side of military institutions.[11] War is a 'competition in death and destruction', in the words of Henry Shue, and these individuals deliberately forego opportunities to score points for their own team.[12]

The reasons behind non-firing/misfiring are too complex for a full exposition here.[13] But a likely part of the explanation is that, for most ordinary people, killing is psychologically very difficult. This might be because humans are naturally averse to killing members of their own species. Or it might be because some such aversion is socially inculcated into us. Either way, it stands to reason that combat training is designed to make killing psychologically easier. As Jessica Wolfendale notes, one of the main goals of military conditioning has always been 'to eradicate the moral and emotional distress associated with obedience to destructive authority'.[14] A couple of strategies are standardly employed to achieve this end: the performance of killing is made *routine*, and the victims are *dehumanized*. In the not-too-distant future combatants might also be

[9] S.L.A. Marshall, quoted in David Grossman, *On Killing: The Psychological Cost of Learning to Kill in War and Society*, Boston, MA: Little Brown and Co, 1995, p. 250.
[10] S.L.A. Marshall, *Men Against Fire: The Problem of Battle Command in Future War*, Washington, DC: Infantry Journal Press, 1947. For an overview of some of the criticisms see Roger J. Spiller, 'S.L.A. Marshall and the Ratio of Fire', *The RUSI Journal*, Winter, 1988, pp. 63–71.
[11] See Joanna Bourke, *An Intimate History of Killing: Face-to-Face Killing in Twentieth Century Warfare*, London: Granta Books, 1999, p. 73.
[12] Henry Shue, 'Last Resort and Proportionality', in Seth Lazar and Helen Frowe (eds.), *The Oxford Handbook of Ethics of War*, New York: Oxford University Press, 2018, p. 273.
[13] Apparently, some passive combat personnel have explained that they held their fire because they feared being rebuked for wasting ammunition on targets that were not clearly visible. For more see Bourke, *An Intimate History of Killing*, pp. 77–8.
[14] Jessica Wolfendale, *Torture and the Military Profession*, Houndmills and New York: Palgrave Macmillan, 2007, p. 128.

emotionally *anaesthetized* by pharmacological means. More on this shortly.

Militaries have long relied on repetitive drills to make the act of killing feel routine. A Canadian First World War soldier explained: 'Mechanically we stabbed a dummy figure. Mechanically we would stab and stab again a breathing human frame.'[15] But these drills underwent a significant transformation after the world wars. Whereas basic training may have once involved shooting at a paper target or bayonetting a burlap sack, nowadays the drills are designed to look, and feel, more like the real thing. Dave Grossman describes some of the more interesting makeshift innovations in this space, like putting enemy uniforms on balloons filled with fake blood, or using heads of cabbages covered in tomato sauce as targets. A trainer at one of the camps using such devices explained: 'When you look through that scope, I want you to see a head blowing up.'[16] The idea is to recreate the experience of killing as closely as possible, and to have soldiers relive that experience as often as possible before going into battle so that, once they get there, they are able to use lethal force without hesitating. One US soldier described his first kill as follows: 'Two shots. Bam-Bam. Just like we had been trained in "Quick-Shoot". When I killed, I did it just like that. Just like I'd been trained. Without even thinking.'[17] This is precisely the kind of automatic conditioned response that drill training aims to instil.

Advanced computer simulations are taking things to the next level. The trainee enters a highly immersive virtual reality with what looks and feels like a real rifle, where he shoots at screens projecting high-resolution images of the enemy that he will soon be facing. Some of the latest state-of-the art simulators recreate the theatre of battle down to its details and allow multiple trainees to coordinate complicated missions and respond to an assortment of specific frontline scenarios—IED explosions, ambushes, etc.[18] Hamza Shaban, technology writer for *The Atlantic*, describes one such war theatre simulator as 'a primitive

[15] Bourke, *An Intimate History*, p. 98.
[16] Quoted in Wolfendale, *Torture in the Military Profession*, p. 137.
[17] Grossman, *On Killing*, p. 128.
[18] See Jose Antonio Vargas, 'Virtual Reality Prepares Soldiers for Real War', *Washington Post*, 14 February 2006; and Jeff Sparrow, 'Killing Soldiers' Humanity', *The Age*, 4 June 2007.

version of *Star Trek's* Holodeck or the *X-Men's* Danger Room'.[19] By replicating the environment and the experience in this way, the hope is that trainees can make a seamless transition from the simulated war to the real one. Lt. Col. Scott Sutton, director of the technology division of Quantico Marine Base, is confident that it is working. The current generation of soldiers, he thinks, 'probably feel less inhibited, down in their primal level, pointing their weapons at somebody... [which] provides a better foundation for us to work with'.[20]

In addition to making killing routine, militaries deploy rhetorical devices that *dehumanize* (and sometimes demonize) the adversary. Informally, soldiers might refer to enemy combatants as 'commies' or 'huns' or 'gooks' or 'sand monkeys', rather than men and women. Describing people in such derogatory terms makes it psychologically easier to kill them. But even the language formally adopted by military organizations lends itself to this result. Soldiers are not ordered to kill people; they are ordered to 'service targets', or to 'neutralize' them. When all targets are serviced the area is 'clear' or 'cleansed'. Killing the wounded is 'checking'. Arial bombing in preparation for a ground assault is called 'softening up'. The function of such euphemisms is to allow unpleasant things to be communicated without the unpleasantness of conjuring up mental pictures of them.[21]

Arguably, the current trend of attaching highly moralized labels to military operations—Operation Just Cause; Operation Enduring Freedom; Operation Valiant Guardian; Operation Iron Justice—also contributes to enemy dehumanization. Philosopher A.J. Coates suggests, I think plausibly, that the more soldiers think of themselves as the defenders of justice, good, and civilization, (as opposed to mundane national interests), the more likely they are to 'simplify the moral boundaries of the conflict', and to perceive the enemy as the embodiment of injustice, evil, and barbarism; as an opponent that is not deserving of the respect that is

[19] Hamza Shaban, 'Playing War: How the Military Uses Video Games', *The Atlantic*, 10 October 2013, available at: https://www.theatlantic.com/technology/archive/2013/10/playing-war-how-the-military-uses-video-games/280486/, last accessed November 2018.
[20] Quoted in Vargas, 'Virtual Reality Prepares Soldiers for Real War'.
[21] William J. Astore, 'All The Euphemisms We Use for War', *The Nation*, 15 April 2016.

usually owed to human beings.[22] Thus militaries might facilitate the dehumanization of enemy fighters not just by their use of sterile language ('service the target'), but perhaps also, paradoxically, by their use of moral concepts and categories.

In the near future these familiar methods of *routinization* and *dehumanization* may be supplemented by chemical interventions that insulate soldiers from the moral and emotional stressors of war-fighting. The beta-blocker Propranolol, for instance, has been tested for use in the treatment of combat-induced mental afflictions such as post-traumatic stress disorder (PTSD).[23] The drug works by paralysing the emotions; under its influence a person exposed to a disturbing event remembers the raw details of that event, but does not experience any emotion in response to it. The images and memories are rendered 'emotionally toothless'.[24] Former Chairman of the US President's Council on Bioethics, Leon Kass, memorably described Propranolol as 'the morning-after pill for just about anything that produces regret, remorse, pain, or guilt'.[25] Barry Romo, a national coordinator for Vietnam Veterans Against the War, called it the 'devil pill', the 'monster pill', and the 'anti-morality pill'.[26]

This is hyperbole, but underneath it is a legitimate concern, which brings us back to where we started. We would expect a morally healthy person who kills another human being to experience some anguish or sorrow—a 'frisson of horror' as O'Donovan says. This is even if the killing is ethically and legally justified. So, if administering Propranolol

---

[22] Anthony J. Coates, 'Humanitarian Intervention: A Conflict of Traditions', in Terry Nardin and Melissa S. Williams (eds.), *NOMOS XLVII: Humanitarian Intervention*, New York and London: New York University Press, 2006, p. 76.

[23] Jessica Wolfendale, 'Performance-Enhancing Technologies and Moral Responsibility in the Military', *The American Journal of Bioethics*, vol. 8, no. 2, 2008, p. 30. Xenon gas has been used to successfully inhibit emotional memory recall in rats, and it is now being considered for PTSD treatment in humans. See E.G. Meloni, T.E. Gillis, J. Manoukian, and M.J. Kaufman, 'Erasing Memories with Gas: Xenon Impairs Reconsolidation of Fear Memories in a Rat Model of Post-Traumatic Stress Disorder (PTSD)', *PLOS ONE*, vol. 9, no. 8, 2014, pp. 1–8.

[24] Penny Coleman, 'Pentagon, Big Pharma: Drug Troops to Numb Them to Horrors of War', *Alternet.org*, 9 January 2008.

[25] Kass has also spoken out against other kinds of military conditioning aimed at making soldiers more resilient. During the Gulf war American soldiers were apparently put through desensitization training to enable them to hear women being raped and tortured without breaking. Kass said of this: 'It's a deformation of the soul of the first order. I cannot speak about it without outrage.' Erik Baard, 'The Guilt-Free Soldier', *The Village Voice*, 21 January 2003.

[26] Quoted in Baard, 'The Guilt-Free Soldier'.

to soldiers means that they can kill and recall killing without experiencing any emotional sting, is this substance not damaging to their moral health?[27] Penny Coleman thinks so. She describes the proposed administration of Propranolol to soldiers as 'a form of moral lobotomy' that 'medicates away one's conscience'. Coleman is worth quoting at length in this connection:

> I cannot imagine what aspects of selfhood will have to be excised or paralyzed so soldiers will no longer be troubled by what they, not to mention we, would otherwise consider morally repugnant. A soldier who has lost an arm can be welcomed home because he or she still shares fundamental societal values. But the soldier who sees her friend emulsified by a bomb, or who is ordered to run over children in the road rather than slow down the convoy, or who realizes too late that the woman was carrying a baby, not a bomb—if that soldier's ability to feel terror and horror has been amputated, if he or she can no longer be appalled or haunted, something far more precious has been lost. I am afraid that the training or conditioning or drug that will be developed to protect soldiers from such injuries will leave an indifference to violence that will make them unrecognizable to themselves and to those who love them.[28]

All I have said so far is that emotional sensitivity to killing is an indicator of moral goodness, and that military conditioning aims to reduce this sensitivity. If this is correct, however, then it seems that military conditioning is intended to abrade virtue; it aims to make people *less good* in one respect. This is not to say that those who undergo the conditioning deserve censure; in fact it may be that we owe them appreciation for this sacrifice. But if we accept that morally healthy people cannot kill and maim without emotional distress, then we have got to accept that individuals successfully conditioned to kill and maim without distress

---

[27] For a more thorough ethical analysis of this issue, see Michael Henry, Jennifer R. Fishman, and Stuart J. Youngner, 'Propranolol and the Prevention of Post-Traumatic Stress Disorder: Is it Wrong to Erase the "Sting" of Bad Memories?', *The American Journal of Bioethics*, vol. 7, no. 9, 2007, pp. 12–20.
[28] Coleman, 'Pentagon, Big Pharma'.

have been morally damaged. This might even be a variant of what psychologists and military ethicists are now calling 'moral injury'.[29]

Moral Injury

While combat-induced post-traumatic stress disorder has received a considerable amount of scholarly attention, until recently relatively little had been paid to the so-called moral injuries sustained by combatants. The nascent literature on this topic usually runs together two distinct phenomena. A *Huffington Post* essay by Pulitzer Prize winning journalist David Wood will serve as our example.

Wood tells one story of an American soldier in Iraq involved in a firefight with insurgents. Some of the insurgents attack the soldier while shielding themselves behind innocent civilians. The impulse of self-preservation kicks in, the soldier fires back, and some of the human shields are killed. Upon his return to the United States the veteran's wife hands him his newborn baby daughter as he comes off the plane, but he cannot bear to hold her. The veteran feels so morally impure as a result of having killed those civilians that he fears he will contaminate his child.[30] Here the moral emotions (guilt, shame) are so intensely engaged that the individual has become dysfunctional. Wood characterizes this soldier as morally injured.

A more well-known example comes from the Second World War. Colonel Paul Tibbitts, the pilot who dropped the atomic bomb on Hiroshima, was by most accounts untroubled by what he had done. In the years that followed he even participated in re-enactments of the bombing in front of audiences at model aircraft shows. By contrast, the man who flew the reconnaissance plane over Hiroshima immediately before the bombing—Major Claude Eatherly—could hardly live with himself afterwards. He came home and spoke out in support of pacifist groups, donated part of every paycheck to a fund for children in Hiroshima, and sent letters of apology to the victims and their families.

---

[29] The following section builds on a distinction that I first drew in Ned Dobos, 'Moral Trauma and Moral Degradation', in Tom Frame (ed.), *Moral Injury Unseen Wounds in an Age of Barbarism*, Sydney: NewSouth Press, 2015.
[30] David Wood, 'Healing: Can We Treat Moral Injury?', *Huffington Post*, 20 March 2014.

He was haunted by nightmares, attempted suicide, and underwent psychiatric treatment.[31] He even committed petty, senseless crimes for no gain, apparently in 'a desperate attempt to prove his guilt to himself and to his fellow men, who too easily had classified him as a guiltless, even gilded hero'.[32] Eatherly's inflamed conscience consumed him for the rest of his life.

Consider now another US soldier characterized by Wood as morally injured: Stephen Canty, who describes as follows what happened after he shot an Afghan man in the back on his second deployment:

> One of the bullets bounced off his spinal cord and came out his eyeball, and he's lying there in a wheelbarrow clinging to the last seconds of his life, and he's looking up at me with one of his eyes and just pulp in the other … I just stared down at him … and walked away. And I will … never feel anything about that. I literally just don't care whatsoever … I think I even smiled.

Canty continues:

> You learn to kill, and you kill people, and it's like, I don't care. I've seen people get shot, I've seen little kids get shot. You see a kid and his father sitting together and he gets shot and I give a zero fuck.[33]

Wood characterizes both the guilt-ridden soldier from the first example, and Canty, as morally injured, but clearly there is a world of difference between them.

The first example involves an arousal of the moral emotions to such an extent that they become debilitating. The soldier feels so bad about his actions that he struggles to function or to live a flourishing life upon his return from duty. The experience of war has aggravated the moral emotions to pathological levels. Let us call this variety of moral injury

---

[31] Jonathan Glover, *Humanity: A Moral History of the 20th Century*, 2nd Edition, London and New Haven, CT: Yale University Press, 2012, pp. 100–1.
[32] Gunther Anders and Claude Eatherly, *Burning Conscience: The Case of the Hiroshima Pilot, Claude Eatherly, Told in his Letters to Gunther Anders*, New York: Monthly Review Press, 1962, p. 52.
[33] David Wood, 'The Grunts: Damned if they Kill, Damned if they Don't', *Huffington Post*, 18 March 2014.

moral trauma. Dawn Weaver, a psychiatric nurse for the US military, describes the typical experience of the morally traumatized like this: 'when they come home, they are so horrified by what their primal brain had them do [...] that they find themselves absolutely reviled, repugnant. They can't tolerate themselves.'[34] The second kind of moral injury, embodied by Canty, involves a corrosion of the moral emotions. Canty does *not* feel emotionally troubled by what he has done, but we cannot help but feel that he *should.* Here the individual fails to manifest the moral emotions in an appropriate way. There is no 'proper affect'. We can call this *moral degradation.*

A soldier that suffers moral trauma *feels* like a worse/less virtuous person than he was prior to the injury. A soldier that suffers moral degradation *is* a less virtuous person in one respect. Soldiers in war must sometimes do terrible things, but the likes of Canty no longer experience these things *as* terrible. The silence of their emotions—their indifference—is their injury.[35]

For present purposes I am content simply to highlight that moral injury comes in these two distinct forms, of trauma and degradation. But part of me thinks that only the latter counts as moral injury *properly speaking.* Wood defines moral injury as 'damage to a person's moral foundation'.[36] Tyler Boudreau similarly talks of 'damage done to our moral fiber'.[37] Neilsen et al. define it as a condition that 'reduces the functioning or impairs the performance of the moral self'.[38] Stephen Canty meets this definition. His moral compass has become unresponsive. But we cannot say the same for the likes of Major Eatherly, the aforementioned Hiroshima reconnaissance pilot. Guilty feelings, however acute and debilitating, do not indicate that one's moral foundation has been compromised. On the contrary, they can serve as evidence that

[34] Quoted in Sarah J. Hautzinger and Jean Scandlyn, *Beyond Post-Traumatic Stress: Homefront Struggles with the Wars on Terror*, London: Routledge, 2016, pp. 66–7.
[35] To be entirely devoid of moral feelings is to be 'morally dead' according to Kant. Jeffrie G. Murphy, 'Moral Death: A Kantian Essay on Psychopathy', *Ethics*, vol. 82, no. 4, July 1972, p. 284. Moral degradation can be understood as an injury that edges one closer to this state.
[36] Wood, 'The Grunts'.
[37] Tyler Boudreau, 'The Morally Injured', *The Massachusetts Review*, vol. 52, no. 3–4, 2011, p. 749.
[38] R. Nielson, A. Macdonald, E. Scarr, H. Smith, T. Frame, and C. Roberts, 'Moral Injury from Theory to Practice: A Research Report Prepared for the Centre for Defence Leadership and Ethics, Australian Defence College', Canberra, 2016, p. 35.

one's moral senses are still very much active. A letter of consolation written to Eatherly makes this point especially well. He had expressed frustration and hopelessness at the impossibility of atoning for his involvement in the atrocity. In response, Gunther Anders wrote this: 'That you, since your efforts cannot succeed, react panically and unco-ordinatedly, is comprehensible. One could almost say that it is proof of your moral health. For your reactions prove that your conscience is on guard.'[39]

Let us pause now to take stock. I have said that, even when killing is justified, it is a sign of good moral character if the killer experiences some anguish or distress. The absence of such feelings—an emotional indifference or numbness to killing—is a morally degraded state to be in, arguably a form of moral injury. But combat training aims to cultivate precisely this kind of indifference, in the name of making soldiers more resilient and effective. The conclusion this brings us to is that military training is morally injurious, not by accident but by design. One kind of moral injury (moral trauma) happens primarily during combat. The other kind (moral degradation) is pre-inflicted on soldiers in preparing them for combat, though of course their combat experiences might always aggravate it.

To be clear, none of this is meant to suggest that those who undergo military conditioning pose a danger to the civilian society to which they belong. Even if combat training does desensitize them to violence, soldiers are also taught to respect authority, to follow rules, to exercise self-restraint, and so on. This will probably be enough to prevent most veterans from using violence illicitly outside the context of war *even if* they have been emotionally numbed to it. The conditioning that inflicts the moral injury can also keep it from becoming outwardly symptomatic after soldiers return to civilian life. Thus the position I am advancing here should not be confused with what Joanna Bourke calls the 'brutalization thesis'. This is the view that military training and combat instil 'violent habits' that die hard, or not at all, such that returning military personnel pose a danger to their parent society.[40]

---

[39] Anders and Eatherly, *Burning Conscience*, p. 4.
[40] In earlier historical periods some people were worried enough about this to propose that veterans be segregated off from the rest of the community. At the end of the Second World War, for instance, one prominent American suggested that veterans be confined to 'reorientation camps' for a while—somewhere in the Panama Canal Zone—and upon release be required to

Bourke's research shows that worries about brutalization peaked during the Vietnam War and then receded. But the war on terror—which began shortly after the publication of Bourke's monograph—has awakened these concerns once again. *Beyond Post-Traumatic Stress* by Sarah Hautzinger and Jean Scandlyn is a recent case in point. The authors tell the story of the 2nd Battalion, 12th Regiment of the US Army (better known as the 2-12th). Its members are alleged to have been involved in various war crimes while on tour in Iraq, including the killing of unarmed civilians, torture (an Iraqi captive had his face skinned off while his hands were tied behind his back), and the mutilation of corpses. One member of the regiment reportedly kept a running tally of all the dogs he managed to kill while out on patrol.[41] Another—Kenneth Eastridge—fired 1700 rounds at Iraqi civilians against orders. He estimated that 'not that many, maybe a dozen' were killed, and later elaborated that 'it doesn't really matter to me [...] They're not humans; they're not like us.'[42]

The delinquency didn't end when the deployments did. One 2-12th soldier killed his wife (and then himself) after an Iraq tour. Eastridge and two others from the 2-12th were involved in a spate of robberies, assaults, and killings around Colorado Springs. One evening the trio decided to rob a 19-year-old woman walking to a bus stop. One of them ran her down with the car, before another stabbed her six times, puncturing a lung, and cutting her left eye open. Shortly after these three were arrested, two other members of the 2-12th were arrested for driving around town randomly firing at people with an AK-47. They shot an army captain, and a couple out posting garage sale signs. Then another former 2-12th soldier was charged with beating his girlfriend to death. Later two more were charged, one for shooting a pregnant woman in the thigh at a party.[43]

Members of the 2–12th were repeatedly exposed to intense combat. Some suffered PTSD, had criminal histories, drug and alcohol problems,

---

wear clearly visible identification patches, to remind civilians that they need to be vigilant of the danger. See Bourke, *An Intimate History of Killing*, p. 352.

[41] See Hautzinger and Scandlyn, *Beyond Post Traumatic Stress*, p. 90.
[42] Hautzinger and Scandlyn, *Beyond Post Traumatic Stress*, p. 77.
[43] Hautzinger and Scandlyn, *Beyond Post Traumatic Stress*, pp. 75–80.

and pre-existing behavioural health issues. All of these factors likely contributed to their depraved behaviours in Iraq and at home, but Hautzinger and Scandlyn suggest that their military training probably played a role as well. 'Like the bad-apples thesis', they write, 'treating PTSD itself as explanatory is too simplistic and reductive [...] Instead, the interplay between multiple factors requires attention: yes, consider combat/violence exposure, but also conditioned perpetration of violence.'[44] The suggestion seems to be that members of the 2-12th had been brutalized by their military conditioning and experience, which made them a danger to the communities to which they returned.

The obvious problem with this view is that there are plenty of cases of civilians with no military background committing equally horrific crimes, and it is difficult to say whether combat training makes people *more likely* to engage in such behaviours once all confounding variables are controlled for. But that is not what I am saying anyway. I have argued only that military conditioning aims to inflict a kind of moral injury—specifically what I have labelled 'moral degradation'—which consists of a weakening of the emotional inhibitions against killing and maiming. This does not entail any predictions about whether veterans are more or less likely to use violence illicitly once they return to civilian life.

In what remains I want to consider two responses to the claim that military conditioning is morally damaging. The first says that although combat training can affect an enduring state of emotional indifference or coldness towards lethal violence, it need not. When done correctly, it will not extinguish the trainee's emotional responsiveness to killing; it will only produce a limited and temporary suspension of that responsiveness. This being the case, military training ought not to be considered morally injurious.

Dehumanization Done Right?

Adam severs his spinal cord in a car accident, leaving him paralysed from the waist down. Eve undergoes a medical procedure during which she is administered a spinal anaesthetic, paralysing her from the waist down.

---

[44] Hautzinger and Scandlyn, *Beyond Post Traumatic Stress*, p. 93.

Even though both have been left incapable of walking, we would say that Adam has been injured but Eve has not. Clearly there are several important differences between these two cases, but the most salient is that Eve's state of paralysis, unlike Adam's, is temporary. Once the anaesthetic wears off, she will regain the use of her legs. Military training and socialization, one might argue, is like this. To the extent that it works, it does not leave the soldier permanently desensitized or indifferent to the suffering of others; it leaves him temporarily impervious to the emotions ordinarily triggered by the suffering of others, so as to enable him to do his job effectively. The 'virtue of proper affect' is still there, just momentarily supressed.

This seems to be the view taken by Shannon French and Anthony Jack in a recent essay.[45] Their focus is specifically on enemy dehumanization. As we have seen, this is one of the standard methods used by military institutions to psychologically prepare their personnel to kill people. French and Jack admit that this is indispensable: 'Given the inevitability that our troops will be required to commit acts of violence towards others, [dehumanization] is a necessary psychological strategy that can both allow them to perform their duties well and also safeguard them from the perils of psychological disintegration.'[46] The authors insist, however, that the dehumanization process can be managed so that the resulting emotional detachment is limited to enemy combatants, not the enemy population as a whole, and, importantly, to ensure that it is reversible *post bellum*. If this is right, then military training can be conducted in a way that produces a time-limited suspension of sympathy towards a narrowly circumscribed group of people, rather than the more permanent and more generalized loss of sympathy characteristic of moral degradation.

French and Jack begin by noting that there are two distinct kinds of dehumanization. *Animalistic* dehumanization involves characterizing enemy soldiers as an inferior life form ('gooks', 'Huns', 'vermin', etc.)

---

[45] Shannon E. French and Anthony I. Jack, 'Dehumanizing the Enemy: The Intersection of Neuroethics and Military Ethics', in David Whetham and Bradley J. Strawser (eds.), *Responsibilities to Protect: Perspectives in Theory and Practice*, Leiden: Brill, 2015, pp. 165–95.

[46] French and Jack, 'Dehumanizing the Enemy', p. 172. See also Michael W. Brough, 'Dehumanization of the Enemy and the Moral Equality of Soldiers', in Michael W. Brough, John W. Lango, and Harry van der Linden (eds.), *Rethinking the Just War Tradition*, New York: SUNY Press, 2007, pp. 151–3.

This creates psychological distance by generating contempt, disgust, or hatred. *Mechanistic* dehumanization (or 'objectification'), by contrast, involves equating enemy soldiers with inanimate objects ('neutralize the target').[47] Rather than producing disgust or contempt, this form of dehumanization only produces cold indifference, but again this is enough to achieve the psychological distance necessary to enable soldiers to kill without hesitation or compunction. Michael Brough draws the same distinction with different language. Animalistic dehumanization he calls 'sub-humanization'. This involves perceiving the enemy as 'an animal or insect, or evil, as a monster or demon'. Mechanistic dehumanization he calls 'non-humanization'. This involves perceiving the enemy as 'things neither base nor evil, but also things devoid of inherent worth'.[48]

According to French and Jack, mechanistic dehumanization is preferable for a number of reasons. First, it creates an 'emotional disengagement' that is conducive to sound, sensible decision-making, unlike animalistic dehumanization, which is said to engage parts of the brain that give rise to an 'emotionally dysfunctional cognitive mode'.[49] Second, and relatedly, mechanistic dehumanization is supposedly less likely to produce crimes of rage and indiscriminate or excessive violence in combat. Third, and most importantly for present purposes, French and Jack suggest that mechanistic dehumanization has a less profound and shorter-lasting impact on the soldier's personality and values. It creates a 'careful and limited' disregard for specific others, they say; a 'controlled and limited degree of interpersonal coldness'.[50] This effect is said to be impermanent: 'objectifying [the enemy] is a necessary, *but temporary*, fix' (emphasis added).[51] A mechanistically dehumanized enemy, French and Jack suggest, can be *re*-humanized in the minds of our soldiers once the war is over.

Unfortunately, French and Jack do not give us much reason to share their confidence. It is true that animalistic dehumanization is difficult to

---

[47] See Nick Haslam, 'Dehumanization: An Integrative Review', *Personality and Social Psychology Review*, vol. 10, no. 3, February 2006, pp. 252–64; David Livingstone Smith, 'Dehumanization, Essentialism, and Moral Psychology', *Philosophy Compass*, vol. 9, no. 11, 2014, pp. 819–20.

[48] Brough, 'Dehumanization of the Enemy', pp. 160–1.

[49] French and Jack, 'Dehumanizing the Enemy', p. 186.

[50] French and Jack, 'Dehumanizing the Enemy', pp. 187 and 192.

[51] French and Jack, 'Dehumanizing the Enemy', p. 187.

contain. If a soldier is conditioned to see enemy combatants as an inferior life form, it is likely that this will influence the way he perceives enemy civilians as well, given that they all belong to the same national or cultural group and share salient features. It is not obvious, however, that mechanistic dehumanization is inherently any more resistant to this kind of spread. If a soldier is conditioned to see enemy soldiers as inanimate objects without inherent worth, I imagine he will be more inclined to see enemy civilians also as mere things that clutter the battlespace.[52] The widespread use of expressions like 'collateral damage' to denote civilian casualties suggests that some such mechanistic objectification of civilian lives, not just combatant ones, already happens.[53] Furthermore, if it is difficult to reverse animalistic dehumanization, it is not clear why we should think that mechanistic dehumanization is any more easily undone *post bellum*. As Tom Digby says, 'just as physical fitness for battle cannot simply be turned on or off at a moment's notice, neither can emotional fitness for battle be simply turned on or off like a light switch'.[54] This is presumably true whether we use sub-humanization, or non-humanization, to make our soldiers emotionally fit.[55]

Recent empirical research suggests that the effects on personality of ordinary military training endure far longer than was previously supposed. A study published in *Psychological Science*, for example, shows that military conditioning generally makes people less 'agreeable': less concerned about the feelings of others, less cooperative, and less patient.[56] This change apparently lingers long after the veteran has

---

[52] French and Jack, 'Dehumanizing the Enemy', p. 186. Brough makes a similar point in 'Dehumanization of the Enemy'.

[53] In places, French and Jack do seem to appreciate this point. They admit, for instance, that 'the grotesquely efficient massacres committed in the concentration camps during the Holocaust were primarily conducted through cold, mechanistic objectification'.

[54] Tom Digby, *Love and War: How Militarism Shapes Sexuality and Romance*, New York: Columbia University Press, 2014, p. 57.

[55] Digby's words echo that of the former President of the National Committee for Mental Hygiene in Canada. In 1944 he warned that 'aggressive urges which have been carefully nurtured and developed over a period of years' could not reasonably be expected to 'disappear overnight, leaving a peaceful civilian with no such pressures'. He admitted: 'This changeover in attitude may be very difficult indeed.' Similarly, the eminent psychiatry professors Mardi Horowitz and George Solomon acknowledged that the 'inhibitions to destruction behavior', lost during military conditioning and combat, would be 'difficult to reimpose'. See French and Jack, 'Dehumanizing the Enemy', pp. 351 and 353.

[56] Joshua J. Jackson, Felix Thoemmes, Kathrin Jonkmann, Oliver Lüdtke, and Ulrich Trautwein, 'Military Training and Personality Trait Development: Does the Military Make the Man, or Does the Man Make the Military?', *Psychological Science*, vol. 23, 2012, pp. 270–7.

been re-socialized into civilian life. The lead author of the study, Joshua Jackson, commented in an interview that 'these individuals—who, by and large, did not face any combat—had experiences in basic training that likely shaped the way they approach the world…The changes in personality were small, but over time, they could have important ramifications for the men's lives.'[57] This gives us reason to be sceptical, at least, of the idea that military conditioning need not have lasting effects on the emotional and moral profile of the average soldier.

It is worth emphasizing, moreover, that by French and Jack's own admission, enemy dehumanization does not simply wear off after a period of time has elapsed like an anaesthetic would. Rather, it needs to be actively undone: dehumanization needs to be counteracted by a program of re-humanization, so as to rekindle the emotional responsiveness suspended by military conditioning. I am not aware of any programs for veterans dedicated specifically to this. Investments are made, to be sure, in treating many of the unseen wounds associated with combat, but the emotional insensitivity to violence cultivated during military training does not appear to be among them. One of the instructors at Phan Rang, who was responsible for running American troops through an indoctrination course as they arrived in Vietnam during the war, later admitted that 'whenever I see something about a killing in the paper, I look to see if it was done by a Vietnam veteran'. He explained why: 'We had to *motivate* those kids to kill; we *programmed* them to kill, man…Well, nobody's *unprogramming* them.'[58]

Even if French and Jack are right, then, and the psychological effect of mechanistic dehumanization is reversible, the reality is that little effort is presently made to actually reverse it. If the result is that some veterans never regain those emotional sensitivities we associate with good moral character, then it is difficult to resist the conclusion that those veterans have been left injured by the institution that they serve. Maybe not physically or psychologically, but morally.

---

[57] Association for Psychological Science, 'Does The Military Make The Man Or Does The Man Make The Military?', 17 November 2011, available at: https://www.psychologicalscience.org/news/releases/does-the-military-make-the-man-or-does-the-man-make-the-military.html, last accessed March 2019.

[58] Bourke, *An Intimate History*, p. 352.

There is another counterargument to this view that I now want to consider. It says that even if military conditioning is morally damaging in the way that I have just described, in other ways it is actually morally enhancing, of virtue-promoting. Note that this does not directly challenge my contention, which is only that there is *a respect in which* military conditioning is morally injurious. But it blunts the force of any such conclusion by highlighting that, whatever moral damage is caused by combat training, it is at least partly offset by positive effects on character.

Self-Forgetfulness and Obedience Unto Death

One of the fathers of modern psychology, William James, feared that a world without military conflict could easily degenerate into 'a cattle-yard of a planet' where there is 'no scorn, no hardness, no valour anymore'.[59] James was by no means a militarist—in fact he was a pacifist, and open about it—but he saw in military service one redeeming feature: he thought it promoted virtues that tend to remain dormant, or waste away, in the course of ordinary civilian life. In particular, James's famous essay on the moral equivalent of war emphasizes the virtue of 'hardihood', which he explicitly associates with 'manliness'. Today this attribute goes by the name 'toxic masculinity', and its status as a virtue is dubious. (I will have more to say about this in Chapter 5). Thankfully, hardihood is not the only virtue that James connects to military service. He also notes approvingly that the military is an institution that rewards 'self-forgetfulness' over 'self-seeking'.[60] Most of us would be prepared to accept that self-obsession is a vice, and accordingly, that some willingness to set aside one's private interests for the greater good is an admirable character trait. Thus, to the extent that military conditioning does induce a degree of self-forgetfulness, there is a case to be made that it is morally enhancing.

---

[59] William James, 'The Moral Equivalent of War', *Essays in Religion and Morality*, Cambridge, MA: Harvard University Press, 1982, p. 166.
[60] James, 'The Moral Equivalent of War'.

The devil, however, is in the detail. Militaries do not train soldiers to independently appraise where their service is most needed, to figure out how to render that service most efficiently, and then to set their personal and career aspirations aside in devotion to the task. This is not the kind of 'selfless service' that military conditioning inculcates. Its goal is not to create effective altruists. Instead, the purpose of military conditioning is to instil a habit of what we might call *sacrificial obedience*.

The following excerpt is taken from Admiral Sandy Woodward's memoir *One Hundred Days*. Woodward was a British battle group commander during the Falklands War.

> ...mine-sweepers and their special equipment I did not have, which meant that I would have to use something else—and the hull of a ship was the only suitable hardware available [...] I phoned Commander Craig on the voice-encrypted network and said, 'Er...Christopher, I would like you to do a circumnavigation of East Falkland tonight [...]' He was silent for a few moments and then he said, 'Umm, I would expect you would like me to go in and out of the north entrance a few times, Admiral. Do a bit of zig-zagging.' 'Oh,' I said, feigning surprise and feeling about two inches high. 'Why do you ask that?' 'I expect you would like me to find out if there are any mines there,' he said quietly. I cannot remember what I said. But I remember how I felt. I just mentioned that I thought it would be quite useful [...] He went off to prepare for the possible loss of his ship and people the best way he could. I shall remember him as one of the bravest men I ever met.[61]

Woodward may have felt uncomfortable asking, but there is no question that he expected Commander Craig to do as he was told. This highlights one of the most distinctive features of the military: it is the only social institution that openly expects, and enforces, obedience *unto death*.

Military service is sometimes said to be governed by an 'unlimited liability covenant', so called because under the terms of the covenant

[61] Admiral Sandy Woodward, *One Hundred Days: The Memoirs of the Falklands Battle Group Commander*, London: Harper Collins, 1992, pp. 202–3.

there are no limits to the sacrifice that a soldier can legitimately be ordered to make.[62] This finds expression in instruments like the Uniform Code of Military Justice (UCMJ) in the United States, according to which it is a crime for a soldier to disobey a directive from a superior unless it is clearly unlawful. This qualification is usually interpreted narrowly to cover orders to commit war crimes or to victimize civilians, not orders that would require sacrifice of life or limb. Under the UCMJ, a soldier who disobeys an order simply because it demands self-sacrifice is liable to punishments up to and including execution.[63] In other words, soldiers are afforded some right of conscientious disobedience, but no right of self-preserving disobedience, at least not during wartime.[64] This arrangement is by no means idiosyncratic to the US. In most countries professional soldiers are expected to obey all orders except for criminal ones.

Things are very different in civilian workplaces, where there are usually laws protecting workers who refuse to comply with unsafe directives on the job. In Australia, the right to refuse hazardous work is given to employees by the *Work Health and Safety Act* (2011). In the United States, the *Occupational Safety and Health Act (1970)* grants workers a right to disobey a superior and request an official safety inspection if they believe that an 'imminent danger' exists, where this is defined in terms of a reasonable expectation 'of death or serious physical harm'.[65] The Act protects employees who exercise this right from discharge or retaliation. In other words, civilian workers—unlike soldiers— enjoy an inalienable right of self-preservation, which means they cannot be obligated to obey unto death. Directives that are suicidal, for want of a better term, may always be refused. Importantly, this right applies even in inherently dangerous civilian occupations. A high-rise construction

---

[62] The UK's Military Covenant similarly states that British soldiers must 'forego some of the rights enjoyed by those outside the Armed Forces', and that they have 'an unlimited liability to give their lives'.
[63] See The Uniform Code of Military Justice, §890 Art. 90, 'Assaulting or Wilfully Disobeying a Superior Commissioned Officer', and §892 Art. 92, 'Failure to Obey Order or Regulation'.
[64] For an ethical analysis of this feature of military service, see Ned Dobos, 'Punishing Non-Conscientious Disobedience: Is the Military a Rogue Employer?' *Philosophical Forum*, vol. XLVI, no. 1, 2015, pp. 105–19.
[65] Ruth R. Faden and Tom L. Beauchamp, 'The Right to Risk Information and the Right to Refuse Workplace Hazards', in Tom Beauchamp, Norman Bowie, and Denis G. Arnold (eds.), *Ethical Theory and Business*, 8th International Edition, Upper Saddle River, NJ: Pearson, 2008, p. 134.

worker may have agreed to a risky job, but this does not bind him to follow orders where it is foreseen that the harm risked will materialize. If the worker arrives on site one morning and is ordered by his foreman to climb an obviously unstable scaffold in strong winds, he is within his rights to refuse, morally and legally, on the grounds that death or serious injury is the reasonably foreseen outcome of compliance.

Now there may be occasions where a soldier does refuse an imminently dangerous directive and needs to be compelled into self-sacrifice. We have all heard stories of the Red Army's barrier troops, who were stationed behind the frontline during battle in order to apprehend or shoot any Soviet soldier attempting to retreat without orders. These days, however, there is probably less need for any such enforcement mechanism, since professional soldiers are rigorously conditioned to obey without self-regard. Being told what to do, and doing it without a fuss, quickly becomes an unremarkable feature of daily life for recruits into professional armed forces. Everything from what they eat, to when and where they sleep, what they wear, which events they attend, who they date, which pharmaceuticals they take, how their hair is groomed, how their jewellery is worn, and other such decisions that are usually the sovereign domain of the competent adult, are subject to the approval of superiors in most militaries. In some ways it is not dissimilar to the treatment of children in school. Hence one author writes of the *infantilization* of soldiers.[66] Another writes of their borderline *enslavement*.[67] Michael Walzer talks of their *servitude*.[68] Henry Thoreau memorably said of soldiers that they serve the state 'not as men mainly, but as machines, with their bodies'.[69]

In addition to this, rank and authority are heavily emphasized in military settings. Stanley Milgram's famous experiments give us an insight into the important role that this plays in achieving obedience.

[66] See Bruce Flemming, 'The Few, The Proud, The Infantilized', *The Chronicle*, 8 October 2012.
[67] See David Garran, 'Soldiers, Slaves and the Liberal State', *Philosophy and Public Policy Quarterly*, vol. 27, no. 1/2, Winter/Spring, 2007.
[68] Michael Walzer, *Just and Unjust Wars: A Moral Argument with Historical Illustrations*, New York: Basic Books, 1977, p. 35.
[69] Henry David Thoreau, 'Civil Disobedience', in *The Writings of Henry David Thoreau*, vol. 4, Boston, MA: Houghton Mifflin, 1906, p. 359.

The participants in those experiments showed a willingness to administer painful electric shocks to their fellow human beings despite their own moral reservations and emotional disquiet. When afterwards asked why, they almost always alluded to the experimenter's position of authority over them. This made them feel that they had no meaningful choice in the matter. Remarks such as 'I *wouldn't* have administered the electric shocks *if it were up to me*' were apparently common.[70] Milgram's experiments lend support to the idea that there is an innate human tendency to obey authority figures. The military environment is designed to fertilize this tendency. It does so through the use of insignias, badges, stripes, and other visible symbols of rank; through saluting rituals; through the separation of the enlisted from the commissioned, and so on. The purpose of all this is to continuously remind military personnel of their position in a hierarchy, and to render as conspicuous as possible the established legitimacy of the authority to which they are subject.

Group bonding and peer pressure also play a role in cultivating the habit of obedience. The military is sometimes referred to as a 'greedy institution' because of how much it demands of its members.[71] A civilian worker who starts a new job will typically still go home to his family in the evening, still go out with his friends on Saturday, still attend his church on Sunday morning, and so on. By contrast, new recruits into the military can spend almost all of their time together, in class, on the parade ground, in the mess hall, in the barracks, etc. Their lives are totally consumed by the institution—this is the sense in which it is 'greedy'. This quickly creates deep personal bonds between members of the armed forces, and also remakes their self-conceptions—they start to identify very strongly *as military* almost immediately. The fear of being excluded invariably follows, and the behavioural consequence of this is predicable: conformity.[72] Disobedience carries the risk that one will be perceived as disloyal, as lacking trust in other members of the group, or as lacking devotion to their common cause. This fear of exclusion creates a powerful incentive to do as one is told.

---

[70] Wolfendale, *Torture*, p. 147.
[71] Mady Wechsler Segal, 'The Military and the Family as Greedy Institutions', *Armed Forces and Society*, vol. 13, no. 1, Fall 1986, pp. 9–38.
[72] For fuller discussion see Wolfendale, *Torture*, pp. 131–4.

Militaries have also been known to use humiliation and cruelty to achieve sacrificial obedience. The following testimonial from a soldier training in the British Army in 1919 gives us a lucid sense of it:

> To be struck, to be threatened, to be called indecent names, to be drilled by yourself in front of a squad in order to make a fool of you, to do a tiring exercise and continue doing it whilst the rest of the squad does something else; to have your ear spat into, to be marched across parade-ground under escort, to be falsely accused before an officer and silenced when you try to speak in defence—all these things take down your pride, make you feel small, and in some ways *fit you to accept the role of cannon-fodder* on the battle-ground.[73]

Early in the twentieth century the German sociologist Karl Liebknecht argued that this kind of cruel and degrading hazing—or 'bastardization' as Australians would call it today—is a permanent feature of military socialization, not a contingent one that might be corrected through appropriate oversight and reform:

> [All] kinds of refined and horrible methods of ill treatment belong to the stock-in-trade of the present-day military education system ... The ill-treatment of soldiers springs from the very essence of capitalist militarism. The human material is for the most part, as far as the mind is concerned, and to an even greater extent as far as the body is concerned, not fitted for the demands made upon it by military life ... [Therefore] it is necessary to tear out a part of the soul of these 'fellows', and instil a new spirit of patriotism and loyalty to the crown. All these tasks cannot be solved by even the cleverest instructors ...[74]

What Liebknecht suggests is that the particular attributes necessary for competent military service cannot be produced through ordinary training and education. Some kind of bastardization, he thinks, is indispensable to the project of maintaining a functional war-machine.

---

[73] Quoted in Bourke, *An Intimate History*, p. 80, emphasis added.
[74] Karl Liebknecht, *Militarism and Anti-Militarism*, Grahame Lock (trans.), Cambridge: Rivers Press Limited, 1973, section 4. Full text available at: http://www.marxists.org/archive/liebknecht-k/works/1907/militarism-antimilitarism/index.htm, last accessed July 2018.

Accordingly, Liebknecht describes the military establishment as 'a penitent *but incorrigible* sinner' in connection with the humiliation of recruits.[75] I doubt that this is true. Many professional militaries have made sustained efforts to eliminate hazing with no obvious loss of capability. It seems the (relatively) more salubrious methods mentioned above—repetitive drills, group bonding etc.—can do the trick of instilling the habit of unreflective obedience that militaries strive for.[76]

Whichever methods are relied upon, the intention is to produce soldiers who will obey all lawful orders, including imminently dangerous ones that are reasonably expected to result in serious injury or death. In other words, the aim of military conditioning is to create a disposition towards sacrificial obedience. Once we appreciate that *this* is the nature of the 'self-forgetfulness' that militaries try to induce, however, I think the claim that military training is morally enhancing becomes considerably less plausible.

Self-regard is a property to which Aristotle's doctrine of virtue as a mean applies: too much of it (arrogance, conceit) is a vice, but so is too little.[77] Consider people who are willing to harm or humiliate themselves for the amusement of others, or people who always put the needs of others before their own, regardless of how much it costs them and how negligible the advantage to the beneficiary. These people show an excessive and improper lack of self-regard.[78] The fact that they have internalized a disposition to behave as they do does not make them better or more virtuous human beings. On the contrary, their 'self-forgetfulness' shows an objectionable lack of self-respect. It is hardly a stretch to say the same about an individual who has been conditioned to immediately obey all orders, even those that, if complied with, are reasonably expected to result in life-threatening injury or death. This individual has internalized a disposition to treat his own life as an expendable resource; he stands ready to dispose of himself without question at the behest of his superior.

---

[75] Liebknecht, *Militarism and Anti-Militarism.*

[76] Jessica Wolfendale says 'the *primary aim* of actual military training is to cultivate the habits of unreflective obedience' (emphasis added). Wolfendale, *Torture*, p. 127.

[77] Aristotle, *Nicomachean Ethics*, Book 2, any edition.

[78] Improper lack of self-regard can take various different forms. Kalynne Hackney Pudner distinguishes between self-abnegation, self-effacement, self-immolation, and self-donation. See her essay 'What's So Bad about Self-Sacrifice?', *Proceedings of the American Catholic Philosophical Association*, vol. 81, 2007, pp. 241–50.

At the very least I think we can say that it is an open question whether this is consistent with proper self-regard. For this reason I am not convinced that the self-forgetfulness typically cultivated by militaries constitutes a virtue that can offset the moral damage caused by combat training.

Conclusion

Desensitizing soldiers to lethal violence might well be justified, all things considered, to protect them from psychological breakdown and/or to increase their effectiveness. Nothing I have said denies this. But regardless of whether it is justified, the reality of it alone suggests that there is something uniquely troubling about the profession of arms. In most occupations the purpose of training is, in part, to minimize injury to personnel. This is equally true in the military. But it is also true that in the military, the training is itself injurious. Military conditioning aims to make people more comfortable with killing and maiming than they would otherwise be, so that they can participate in the horrors of war without being too horrified by them to continue. But to the extent that this conditioning works, leaving the soldier emotionally numbed enough to inflict suffering on others without suffering himself, his moral qualities are degraded. This infliction of moral injury should be counted as one of the costs of maintaining a military establishment, but it seldom is.

2

The Coup Risk

Introduction

It is not uncommon for the armed forces of a country to turn against the government that they are supposed to protect. Wherever there is a military there is a risk of a coup. Since 1950 there have been 232 of them in ninety-four countries, and this is only counting the successful ones where an incumbent government was unseated.[1] If we add the failed attempts, the number more than doubles to 475.[2] The coup risk is a function of what Peter Fever famously called the 'civil–military problematique': armed forces with the means to defend their state invariably have the means to attack it as well.[3]

In some places the risk of a coup is so pronounced that it has become a foremost consideration in military spending decisions. How much is allocated to the armed forces is not determined by a sober assessment of what is needed to protect against aggressive outsiders. Rather, it is based on estimates of how much is needed to buy off military elites in order to deter them from challenging the civilian authorities.[4] Many governments also feel the need to engage in so-called 'coup-proofing' strategies. For instance, it is common to split up the air, land, and sea

---

[1] Erik Meyersson, 'Turkey and the Economics of Coups', *Harvard Business Review*, 22 July 2016.

[2] Adam Taylor, 'The World of Coups Since 1950', *The Washington Post*, 22 July 2016.

[3] Peter Feaver, 'Civil-Military Relations', *Annual Review of Political Science*, vol. 2, no. 1, 1999, pp. 211–41. Or as Patricia Shields puts it: 'the institution created to protect the polity must become powerful enough to threaten the polity'. Patricia M. Shields, 'Civil-Military Relations: Changing Frontiers', *Public Administration Review*, vol. 66, 2006, pp. 925. James Pattison writes: 'In short, there needs to be protection *by* the military, but also protection *from* it', *The Morality of Private War: The Challenge of Private Military and Security Companies*, Oxford: Oxford University Press, p. 74.

[4] See Paul Collier and Anke Hoeffler, 'Military Spending and the Risks of Coups d'États', unpublished manuscript, Department of Economics, Oxford University, available online at: citeseerx.ist.psu.edu/viewdoc/download?doi=10.1.1.521.8028&rep=rep1&type=pdf.

Ethics, Security, and The War-Machine: The True Cost of the Military. Ned Dobos, Oxford University Press (2020).
© Ned Dobos.
DOI: 10.1093/oso/9780198860518.001.0001

services, and to foster a certain competitiveness among them. One rationale for this, apparently, is to create 'cohesion obstacles' that make it more difficult for the branches of the military to coordinate a domestic political intervention against the state.[5] In other places, states coup-proof by 'stacking'—filling the military with people from the same ethnic or cultural group as those that hold political office, since they are presumed to be more loyal.[6]

It is hardly surprising that civilian political leaders take these measures; military coups are usually very bad news for them both professionally and personally. But what is at stake for the citizens of the polity? Why should they take the prospect of a coup seriously?

A military regime that comes to power via a coup might turn out to be a benevolent dictatorship, but history tells us that is unlikely. Usually, such governments are characterized by violence and repression. Christopher Finlay suggests that this may be a by-product of military training and socialization:

> … political philosophers have sometimes mistakenly regarded societies as akin to some sort of raw material that it is the task of the political leader to refashion: if people are the wood, and leaders are the carpenters, then the means of fashioning will be modelled on the bladed and blunt-force instruments typical of that craft. The analogy leads to a conflation of politics, power, and the application of force. As 'managers of violence' (Samuel Huntington's expression), military officers seem likely to share this misconception. To a general with a hammer, everything will tend to look like a nail. Officers will view the task of reforming the state as being susceptible to the tools in which they have greatest expertise.[7]

[5] Jonathan Powell, 'Determinants of the Attempting and Outcome of Coups d'État', *Journal of Conflict Resolution*, vol. 56, 2012, p. 1022.

[6] Aaron Belkin and Evan Schofer, 'Toward a Structural Understanding of Coup Risk', *Journal of Conflict Resolution*, vol. 47, no. 5, 2003, p. 596.

[7] Christopher J. Finlay, 'Just and Unjust Coups d'État? Zimbabwe and the Ethics of Military Takeover', *Stockholm Centre for the Ethics of War and Peace*, available at: http://stockholmcentre.org/just-and-unjust-coups-detat-zimbabwe-and-the-ethics-of-military-takeover/, last accessed 16 December 2019.

Finlay is surely onto something. Military officers, conditioned as they are to rely on coercive force and domination to achieve their objectives, will probably rely on these same instruments when it comes to governing. But there is more to the story than this.

The so-called 'civil–military gap' that tends to open up in societies with standing armies, I will argue, often leaves military personnel with the same kinds of attitudes towards the civilian masses that are good predictors of oppression when found in governments. Given this, we can reasonably anticipate that a military regime that seizes power via a coup will neither express the shared values of its citizens nor govern them benevolently. If these are plausible suppositions, then citizens should take the risk of a coup seriously for largely the same reasons that they take the risk of foreign aggression and occupation seriously: both can be expected to compromise their *communal self-definition* and their enjoyment of *human rights* (even if neither is guaranteed to do so).

Of course, some societies are not as coup-prone as others. To that extent their citizens have less reason to fear the military. Having said that, in the final section of the chapter I warn against any generalization to the effect that certain kinds of societies—such as economically prosperous ones, or democracies—are impervious to domestic political interventions by the military. If the developed world's most recent coup event taught us anything, it is that certain structural features may reduce the chances of a coup happening, but never all the way to zero. In 2006, mathematical political forecasts put the likelihood of an attempted coup in Turkey at 2.5 per cent—or 'very unlikely'—and yet we saw it come to pass, barely a decade later.[8]

Foreign Occupation, Self-Definition, and Human Rights

Imagine that the democratically elected government of Country A is overthrown by the armed forces of neighbouring State B. The attackers

---

[8] Max Fisher and Amanda Taub, 'Turkey Was an Unlikely Victim of an Equally Unlikely Coup', *New York Times*, 16 July 2016, available at https://www.nytimes.com/2016/07/17/world/europe/turkey-was-an-unlikely-victim-of-an-equally-unlikely-coup.html?_r=0.

take control of the political institutions of Country A and remove from power the men and women who occupy its offices, seizing those positions for themselves. The people of Country A cannot know for sure what the new regime has in store for them, but I think they can reasonably assume a couple of things. The first thing they can assume is that the new regime, coming from a foreign culture, will not embody their shared values nor express their political will in the same way that the ousted democratically elected government did. In other words, the people of Country A can expect their *communal self-definition* to be compromised. The second thing they can expect is a certain amount of oppression and mistreatment, simply because the representatives of the new regime will see them as 'other' (probably lesser) human beings. In other words, the people of Country A can expect their *human rights* to deteriorate

When political institutions 'express the inherited culture' of the people subject to them, and the government rules the people 'in accordance with their traditions', there is what Michael Walzer calls a 'fit' between the rulers and the ruled.[9] This 'fit' ensures that the people are *self-defining*, in the sense that their shared customs and values are reflected in their political configurations.

There are a few different accounts of what makes communal self-definition so important. Yael Tamir seems to think that individual self-esteem depends on it. 'When individuals are able to identify their own culture in the political framework', she writes, 'individuals come to see themselves as the creators, or at least the carriers, of a valuable set of beliefs'.[10] The implication is that if people *cannot* see their values and traditions manifested in their political arrangements, they may come to adopt a depreciatory image of themselves.[11] My colleague Deane-Peter Baker takes things a step further. Following Martha Nussbaum, he first posits that to live a truly human life people must realize certain distinctly human capabilities. Baker then argues that the full realization of these

---

[9] Michael Walzer, 'The Moral Standing of States: A Response to Four Critics', *Philosophy and Public Affairs*, vol. 9, no. 3, 1980, pp. 209–29.

[10] Yael Tamir, *Liberal Nationalism*, Princeton, NJ: Princeton University Press, 1993, p. 72.

[11] For more on this point, see Will Kymlicka, *Multicultural Citizenship: A Liberal Theory of Minority Rights*, Oxford: Clarendon Press, 1995, p. 89; and Peetush, A.K., 'Cultural Diversity, Non-Western Communities, and Human Rights', *The Philosophical Forum*, vol. 34, no. 1, 2003, pp. 1–19.

capabilities is only possible when the political forms people live under reflect their conceptions of the good, their exercise of practical reason, and their culturally particular ways of relating. On this view, communal self-definition is essential not only if people are to live dignified lives, but if they are to live genuinely human lives at all.[12]

Foreign occupiers will sometimes make an effort to 'fit' with the communities they conquer, in the above sense. Michael Hechter provides several historical examples of alien rulers adopting (or mimicking) the cultural forms and institutions of the native societies they had subdued. According to Hechter, these rulers were attempting to 'diminish their alienness in the eyes of the ruled', so as to placate any resistance.[13] Even in these cases, however, a close fit between the people and the government was seldom achieved. Foreign invaders invariably bring with them their own inherited culture, and this invariably influences the shape of the political arrangements they impose on the occupied land. This being the case, one thing that people on the receiving end of foreign occupation can expect is a loss of communal self-definition.

But that is not all. In his book *Humanity: A Moral History of the 20th Century*, Jonathan Glover asks how it is that some people, despite being naturally inclined to feel sympathy for others and to respect their dignity, can bring themselves to seriously mistreat their fellow human beings. His answer is that the 'human responses' of sympathy and respect, which normally function as moral restraints, 'fail sometimes by being neutralized or anaesthetized, and sometimes by being overwhelmed by other factors'.[14] For instance, sympathy is weakened by physical distance, and its inhibiting force is diminished when there are many people involved in inflicting some harm, since responsibility gets fragmented in these cases. More importantly for our purposes, the human responses are only fully engaged in relation to people that we perceive as fully-fledged human beings *just like us*. When people are presented, and

[12] Deane-Peter Baker, 'Defending the Common Life: National Defence After Rodin', *Journal of Applied Philosophy*, vol. 23, no. 3, 2006, pp. 259–75.
[13] Michael Hechter, *Alien Rule*, New York: Cambridge University Press, 2013, p. 2.
[14] Jonathan Glover, *Humanity: A Moral History of the 20th Century*, New Haven, CT and London: Yale University Press, 2012, p. xix.

perceived, as fundamentally different or 'other', our sense of fellow-feeling towards them is diluted, weakening our natural inhibitions against mistreating them.

There are plenty of historical examples of this tendency to treat the 'other' worse than we treat our own. In 1139, the Lateran Council sanctioned the use of crossbows against infidels but not against fellow Christians. In the 1800s soft-nosed dum-dum bullets, 'designed not just to penetrate the body but to tear it apart', were developed by the British for use in colonial wars but not in European wars. In the Second World War, the Germans adopted radically different rules of engagement on the Eastern and Western Fronts. They recognized the common humanity of the English and Americans, but not of the Slavic Russians. Similarly, the Americans tended to treat German soldiers in accordance with the rules of war, while the bodies of Japanese combatants were regularly mutilated.[15]

Going back further, Plato observed that when the Greeks of his time fought other Greeks, 'they quarrel as those who intend someday to be reconciled'. As a result

> they will not devastate Hellas, nor will they burn houses, nor ever suppose that the whole population of a city—men, women, and children—are equally their enemies, for they know that the guilt of a war is always confined to a few persons and that the many are their friends.[16]

In stark contrast, when the ancient Greeks faced the Barbarians, they would tend to fight with greater savagery and ruthlessness, and to pay less regard to the distinction between combatants and non-combatants. According to Anthony Coates, this was due precisely to the 'fundamental Otherness' of the Barbarians, which served to weaken the self-restraint that Greek warriors would show in battle against other Greeks, whom they perceived to be 'by nature friends'.[17]

---

[15] Anthony J. Coates, 'Culture, the Enemy and the Moral Restraint of War', in Richard Sorabji and David Rodin (eds.), *The Ethics of War: Shared Problems in Different Traditions*, Aldershot: Ashgate, 2006, pp. 213–14.

[16] Quoted in Coates, 'Culture, the Enemy and the Moral Restraint of War', p. 212.

[17] Coates, 'Culture, the Enemy and the Moral Restraint of War', p. 212.

With these admittedly cursory observations made I am prepared to submit the following: If a foreign invader succeeds in deposing our appointed leaders and imposing his own rule, we should expect to be mistreated, oppressed, and neglected, because to the conqueror we are 'other'. Of course, this is not guaranteed to happen, but there is reason to anticipate that it will, and we should never be surprised when it does. I do not think this is particularly controversial. The victims of foreign aggression and occupation can reasonably assume that there will be ongoing violations of their human rights, over and above any loss of communal self-definition.

I do not mean to suggest that these are the only reasons for the general antipathy towards foreign occupation. I do, however, think that these are the only unequivocally good reasons. For some readers, perhaps, the mere prospect of being governed by persons who are not members of their own national/cultural group will be deeply disagreeable in and of itself, independently of whether it is likely to result in any further undesirable consequences. I am not so sure that this kind of groundless aversion to rule by foreign nationals is sensible and justified. On the other hand, the fact that such rule predictably leads to a loss of communal self-definition, oppressive government, and ongoing human rights abuses, is clearly a good reason for objecting to it.

Next, I want argue that when a society's military stages a coup against the civilian authorities, the citizens of that society can reasonably expect these same results.

The Civil–Military Gap

Conscription is gradually being consigned to history. A standing army of professional volunteers is the new norm. In one way, this represents moral progress—the end of forced labour as an arrangement for national defence. Professionalization comes at a cost, however.

Where conscription is properly implemented, the armed forces should come to mirror society demographically—we should expect to find people of all races, religions, and economic classes serving, roughly in proportion to their numbers in the general population. This has the effect of 'infusing familiarity' with the military across all sectors of society.[18] Furthermore, insofar as conscripts return to civilian life once hostilities cease, they are less likely to end up feeling detached from their parent society. The conscript arrangement thus produces 'citizen-soldiers': combatants who see themselves as part of the community they serve, and who are accepted as such by that community.[19] Where there is a professional standing army, by contrast, the military and civilian worlds tend to drift apart. Journalist Arthur Hadley once called this 'The Great Divorce'.[20] Sociologists today usually call it the 'civil-military gap'. It can be broken down into several components, which tend to be mutually reinforcing.[21]

There is a *demographic* gap, meaning that the military fails to reflect the composition of its parent society in the way just described. (For example, in the US only 13 per cent of military personnel identify as Democrats, whereas in the general population Democrats slightly outnumber Republicans. Only 15 per cent of the US military is female, compared to half the civilian population).[22] Second, there is a *policy preference gap*. Again, take the United States. Military elites there generally believe that the armed forces should only be used to protect the nation and its interests, whereas civilian elites have a greater appetite for peacekeeping and humanitarian operations. Then there is what Rahbek-Clemmensen et al. call an *institutional* gap, referring to a lack of meaningful interaction—and sometimes antagonism—between the military establishment and other powerful social institutions, such as the media, civilian courts, and universities.[23] Finally, and most importantly for our purposes, there is a *cultural* gap: civilian and military populations develop different (and often incompatible) sets of values, ideologies, and attitudes.

---

[18] Linn K. Desaulniers, 'The Gap That Will Not Close: Civil-Military Relations and the All-Volunteer Force', *Master of Military Studies, US Marine Corps Command and Staff College*, 4 May 2009, p. 5, available at: http://www.dtic.mil/dtic/tr/fulltext/u2/a513806.pdf.

[19] See Cheyney Ryan, *The Chickenhawk Syndrome: War, Sacrifice, and Personal Responsibility*, Lanham, MD: Rowman and Littlefield, 2009, especially chapter 2: 'The Rise and Fall of the Citizen-Soldier; or, Bye Bye, Elvis'.

[20] Arthur Hadley, *The Straw Giant*, New York: Random House, 1986, p. 274.

[21] Here I am following Jon Rahbek-Clemmensen, Emerald M. Archer, John Barr, Aaron Belkin, Mario Guerrero, Cameron Hall, and Katie E. O. Swain, 'Conceptualizing the Civil-Military Gap: A Research Note', *Armed Forces and Society*, vol. 38, no. 4, 2012, pp. 669–78.

[22] Rahbek-Clemmensen et al., 'Conceptualizing the Civil-Military Gap', p. 673.

[23] Rahbek-Clemmensen et al., 'Conceptualizing the Civil-Military Gap', p. 673.

The cultural gap is especially pronounced in liberal-democratic societies, and that should come as no surprise. As Richard Kohn writes, 'the military is, by necessity, among the least democratic institutions in human experience; martial customs and procedures clash by nature with individual freedom and liberty'.[24] This is why Richard Wrona Jr. uses words like 'inherent' and 'insurmountable' to describe the ideological differences between liberal-democratic civil society and the military.[25] A society organized around military values and principles, Wrona thinks, cannot be liberal-democratic, while a military organized around liberal-democratic values cannot be effective. Samuel Huntington is of much the same view. Hence, in *The Soldier and the State*, he warns against any 'fusionist' program aimed at imbuing the military with the norms of its parent (liberal) society, arguing that this threatens to undermine operational effectiveness. We should not be trying to close the civil-military gap on this view; we should be doing what we can to accommodate it. To say that the military has a right to be different does not go far enough. The military *needs* to be culturally different from liberal society, to competently perform the functions that justify its existence in the first place.[26]

Note that a cultural gap between soldiers and civilians does not mean that the two groups share no values whatsoever. As we will see in Chapter 5, as long as a permanent military establishment is present, some of the values that are cultivated in it, and celebrated by it, are bound to spill over into civilian society and its institutions. This causes problems of a different kind, and I will have more to say about this later in the book. For the time being, the cultural gap can be understood as referring simply to the distance between the collectivist and conservative values of the military, and the individualist, liberal values that usually prevail among the masses in democratic countries.

There is mounting evidence that some such gap exists in most liberal-democratic states. In France, the values upheld by the military—sacrifice,

[24] Quoted in Deane-Peter Baker, 'Civil-Military Relations', in Deane-Peter Baker (ed.), *Key Concepts in Military Ethics*, handbook, Sydney: UNSW Press, 2015, p. 45.

[25] Richard M. Wrona Jr., 'A Dangerous Separation: The Schism between the American Society and Its Military', *World Affairs*, vol. 169, no. 1, Summer 2006, pp. 31 and 26.

[26] Samuel P. Huntington, *The Soldier and the State: The Theory and Politics of Civil-Military Relations*, Cambridge, MA: Harvard University Press, 1957.

patriotism, civic duty, order, and discipline—are ranked *least* important by the civilian population. The civilians value human rights, justice, and individual freedom above all else.[27] In South Africa, military officers are much more likely than civilians to insist that traditionalism, love of country, and comradeship be taught in schools.[28] In Germany, the self-conceptions of military personnel are intimately bound up with their nation-state, while civilians there are more cosmopolitan; they identify as members of the world community (or Europe at least).[29] Hew Strachan has published on the civil-military gap in Britain;[30] Margaret Daly Hayes has investigated its manifestation across Latin America and the Caribbean;[31] and there is an abundance of literature on the United States.[32]

It is worth adding that there are a number of trends currently underway in many of these countries that are only likely to reinforce, and may even have the effect of widening, the civil-military gap over the coming decades.

One is privatization. Increasingly it is private corporations that are being tasked with servicing and repairing military hardware, staffing mess halls, and so on. The result is that fewer uniformed military personnel than ever before are serving in occupations that have civilian equivalents. Soldiers are specializing in military activities, and cultivating military skills that are not readily transferrable to the civilian sector.[33] This could not only deepen the isolation of soldiers from civilian society,

---

[27] Pascal Vennesson, 'Civil-Military Relations in France: Is There a Gap?', *Journal of Strategic Studies*, vol. 26, no. 2, 2003, pp. 37–8.

[28] Lindy Heinecken, Richard Gueli, and Ariane Neethling, 'Defence, Democracy and South Africa's Civil-Military Gap', *Scientia Militaria: South African Journal of Military Studies*, vol. 33, no. 1, 2005, p. 124.

[29] Sabine Collmer, 'The Cultural Gap between the Military and the Parent Society: The German Case', in Giuseppe Caforio and Gerhard Kümmel (ed.) *Military Missions and their Implications Reconsidered: The Aftermath of September 11th* (Contributions to Conflict Management, Peace Economics and Development, Volume 2), Bingley: Emerald Group Publishing Limited, 2006, p. 122.

[30] Hew Strachan, 'The Civil-Military "Gap" in Britain', *Journal of Strategic Studies*, vol. 26, no. 2, 2003, pp. 43–63.

[31] Margaret Daly Hayes, *Addressing the Civil-Military Gap in Latin America and the Caribbean*, PhD Dissertation, Centre for Hemispheric Defense Studies, 2008.

[32] A study by Andrew Scobell of the RAND Corporation also suggests that there are 'significant differences' between the values and attitudes of Chinese soldiers and civilians. Andrew Scobell, 'Is There A Civil-Military Gap in China's Peaceful Rise?', *Parameters*, vol. XXXIX, no. 2, Summer 2009, p. 6.

[33] Thomas E. Ricks, 'The Widening Gap between Military and Society', *The Atlantic*, July 1997, available at: www.theatlantic.com/magazine/archive/1997/07/the-widening-gap-between-military-and-society/306158/.

but also prolong it, by impeding veteran reintegration into civilian industries and economies after their discharge. Another factor exacerbating the cultural gap is physical separation. Due to security concerns, military establishments are usually closed to the public, and it is increasingly difficult for visitors to gain access. This limits opportunities for interaction between the armed services and the societies they attach to.

Third, militaries are increasingly engaged in counter-insurgency, counter-terrorism and peacekeeping operations, all of which 'put a premium on the skill and self-reliance of the small patrol'. The effect, according to Hew Strachan, is to 'entrench the values of the group, the section or platoon, as the bedrock of morale', strengthening the sense of distinctiveness felt by military personnel.[34] Fourth, continuous postings to different locations make it difficult for military personnel and their families to ever become firmly embedded in a local civilian community.[35] Finally, the notion that being a professional soldier means being politically neutral can lead to a general disengagement from the concerns that preoccupy the wider public.[36] A student at the Royal Military College in Canada admitted to one of its researchers that she did not understand this 'politics thing', did not think it relevant, and had no intentions of ever voting in her country's democratic elections.[37]

None of this is to say that we are completely powerless to resist the widening of the gap, or that we can do nothing at all to counteract it. Christopher Dandeker argues that some civilian norms can be accommodated by the military without any loss of operational effectiveness. Some can even be 'embraced with enthusiasm' he reckons.[38] The zero-tolerance attitudes towards bullying and harassment, found in most civilian workplaces nowadays, are offered up as one example. Still, Dandeker is adamant that other liberal values are 'divergent from military requirements' and must be resisted lest the armed forces become impotent. He concentrates curiously on the full integration of women,

[34] Strachan, 'The Civil-Military "Gap" in Britain', pp. 47–8.
[35] Strachan, 'The Civil-Military "Gap" in Britain', p. 53.
[36] Strachan, 'The Civil-Military "Gap" in Britain', pp. 53–4.
[37] Quoted in Donna Winslow, 'Canadian Society and its Army', *Canadian Military Journal*, Winter 2003–2004, p. 19, available at: http://www.journal.forces.gc.ca/vo4/no4/doc/military-socio-eng.pdf
[38] Christopher Dandeker, 'On the Need to be Different: Military Uniqueness and Civil-Military Relations in Modern Society', *The RUSI Journal*, vol. 146, no. 3, 2001, pp. 4–9.

but also mentions in passing the adoption of individualistic principles that threaten to 'erode the value of military self-sacrifice at the core of fighting the spirit'.[39]

Civilian society can also work to reduce the gap from its end, by culturally assimilating to its armed forces. Huntington seems to recommend something along these lines. 'Today America can learn more from West Point than West Point from America [...] If the civilians permit the soldiers to adhere to the military standard, the nations themselves may eventually find redemption and security in making that standard their own.'[40] In a liberal country, however, the scope for any such cultural assimilation is decidedly limited. That is because there are certain normative commitments that *define* liberal societies—the commitment to equal rights and protections, for example. This is not a mere preference; it is an identity-grounding aspiration, in the sense that we could not abandon the project of realizing equal rights while still properly calling ourselves 'liberal'.[41] Any cultural assimilation of a liberal society to its military of the kind Huntington recommends must take place within the parameters set by the defining normative commitments of that society.

The upshot, to put it crudely, is that as long as we want our civilian society to remain liberal, and our military to remain effective, there will be a cultural gap between them that cannot be fully closed.

Warrior-Class Consciousness

The cultural gap discussed above tends to give rise to what we might call *warrior-class consciousness*. This is where soldiers come to think of themselves as a distinct caste within society. Over time, the feeling of being separate can mutate into feelings of alienation, contempt, and even hostility towards the civilian 'other'.

American journalist Thomas Ricks found evidence of this among US Marines in the 1990s; he described it as their 'private loathing for public

[39] Dandeker, 'On the Need to be Different', p. 9.
[40] Huntington, *The Soldier and the State*, p. 466.
[41] Shmuel Nili, 'Integrity, Personal and Political', *Journal of Politics*, vol. 80, no. 2, 2018, p. 433.

America'.[42] Even after a relatively short period of time in the service, Ricks observed that some Marines started looking at old non-military friends and colleagues with a certain disdain and avoiding social encounters with them.[43] The contempt can extend to spouses and other family members too. We see this in the popular military comic strip *Terminal Lance*, created by a former US Marine. Comic #56 depicts a 'creature of lore' called 'Dependapotamus'. The caption reads: 'Much like a tick or leach, the creature will engorge itself into gluttony through the benefits and steady paychecks offered by the unsuspecting Marine.' The cartoon depicts a soldier's wife sitting idly on the couch nagging him about his next promotion, while the infant children amuse themselves nearby.[44] The contempt for civilian society even comes through in some of the official literature. One edition of *General Military Subjects*—a textbook used to train US recruits—states that the job of the drill sergeant is to undo 'eighteen years of cumulative selfishness and Me-ism'.[45]

According to Ricks, what makes public America so despicable in the eyes of the Marines is the set of values it upholds: individualism, hedonism, and consumerism. These values are not only different from the Marine corps' values of unity, self-discipline, and sacrifice; they are contradictory sets. Retired US Admiral Stanley Arthur observes that, consequently, 'more and more, enlisted [men and women] as well as officers are beginning to feel that they are special, better than the society they serve'.[46] Major Linn Desaulniers notices this too. He suggests that the dedication to selfless service underlies a perception among US military men and women that they are of 'a higher calibre' than the people they are meant to be protecting.[47] Carl Forsling, a former US Marine, recently coined the term 'veteran superiority complex' to describe this phenomenon.[48] Union boss Eugene Debs, writing over a

---

[42] Ricks, 'The Widening Gap'.

[43] Ole R. Holsti looks at the empirical evidence supporting Ricks's claims. See 'A Widening Gap Between the US Military and Civilian Society? Some Evidence, 1976–96', *International Security*, vol. 23, no. 3, Winter 1998–99, pp. 5–42.

[44] See https://terminallance.com/2010/08/06/terminal-lance-56-myths-and-legends-ii-the-dependapotamus/, last accessed January 2020.

[45] Quoted in Ricks, 'The Widening Gap'.

[46] Quoted in Ricks, 'The Widening Gap'.   [47] Desaulniers, 'The Gap', p. 22.

[48] Carl Forsling, 'Selfless Service and the Veteran Superiority Complex', *Task and Purpose*, 28 March 2019, available at: https://taskandpurpose.com/vet-superiority-complex.

century ago, memorably lampooned West Point for producing graduates afflicted with some such condition:

> It has long been known that the influence of West Point upon society has been vicious in the extreme. As a general proposition, the graduates of that institution are insufferable snobs. They have the idea drilled into them that they constitute a ruling class. They are supported off the earnings of the people, and acquire a strut and swagger indicative of feelings of superiority...West Point annually inflicts upon the country a horde of these gold-lace parasites...[49]

These feelings of superiority do not appear to be confined to American military professionals. Strachan finds much the same thing among the British armed force. Its members are said to 'see civilians as venerating individualism over cohesion, as mentally soft and physically feeble, and as expecting the armed forces to incorporate personnel policies wholly inappropriate to fighting formations'.[50] This expectation breeds resentment. Not only are civilians seen as having detestable values; they are accused of interfering with the military and endangering its members by trying to impose those values on the armed forces, which leads to my next point.

Class-conscious soldiers tend to see civilians as 'other', and sometimes lesser. But they can even come to think of civilians as a kind of *enemy*.

When we talk about the character of a nation or political community, we might simply mean the traits and values that happen to be predominant among its present members. But that is not the only way to think of it. An alternative view attributes to nations some true essence—a 'permanent spiritual structure'—that is independent of the values and attitudes of living members.[51] When a proponent of the first view describes Australia as compassionate, what he means is that Australian people, and/or our leaders, generally show compassion. When a proponent of the latter view says that Australia is compassionate, he means that

---

[49] Eugene V. Debs, 'Standing Armies', *Locomotive Firemen's Magazine*, vol. 9, no. 8, August 1885, pp. 471–3.
[50] Strachan, 'The Civil-Military "Gap" in Britain', p. 43.
[51] Edward Luttwak, *Coup d'État: A Practical Handbook*, Revised Edition, Cambridge, MA: Harvard University Press, 2016, p. 9.

compassion is part of the 'Aussie spirit', or something along those lines. Importantly, this latter view makes it conceptually possible for a nation to have values that are not shared by its members. If most Australians become cold-hearted, on this view, that does not mean that Australia is no longer compassionate. It just means that most Australians have somehow become un-Australian.

Where there is a cultural gap, military personnel will often regard their values as being not only better than, but also *truer to*, their country's real essence. A Quantico survey with US lieutenants revealed that a large majority of them—81 per cent—believe that military values are more in line with those of the Founding Fathers than are the values of America's civilian society.[52] Similarly, the Spanish army has long regarded itself as the keeper of the 'essential Spain', bound to protect it against the government and, if necessary, the Spanish people.[53] This kind of thinking can transform the civilian population into a kind of enemy. No longer are civilians simply 'other' and of 'lower calibre'; they also threaten the spiritual structure of their country by leading it away from its true values.

At the beginning of this chapter I argued that foreign occupation is an evil for two reasons. It typically results in a lack of 'fit' between the rulers and the ruled, or a loss of communal self-definition, and there are usually ongoing human rights abuses. The loss of communal self-definition is to be expected because of the cultural differences that are bound to exist between the conquering regime and the native population it subdues. And the human rights abuses are to be expected because of the 'othering' that such cultural differences give rise to. Over the last two sections I have suggested that, where there is a civil-military gap, soldiers and civilians belonging to the same polity will also be culturally divided, and the former can also come to regard the latter as 'other', lesser, and sometimes dangerous. The same predictors of alienation and oppression are in place. Given this, I submit that citizens should take the risk of a coup seriously for largely the same reasons that they already take the risk of foreign occupation seriously. In either event, the likely result for the people is a government that violates their rights, and one whose values do not align with their own.

---

[52] Ricks, 'The Widening Gap'.   [53] Luttwak, *Coup d'État*, p. 9.

Co-nationality and the Human Responses

At this point one might interject that even if the cultural gap does result in military personnel 'othering' their civilian counterparts in the way that I have described, there will still be a recognition of shared nationality at least, and this will keep the human responses of coup-makers partially engaged vis-à-vis the civilian population. On the other hand, since foreign invaders do not even belong to the same national/political group as the subdued natives, the 'othering' will run deeper in this case. As a result, foreign occupiers can be expected to treat their subjects *worse* than coup-makers normally would. This line of reply concedes that military regimes that come to power via coup will probably engage in oppression, but it says that the oppression of foreign aggressors is likely to be more severe. Hence there is good reason for us to take greater precautions against the latter, even if that means increased exposure to the former.

All I can say in response is that history gives little or no support to the idea that co-nationality inhibits oppression and human rights abuses in the way that this suggests.

The military dictatorship that ruled Brazil from 1964 to 1985 used arbitrary arrest, imprisonment without trial, torture, rape, and castration to repress political opponents.[54] In Chile under Augusto Pinochet's military dictatorship, thousands of people were tortured, executed, and 'disappeared'. In Argentina, up to 30,000 people are estimated to have been killed or tortured by the military junta that came to power in 1976, after a successful coup against Isabel Person. The targets were people suspected of having left-wing views. This included not only militants and guerrillas, but also many young students, trade unionists, writers, jour-nalists, artists, and even a couple of nuns.[55] Pregnant women were

[54] Archdiocese of São Paulo, *Torture in Brazil*, Austin, TX: University of Texas Press, 1998. Dilma Rousseff—a former Marxist who would become Brazil's president in 2011—was among the victims.Jonathan Watts, 'Brazil President Weeps as she Unveils Report on Military Dictatorship's Abuses', *The Guardian*, 11 December 2014, available at: https://www.theguardian.com/world/2014/dec/10/brazil-president-weeps-report-military-dictatorship-abuses.

[55] Alfonso Daniels, 'Argentina's Dirty War: The Museum of Horrors', *The Telegraph*, 17 May 2008, available at: https://www.telegraph.co.uk/culture/3673470/Argentinas-dirty-war-the-museum-of-horrors.html; 'Former Argentine Junta Officers Held', *Al Jazeera*, 26 July 2003, available at: https://www.aljazeera.com/archive/2003/07/20084915434437332.html; 'France

apparently spared, until they gave birth. Then they were killed and their children given over to childless military families.[56] The Indonesian military, with the help of vigilantes, is estimated to have killed *at least* half a million of its own citizens in the space of a year or so, between 1965 and 1966. A CIA report from later that decade described it as 'one of the worst mass murders of the 20th Century'.[57] Others were detained in a vast network of prisons and concentration camps, where they faced extraordinarily inhumane conditions.[58] Many died from malnutrition and beatings after a short period in detention. Once again, suspected communists and communist sympathizers were the targets.

These are the very worst kinds of human rights abuses imaginable, and yet in all of these cases the victims belonged to the same national/political group as the military personnel that persecuted them. They were not racially or ethnically other, but they were culturally and ideologically other, and this was enough to silence the human responses that might otherwise have inhibited interpersonal cruelty. Perceptions of shared nationality with the military did nothing to protect the citizens from the atrocities. I see no reason, then, to assume that the severity of human rights abuses under military rule will vary depending on whether the military is *ours* or *theirs*. Any such assumption can only be an article of faith.

Nowhere is 'Coup-proof'

The conclusion this brings us to is that, *if the two events are equally likely to transpire*, a domestic coup and a foreign invasion are equally serious

---

Demands Argentine Extradition', *BBC News*, 26 July 2003, available at: http://news.bbc.co.uk/2/hi/americas/3098031.stm.

[56] Uki Goñi, 'How an Argentinian Man Learned His "Father" May Have Killed his Real Parents', *The Guardian*, 22 July 2016, available at: https://www.theguardian.com/world/2016/jul/22/argentinian-stolen-baby-guillermo-perez-roisinblit.

[57] Quoted in David F. Schmitz, *The United States and Right Wing Dictatorships*, Cambridge: Cambridge University Press, 2006, p. 48.

[58] Mark Aarons, 'Justice Betrayed: Post-1945 Responses to Genocide', in David A. Blumenthal and Timothy L. H. McCormack (eds), *The Legacy of Nuremberg: Civilising Influence or Institutionalised Vengeance?*, Leiden and Boston, MA: Martinus Nijhoff Publishers, 2007, p. 80.

threats to the citizens of a polity, since both events can be expected to undermine communal self-definition and the enjoyment of human rights. Needless to say, however, the probabilities might not be equal. Sometimes the likelihood of a domestic coup happening will be substantially lower than the likelihood of a foreign attack, in which case the citizens of the polity in question obviously have less reason to worry about it. But I think it would be a mistake for citizens anywhere to assume that they—simply on account of some structural feature of their society, like its democratic institutions— have *no* reason to worry about a coup, as if such features can make their polity completely coup-proof.[59]

If a country is liberal and democratic, this does mitigate the risk of a coup in several ways.[60] First, those who wish to contest the authority of the current regime in a democracy have formally established, peaceful channels through which to do so, and so coup-making is unnecessary. Second, unlike some authoritarian regimes, democratic governments do not routinely conduct purges against military personnel. Members of the military establishment will consequently tend to feel more secure within the democratic status quo, reducing any motivation to disturb it. Third, democratic governments generally enjoy greater 'legitimacy' in the sociological sense of the word. That is, their right to promulgate and enforce laws tends to be more widely accepted. The result is that coups against democratic governments are less likely to attract and retain the support of people outside of the military. This reduces a coup's prospect of success and thereby weakens the incentive to even try it.[61] Finally, in long-established or 'consolidated' democracies at least, the values and norms of the political system are internalized by most people, including those in the armed forces. Once this point is reached, 'the idea of changing government by means of a coup becomes a distant, unimaginable option for political actors'.[62]

As recent events in democratic Turkey (2016), Thailand (2014), Mali (2012), and Honduras (2009) show, however, this guarantees nothing.

---

[59] 'Fundamentally zero' is how Desaulniers describes the chance of a military coup against the US government. 'The Gap', p. 27.

[60] For a full analysis of these, see Curtis Bell, 'Coup d'État and Democracy', *Comparative Political Studies*, vol. 49, no. 9, 2016, pp. 1167–200.

[61] Taeko Hiroi and Sawa Omori elaborate on this point in 'Causes and Triggers of Coups d'État: An Event History Analysis', *Politics and Policy*, vol. 41, no. 1, 2013, p. 42.

[62] Hiroi and Omori, 'Causes and Triggers', p. 45.

Curtis Bell offers an interesting explanation for the surprisingly regular occurrence of coups in democratic countries. The argument, roughly, is that while democratic institutions might reduce the likelihood of a coup in some ways, as outlined above, in other ways democracy actually increases the probability of a coup, and according to Bell the latter factors largely neutralize or cancel out the former.

As noted, democratic governments are less likely than autocracies to purge military elites or to arrest members of the armed forces pre-emptively in anticipation of a challenge.[63] This weakens the motivation to coup, since the military feels less insecure. On the other hand, however, *precisely because* democratic states are unlikely to subject military personnel to these repressive behaviours, if a coup plot were to materialize, it is less likely to be contested or foiled. This *increases* the incentive to coup. Bell therefore concludes that 'democratic constraints have contradictory effects on plotter interests', and consequently democracies are not inherently any less coup-prone than non-democracies.[64] The chances of a coup being *attempted* are roughly the same, and the chances of a coup *succeeding* are actually higher in a democracy—twice as likely in fact, according to Bell.

Edward Luttwak's classic *Coup D'état: A Practical Handbook* is enduringly insightful in this connection. Luttwack's central premise is that when political participation is confined to a small fraction of a population, that society is especially coup-prone.[65] The explanation Luttwak offers is that a politically inactive/indifferent population is unlikely to resist coup-makers, while a politically engaged population probably would. Where only a small elite have political voice, Luttwak writes:

---

[63] Democratic governments are also less likely to engage in 'stacking' and the creation of 'cohesion obstacles' to prevent the services from launching a coordinated domestic intervention. Such strategies may reduce the likelihood of a coup, but they also reduce a military's ability to rebuff external aggressors. Stacking often means failing to appoint the most competent and qualified people to military posts, and service fractionalization impedes not only coup-making, but also effective war-making against outside threats. Democratic governments are less likely to do these things because they are more vulnerable to being politically punished for the loss of military effectiveness that coup-proofing can entail. Ulrich Pilster and Tobias Bohmelt, 'Do Democracies Engage Less in Coup Proofing? On the Relationship Between Regime Type and Civil-Military Relations', *Foreign Policy Analysis*, vol. 8, 2012, p. 358.

[64] Curtis Bell, 'Coup d'État and Democracy', p. 1175.

[65] Luttwak, *Coup d'État*, p. 26.

the masses recognise this and accept the elite's monopoly of power; unless some unbearable exaction leads to desperate revolt, they will accept its policies. *Equally, they will accept a change in government, whether legal or otherwise.* After all, it is merely another lot of 'them' taking over...This lack of reaction from the people is all the coup needs to stay in power.[66]

Now insofar as democracy is defined by mass involvement in the political process, this might seem to imply that democracies are impervious to coup events. But Luttwak stresses that this does not follow. While democratic institutions might *enable* mass political engagement, they do not always guarantee it. Sometimes apathy and inertia can grip the people of even the most mature democracies. When that happens, Luttwak admits, these societies, too, become vulnerable to military take-over. He offers the example of the Algiers putsch of 1958, when a group of senior military figures attempted to topple the elected government of France. But there have been several examples, before that and since then, of coup attempts in democratic states. Indeed, by one count, three out of every four failures of democracy are the result of a successful coup d'état.[67] Marinov and Goemans go so far as to say that 'coup d'état has been (and still is) *the single most important* factor leading to the downfall of democratic governments'.[68]

Luttwak identifies 'economic backwardness' as another coup pre-condition. By this he means underdevelopment and the deprivations that accompany it. The argument is that economically advanced states are less coup-prone for roughly the same reason that mature democracies are: their citizens are politically engaged and therefore will not stand for it. In poor countries, by contrast, where 'the general condition of the population is characterised by disease, illiteracy, high birth and death rates, and periodic hunger', people tend to be too preoccupied to be politically active.[69] Their response to a coup will accordingly be more subdued, and this is favourable to coup-makers. Empirical research

---

[66] Luttwak, *Coup d'État*, p. 24.
[67] N. Marinov and H. Goemans, 'Coups and Democracy', *British Journal of Political Science*, vol. 44, no. 4, 2013, p. 801.
[68] Marinov and Goemans, 'Coups and Democracy', p. 799.
[69] Luttwak, *Coup d'État*, p. 21.

confirms what Luttwack says: economic development is inversely correlated to the risk of a coup. One study suggests that coups are twenty-one times more likely in the poorest countries than in the richest.[70]

Again, however, this does not guarantee anything. Even the richest countries can suffer economic shocks and experience periods of macroeconomic deterioration, leading to runaway inflation or spiralling unemployment. (Indeed such episodes are guaranteed from time to time under capitalism, according to proponents of the 'boom-and-bust' theory.) Luttwak acknowledges that economically advanced states can become coup-prone when things of this nature happen. 'While the political structures of all highly developed countries may seem too resilient to make them suitable targets', he writes, 'if acute enough, even temporary factors can weaken them fatally.'[71] Consider Turkey again. It is a founding member of the OECD, a member of the G20, and has the world's thirteenth largest GDP by purchasing power parity, not to mention thirty-eight billionaires living in Istanbul alone. The World Bank classifies it as an 'upper-middle income country'—hardly an 'economically backward' place. Yet this was not enough to prevent the coup attempt of 2016.

What goes for democracy and economic prosperity, goes for any other feature of a society that one cares to identify: it can mitigate the risk of a military coup, but not eliminate it entirely. 'Brutus'—the American Anti-federalist mentioned in the introduction of this book—understood this. His detractors, like many citizens of economically advanced democracies today, dismissed the prospect of a coup as something that only ever happens to *other* people in *other* countries. Brutus saw this for the short-sighted hubris that it was. He credited the military officers of his time as being true patriots that would not dream of a coup against the civilian authorities. But then he asked:

[A]re we to expect that this will always be the case? Are we so much better than the people of other ages and of other countries, that the same allurements of power and greatness, which led them aside from their duty, will have no influence upon men in our country? Such an idea, is wild and extravagant [...] [T]he passion for pomp, power and

---

[70] Hiroi and Omori, 'Causes and Triggers', pp. 39–64.   [71] Luttwak, *Coup d'État*, p. 18.

greatness, works as powerfully in the hearts of many of our better sort, as it ever did in any country under heaven.[72]

Conclusion

I have argued that the citizens of a militarized polity should take the threat of a coup seriously for largely the same reasons that they take the threat of foreign aggression and occupation seriously: they can reasonably assume that if it were ever to happen, it would undermine their communal self-definition and their enjoyment of human rights.

This conclusion is particularly significant, I think, in countries where the likelihood of a coup is as high, or higher, than the likelihood of a foreign invasion. In these extremely coup-prone states, maintaining a military involves spending lots of public money to make the public no more secure. The threat of alien, oppressive rule is not ameliorated; the source of the threat is simply relocated from outside national boundaries to within. In places like this, militarization is relevantly similar to private gun ownership. The need to protect oneself and one's family from violent intruders is often cited as a justification for keeping firearms in the home. The trouble is that guns purchased to defend families from outsiders are statistically more likely to end up being used by one family member against another, or for suicide.[73] This clearly tells against the standard prudential rationale for gun ownership. The same goes for where the risk of a military coup exceeds the risk of foreign aggression; the solution is worse than the problem.

Even where a coup is significantly less likely than a foreign invasion, however, there is always some risk of it, and this is surely something that needs to be factored into a community's assessment of whether to maintain the status quo, reduce the size of its military establishment, or dismantle that establishment entirely.

---

[72] One might suppose that a coup in the United States today, even if it were attempted, would be bound to fail. But not everybody agrees. See Luke Foster Middup, 'Thinking the Unthinkable: Could There Be a Military Coup in the US?', *The Conversation*, 7 September 2017.

[73] Andrew Anglemyer, Tara Horvath, and George W. Rutherford, 'The Accessibility of Firearms and Risk for Suicide and Homicide Victimization Among Household Members: A Systematic Review and Meta-analysis', *Annals of Internal Medicine*, vol. 160, no. 2, 2014, pp. 101–10.

3

On Fear-Induced Aggression

Introduction

An intuitive argument in favour of standing armies appeals to the idea of deterrence. If we have a military, then we have the means to impose costs of death and destruction on any foreign aggressor who would dare to attack our country. Any such attack is therefore less likely to be worth it for our adversaries, since whatever benefits they expect to reap from their aggression will come at a very high price (compared to the price they would pay in the absence of armed retaliation from our side). This line of argument says that by having armed forces at the ready we discourage our enemies from trying anything untoward, thereby reducing the chances of us ever needing to deploy those forces in the first place. For some thinkers this makes militarization not only sensible, but morally obligatory. Alan Dowd, for instance, says that in a world of 'violent regimes and vicious men', it would be 'criminal', 'sinful', 'inhumane', and 'unchristian' for a state to forego a military deterrent.[1]

Needless to say, though, deterrence is not guaranteed. Even if we are very heavily militarized, a foreign adversary might still attack us because he fails to appreciate just how costly that will be for him. Or, he might accurately forecast the costs, but judge that they are worth sustaining given the considerable benefits on offer. Alternatively, an adversary might recognize that the material benefit-to-cost ratio of an attack is unfavourable, but decide to attack us *anyway*, because he is motivated by non-material considerations like honour, glory, anger, resentment, or some ideological conviction. According to prominent critics of deterrence theory, such as Richard Ned Lebow, it is a mistake to assume that

[1] Alan W. Dowd, 'Shield and Sword: The Case for Military Deterrence', *Providence: A Journal of Christianity and American Foreign Policy*, Fall 2015, pp. 65, 67.

Ethics, Security, and The War-Machine: The True Cost of the Military. Ned Dobos, Oxford University Press (2020). © Ned Dobos.
DOI: 10.1093/oso/9780198860518.001.0001

states are purely rational calculators of material costs and benefits. Emotions play an important role in international relations, just as they do in domestic life.[2]

Worse still, deterrence can sometimes *backfire*. That is, our military can unintentionally provoke the very behaviour that it is meant to forestall.[3] The fundamental problem is that an institution with the means to fend off foreign threats to its own parent society usually also has the means to attack others. This can make those others suspicious, fearful, or even paranoid for their own safety. As Robert Jervis puts it, 'what one state regards as insurance, the adversary will see as encirclement'.[4] In the grip of such fear, militarized state A might come to the view that inaction vis-à-vis militarized neighbour B would be prohibitively risky, and that a first strike against B would therefore be the most prudent course to take. Thus Lebow argues that when we are dealing with 'vulnerable' adversaries—states that are motivated primarily by fear—rather than 'greedy' adversaries that 'seek opportunities to make gains and pounce when they find them', military deterrence is not only pointless but *dangerous*.[5] It intensifies the fear of the adversary, and with it his temptation to strike first.

What this reveals is that militarization involves a kind of trade-off. If we have a military, then other states have less to gain by attacking us, since they will pay a heavy price for doing so. But if we have a military, then other states might also feel that they have more to *lose* by *not* attacking us. The result is that states armed with militaries are less likely to find themselves on the receiving end of 'greedy' or 'opportunistic' aggression, but more likely to find themselves on the receiving end of 'defensive aggression', motivated by fear and feelings of vulnerability. With non-militarized states the trade-off is reversed. The present chapter elaborates on the risk of fear-induced aggression that accompanies

---

[2] Richard Ned Lebow and Janice Gross Stein, 'Rational Deterrence Theory: I Think, Therefore I Deter', *World Politics*, vol. 41, no. 2, January 1989, pp. 209–24.

[3] Richard Ned Lebow, 'Deterrence: A Political and Psychological Critique', in R.N. Lebow (ed.), *Richard Ned Lebow: Key Texts in Political Psychology and International Relations Theory*, Basel: Springer, 2016, section 2.3. See also Michael J. Mazarr, 'Understanding Deterrence', Santa Monica, CA: Rand Corporation, 2018, available at: https://www.rand.org/pubs/perspectives/PE295.html, last accessed November 2018.

[4] Robert Jervis, *Perception and Misperception in International Politics*, Princeton, NJ: Princeton University Press, 1976, p. 64.

[5] Lebow, 'Deterrence: A Political and Psychological Critique', p. 4.

militarization, and argues that certain trends in international relations threaten to exacerbate this danger in the years ahead.

Reciprocal Fear of Surprise Attack

A few years ago researchers in Japan designed an incentivized behavioural experiment to test whether people have any proclivity towards 'defensive aggression'.[6] They called it the Pre-emptive Strike Game (henceforth PSG). Players are paired up, and each is given a red button and a certain amount of money to start with (¥1500). If neither player presses his/her button after one minute, both retain the full endowment. On the other hand if a player does press his/her button, he/she loses ¥100, while the other player loses significantly more—¥1000. At that point the second player's button is deactivated so there is no opportunity for retaliation. Thirty-two participants took part in the experiment. Sixteen of them (50 per cent) pressed their red button, almost always within the first few seconds. The most obvious explanation is that these players were motivated by fear. Even though pressing the button was costly to them, inaction carried the risk of a loss ten times greater. They pushed the button to protect themselves against the worst-case scenario of their counterparty beating them to it and thus depriving them of ¥1000. Nir Halevy explains: 'although neither party has an incentive to launch a surprise attack, they each fear the other's fear, a reciprocal process that gives rise to suspicion, anxiety, and ultimately, defensive aggression'.[7]

At this point one might interject that fear is not the only possible explanation. Perhaps some of the players pushed their button out of spite, or a desire to dominate, or just for fun? To test this hypothesis, the researchers ran a modified version of the game with a unilateral rather than a bilateral condition. In the original bilateral version both players have a red button, while in the unilateral version only one player has a

[6] Dora Simunovic, Nobuhiro Mifune, and Toshio Yamagishi, 'Pre-emptive Strike: An Experimental Study of Fear-Based Aggression', *Journal of Experimental Social Psychology*, vol. 49, no. 6, November 2013, pp. 1120–3.
[7] Nir Halevy, 'Preemptive Strikes: Fear, Hope, and Defensive Aggression', *Journal of Personality and Social Psychology*, vol. 112, no. 2, 2017, p. 225.

button. Here the 'powerful player' (the one with the button) has absolutely nothing to be afraid of—his counterparty lacks the ability to impose costs on him. If the powerful player strikes, therefore, it must be out of hatred or spite or some other motive. The researchers explain: 'this manipulation rids the "powerful player" of a reason to anticipate an aggressive action from his/her opponent and, as a result, provides no reason for this player to act out of self-defense'.[8] In this version of the game, only one of the thirty-two participants decided to push the button, and it happened in the last ten seconds of the experiment. What this suggests is that in the original bilateral version of the PSG, fear is indeed the primary motivator. Most first strikes in the game are instances of anticipatory 'defensive aggression', rather than spiteful, hateful, or 'predatory' aggression.[9]

In the PSG, no player has any reason to believe that any other player is hostile towards him. There is no bad blood among the participants; they do not belong to different social/cultural groups; and they do not have opportunities to provoke and antagonize one another in advance. And yet, in the original version, the participants are fearful enough of being 'attacked' by the other button-wielding players that they strike first half of the time. This fear is not generated by anything the other players say or do, or by their appearances or demeanours, or by any other personal characteristics of theirs. The fear of the other players is due simply to their possession of red buttons that can be used to impose costs. Only those without red buttons are invulnerable to fear-induced defensive aggression.

Military establishments are the big red buttons of the international system.

Depending on their training, organization, logistical arrangements, patterns of troop deployment, operational tactics, and so on, some military forces will be better prepared for offensive expeditionary wars, while others will be optimized for territorial defence. In the former case the military 'posture' of the state is offensive, while in the latter it is

---

[8] Nir Halevy, 'Preemptive Strikes', p. 1121.
[9] See also Robert Böhm, Hannes Rusch, and Özgür Gürerk, 'What Makes People Go To War? Defensive Intentions Motivate Retaliatory and Preemptive Intergroup Aggression', *Evolution and Human Behavior*, vol. 37, 2016, pp. 29–34.

defensive.[10] Even states with defensive postures, though, will still have some offensive *capabilities*. This is partly because military weapons normally have dual uses. As Shiping Tang writes, insofar as most of the items in any arsenal can be employed for both offensive and defensive purposes, even a peace-loving security-seeking state 'will *necessarily* deploy offensive weapons and capabilities'.[11] Admittedly there may be some weapons, such as surface-to-air missiles, that are purely defensive, but no arsenal consists entirely of these.

That being the case, no existing military establishment on Earth is a so-called 'non-offensive defence' institution. This term is used by Bjørn Møller to describe any military that completely lacks offensive capabilities, and that is therefore incapable of aggression against other states. Whether 'non-offensive defence' is feasible, and whether it is an attractive ideal worth aspiring towards, are not questions that I intend to take up here. I am merely pointing out that military organizations *as we know them* are not structurally incapable of aggression, and so there is no such thing as a non-offensive defence establishment in the real world. Even states with the most defensive postures wield offensive capabilities.[12]

The result is a classic security dilemma: by building militaries for their own security, states contribute to the *in*security of others. Lord Grey, the former British foreign secretary, described the dynamics especially well:

> The increase of armaments, that is intended in each nation to produce a consciousness of strength, and a sense of security, does not produce these effects. On the contrary, it produces a consciousness of the strength of other nations and a sense of fear. Fear begets suspicion and distrust and evil imaginings of all sorts, till each government feels it would be criminal and a betrayal of its own country not to take every precaution, while every Government regards every precaution of every other Government as evidence of hostile intent.[13]

---

[10] Shiping Tang, 'Offence-Defence Theory: Towards a Definitive Understanding', *The Chinese Journal of International Politics*, vol. 3, 2010, p. 223.

[11] Shiping Tang, 'Offence-Defence Theory', p. 223; emphasis added.

[12] Bjørn Møller, 'Common Security and Non-Offensive Defence as Guidelines for Defence Planning and Arms Control?', *International Journal of Peace Studies*, vol. 1, no. 2, July 1996, pp. 47, 51.

[13] Quoted in Robert Jervis, *Perception and Misperception*, p. 65.

There are two important claims in this passage. The first is that militarization creates fear. The second is that this fear henceforth warps perceptions of state behaviour. If we fear an agent, we tend to read hostile intent into his innocent and otherwise innocuous conduct. (Imagine if players in the PSG could observe their counterparties servicing and tuning their red buttons, or adding extensions that allowed their buttons to be pushed more quickly, or from multiple different locations). These 'evil imaginings' ramp up the fear and suspicion even more, which leads to further arms acquisition, which creates more fear, and so on in a spiral.

If worst comes to worst, the spiral terminates in one state attacking another not out of hatred or greed or expansionist ambitions, but because it is worried about being attacked itself if it waits: defensive aggression. In Thomas Schelling's words, the 'reciprocal fear of surprise attack' leads to surprise attacks.[14] Rousseau thought that most conflicts start this way:

> ... everyone, having no guarantee that he can avoid war, is anxious to begin it at the moment which suits his own interest and so forestall a neighbour, who would not fail to forestall the attack in his turn at any moment favourable to himself, so that many wars, even offensive wars, are rather in the nature of unjust precautions for the protection of the assailant's own possessions than a device for seizing those of others.[15]

In international relations defensive aggression goes by the name 'preventive war', and there has been plenty of it through history. A.J.P. Taylor goes so far as to suggest that, between 1848 and 1918, '*every* war between Great Powers started as a preventive war, not a war of conquest'.[16] Paul Shroeder says 'preventive wars, even risky preventive wars, are not extreme anomalies in politics...They are normal, even common, tools of statecraft.'[17] Strategic theorist Colin Gray agrees: 'Far from being a

[14] Thomas C. Schelling, *The Strategy of Conflict*, Cambridge, MA: Harvard University Press, 1960, p. 207.
[15] Jean Jacques Rousseau, *A Lasting Peace through the Federation of Europe*, C.E. Vaughan (trans.), London: Constable, 1917, pp. 78–9.
[16] Quoted in Jack S. Levy, 'Declining Power and the Preventive Motivation for War', *World Politics*, vol. 40, no. 1, October 1987, p. 84.
[17] Quoted in Levy, 'Declining Power and the Preventive Motivation for War', p. 84.

rare and awful crime against an historical norm, preventive war is, and has always been, so common, that its occurrence seems remarkable only to those who do not know their history.'[18]

Preventive Wars

The most recent example of preventive war was the US-led invasion of Iraq in 2003. Although there was no reason to believe that Saddam Hussein was preparing an attack on the United States or its allies, the prospect that he might do some day, or that he might supply WMDs to terrorists who would carry out such an attack, created a 'compelling case' for 'anticipatory action to defend ourselves' according to George W. Bush. The president used the language of 'pre-emption' in his justification for the invasion, but insofar as the point was to neutralize an incipient threat before it could be fully formed, rather than to defend against an imminent Iraqi attack, the war was preventive, rather than pre-emptive, properly speaking.[19]

The US is no stranger to preventive strikes, of course. It was on the receiving end in 1941. Worried about Japan's expansionist ambitions, the US Pacific Fleet—which had been stationed on the West Coast of the country—was forwarded to an 'advanced' position at Pearl Harbor, Hawaii. In Japan, this heightened fears that the Americans would attempt to interfere with the Empire's conquest of the Dutch East Indies and its oil fields. To prevent this from happening, the Japanese launched a surprise attack on the re-positioned fleet. The hope was to cripple the US navy, and thus ensure that Japan could continue to pursue its interests in the region unmolested.[20] Again, the strike was not a reaction to evidence of an imminent American attack. It was based on suspicions

[18] Colin S. Gray, *The Implications of Preemptive and Preventive War Doctrines: A Reconsideration*, Strategic Studies Research Institute, US Army War College, July 2007, p. 27.

[19] Charles W. Kegley Jr. and Gregory A. Raymond, 'Preventive War and Permissive Normative Order', *International Studies Perspectives*, vol. 4, 2003, pp. 385–94.

[20] There were, of course, other considerations in play. The point is just that the surprise attack on Pearl Harbor was, at least in part, preventively motivated. See Jules Lobel, 'Preventive War and the Lessons of History', *University of Pittsburgh Law Review*, vol. 68, 2006, pp. 307–40.

of what the US might choose to do with its naval forces at some point in the future.[21]

These are the clearest examples in living memory, but preventive wars date back much further. Indeed we can find examples going back to ancient times. Take the third Punic war (149–146 BC). Carthage was experiencing an economic resurgence at the time, making Rome paranoid that its old foe would soon regain its former strength, that its ambitions would grow in step with its military capabilities, and that this would eventually lead to an attempted conquest of Rome. So worried was Cato the Elder that he ended every speech to the Roman senate with the signoff: 'Carthage must be destroyed!' Rome eventually heeded Cato's advice and annihilated Carthage in an unprovoked attack.[22]

The 'granddaddy of all preventive wars', in the words of Barry Strauss, was the second Peloponnesian War between Athens and Sparta (431–404 BC).[23] Hostilities between the two Greek city-states had been high for a long time, and there were a number of unresolved disputes between them. However as Thucydides points out in his history of the event, this is not ultimately what motivated Sparta's decision to strike first. Rather, the worry was that Athens would become militarily undefeatable before too long, as it was growing more powerful by the day. This created a sense among the Spartans that it was now or never; that delay would guarantee defeat in any future conflict. So Sparta waged war not in retaliation for an Athenian attack, or in anticipation of an intended attack, but to prevent a merely possible future threat from ever materializing.

In each of these cases an attack occurred not *despite* the fact that the target was militarized, but *because* it was militarized. The target's war-making potential helped provoke what it was meant to deter.

To be sure, in each case there were aggravating factors in play that made defensive aggression more likely than it might otherwise have been. In Iraq there were obviously historical enmities between the US

---

[21] This is why Robert Kennedy dismissed the proposal for a preventive attack on Cuban missile bases as 'Pearl Harbor in reverse'. See Arthur Schlesinger, Jr., 'Unilateral Preventive War: Illegitimate and Immoral', *Los Angeles Times*, 21 August 2002.

[22] Kegley Jr. and Raymond, 'Preventive War and Permissive Normative Order', p. 388.

[23] Barry Strauss, 'Preemptive Strikes and Preventive Wars: A Historian's Perspective', *Strategika*, no. 44, August 2017, available at: https://www.hoover.org/research/preemptive-strikes-and-preventive-wars-historians-perspective, last accessed 20 November 2018.

and Saddam Hussein's Ba'ath regime, as well as Hussein's alleged ties to terrorist groups. In the case of Pearl Harbour the movement of the US Pacific Fleet into an advanced position intensified Japanese fears. In the ancient examples, the dominant power felt threatened by a rising challenger, and came to the view that it would be better to fight *now*, under relatively favourable conditions, rather than wait for the adversary to become the dominant power and fight *then*. A rapidly changing power differential contributed to the outbreak of war.

It is important to emphasize, however, that the risk of provoking defensive aggression exists independently of such contingencies. In the original PSG game, every player is at risk of suffering a fear-based preventive attack because (1) He/she has access to a red button that can be used to impose costs on others; and (2) those others cannot be completely certain that the red button will not be used against them first. By the same token, every militarized state bears some risk of being preventively attacked out of fear simply in virtue of its wielding offensive capabilities, together with the fact that its motives are not completely transparent to outsiders. The risk of fear-induced aggression is a function of having a military in an international environment where, to quote John Mearsheimer, 'intentions are impossible to divine with 100 percent certainty'.[24] Other factors might influence the likelihood of the risk materializing, no doubt, but the risk precedes these variables.

Having said that, today fear-induced aggression does not happen nearly as often as we might expect. In the PSG, fear leads to a first strike *half of the time*; every player with a red button faces a 50/50 chance of being targeted in a preventive strike. If states behaved like this, there would be a lot more preventive war. So why isn't there? Indeed, while defensive aggression may have been common once upon a time, it seems to be increasingly rare. Today, Andrew Kydd observes, anticipatory wars 'almost never happen'.[25] What accounts for this?

Here is not the place to attempt a definitive answer, but there are probably several factors that mitigate the danger of defensive aggression among states. The most obvious is the potential for retaliation. Recall

---

[24] John Mearsheimer, *The Tragedy of Great Power Politics*, New York: W.W. Norton, 2001, p. 31.

[25] Andrew Kydd, 'Sheep in Sheep's Clothing: Why Security Seekers Do Not Fight Each Other', *Security Studies*, vol. 7, no. 1, 1997, p. 148.

that in the PSG, once a player strikes, her counterparty's red button is immediately deactivated so there can be no retribution. Suppose instead that built into the game was an indeterminate probability that the counterparty would be able to retaliate, and that this would impose some indeterminate cost on the first striker. In this case, it is plausible to suppose that some of the players who did push their red buttons out of fear would have refrained, for fear of the possibility of revenge. The existence of second-strike capabilities would likely have deterred at least some of the first strikes. We can extrapolate to international relations, and say that since militarized states normally have some second-strike capabilities they are somewhat less likely to be attacked by fearful defensive aggressors compared to players in the original PSG.

But this is not the only factor that explains why there are relatively few preventive wars nowadays. States also form alliances and partnerships, enter into treaties, and establish economic ties. These relationships counteract the fears that might otherwise accompany the build-up of military capabilities. Further, states can and do reveal their peaceful motives to one another in various ways, which reduces fears and uncertainties among them. In the PSG, while players have no opportunity to antagonize one another, they have no opportunity to *reassure* one another of their benign intentions either. States, by contrast, can communicate their peaceful intentions through the use of 'costly signals'— that is, by doing things that aggressive states would not be willing to mimic. For instance, a peaceful security-seeking state might unilaterally reduce the size of its expeditionary forces.[26] This would compromise its ability to conquer other states or annex their territory, and that is precisely the point. By acting in a way that is inconsistent with successful aggression, the state credibly signals to others that it is not aggressive. Signalling operates on the logic that 'if discreet types take different actions, then observers can infer the actor's type from its actions'.[27] Militarized states can credibly demonstrate to others that they are not greedy by doing things that greedy actors never would, such as sacrifice

[26] This is but one way of signalling benign intentions through military policy. Others are discussed in Charles L. Glaser, 'The Security Dilemma Revisited', *World Politics*, vol. 50, no. 1, October 1997, pp. 178–81.

[27] Evan Braden Montgomery, 'Breaking Out of the Security Dilemma: Realism, Reassurance, and the Problem of Uncertainty', *International Security*, vol. 31, no. 2, Fall 2006, p. 158.

concrete military advantages. This can allay the fears of adversaries, and with that reduce the likelihood of provoking fear-based aggression.[28]

We can add that international norms play an important role in tempering the resort to preventive force as a means of self-protection. Norms are 'inter-subjectively shared understandings about the obligations of international actors to behave in specified ways'.[29] They express collective expectations of what is and what is not acceptable in international relations. Since the end of the Second World War the prevailing norm in relation to the preventive use of military force has been unequivocally against it. The UN Charter prohibits the unilateral use of force in all cases except where it is a response to, or where it is taken in anticipation of, an imminent military attack. There is no allowance for the use of force as a way of neutralizing merely possible future threats before they emerge. In other words *reactive* and *pre-emptive* uses of force are allowed, but *preventive* ones are absolutely not.

I suspect that some combination of these factors (signals, relationships, second strike capabilities, and norms) explains why preventive aggression is relatively rare at the international level, compared to in the PSG game, despite the existence of so many red buttons globally.[30] If this is correct, then we have all the more reason to be concerned about a number of recent developments, like the erosion of international partnerships and withdrawals from treaties, and the increasingly combative rhetoric coming from some world leaders. But especially worrying, I think, is the gradual weakening of the norm prohibiting defensive aggression or preventive war.

A New Normative Order?

The United States once championed the norm against preventive military action. Harry Truman labelled preventive war 'the weapon of

---

[28] For more on reassurance see Janice Gross Stein, 'Reassurance in International Conflict Management', *Political Science Quarterly*, vol. 106, no. 3, Autumn 1991, pp. 431–51; and Montgomery, 'Breaking out of the Security Dilemma', pp. 151–85.

[29] Kegley Jr. and Raymond, 'Preventive War and Permissive Normative Order', p. 390.

[30] There may be other factors besides these. Kydd argues that the transparency of democratic politics helps to ensure that security-seeking democratic states are not mistakenly perceived as aggressive or threatening. Kydd, 'Sheep in Sheep's Clothing'.

dictators, not of free democratic countries'. Dwight Eisenhower's National Security Strategy stressed that 'the United States and its allies must reject the concept of preventive war'. The Secretary of State under Eisenhower, John Foster Dulles, said of preventive war that 'it is wholly out of the question as far as the United States is concerned', and that it 'never will be any part of United States foreign policy'.[31] After the 9/11 terrorist attacks, however, things started to change. The National Security Strategy of the Bush administration stated that 'the United States can no longer rely on a reactive posture as we have in the past ... we cannot let our enemies strike first'.[32]

The preventive war against Iraq was initiated shortly thereafter. Despite his opposition to that war, President Obama maintained the course on the policy used to justify it. As the Council of Foreign Relations recognised, Obama's 2010 National Security Strategy did discard some aspects of the Bush strategy it supplanted, but the right to use preventive force unilaterally was not one of them.[33] So far there are no signs that the Trump administration will be reversing this position. Vice President Mike Pence told the UN Security Council not so long ago that 'all options are on the table' in relation to the North Korean threat: 'we are going to achieve the end of a denuclearization of the Korean peninsula—*one way or the other*'.[34]

As Charles Kegley and Gregory Raymond point out, 'when the reigning hegemon promotes a new code of conduct, it alters the normative frame of reference for virtually everyone else. In an anarchical system, what the strongest do eventually shapes what others do.'[35] It should come as no surprise, then, that states less powerful than the US increasingly seem to be following its lead and opening up to the idea of using military force to prevent distant dangers from gathering.

---

[31] All quoted in Kerstin Fisk and Jennifer M. Ramos, 'Introduction: The Preventive Force Continuum', in K. Fisk and J.M. Ramos (eds.), *Preventive Force: Drones, Targeted Killing, and the Transformation of Contemporary Warfare*, New York: NYU Press, 2016, p. 6.

[32] The National Security Strategy of the United States of America, September 2002, p. 15, available at: http://www.state.gov/documents/organization/63562.pdf, last accessed October 2018.

[33] Kerstin Fisk and Jennifer M. Ramos, 'Actions Speak Louder Than Words: Preventive Self-Defense as a Cascading Norm', *International Studies Perspectives*, vol. 15, 2014, p. 169.

[34] Peter Beinart, 'How America Shed the Taboo Against Preventive War', *The Atlantic*, 21 April 2017.

[35] Kegley Jr. and Raymond, 'Preventive War and Permissive Normative Order', p. 391.

A few weeks after the release of the Bush administration's National Security Strategy in 2002, the Indian finance minister stated that 'every nation has that right. It is not the prerogative of any one country. Pre-emption is the right of any nation to prevent injury to itself'. The following year India's foreign minister said that 'India has a much better case to go for pre-emptive action against Pakistan than the US has in Iraq'.[36] In reply, Pakistan's information minister insisted that 'it is India which is a fit case for pre-emptive strikes—there is ample proof that India possesses biological, chemical or other weapons of mass destruction'.[37] In 2003 Russia's defence minister was quoted as saying that 'we cannot absolutely rule out preventive use of force if Russia's interests or its obligations as an ally require it'.[38] Then in 2008 the Russian military's Chief of Staff added that, if it was deemed necessary to defend the country, 'military forces will be used, including preventively, including with the use of nuclear weapons'.[39]

Perhaps even more astonishingly, in 2004 the UN's High Level Panel on Threats, Challenges and Change—which was created by Kofi Annan two years earlier—published a report containing the following passage:

> In the world of the twenty-first century, the international community does have to be concerned about nightmare scenarios combining terrorists, weapons of mass destruction, and irresponsible states and much more besides, which may conceivably justify the use of force, *not just reactively but preventively and before a latent threat becomes imminent.*[40]

It is also telling in this connection that many states are now investing in unmanned aerial vehicles that are equipped for combat, not just for surveillance and reconnaissance. In 2003 only the US, UK, and Israel

---

[36] Fisk and Ramos, 'Actions Speak Louder', p. 173.
[37] Peter Dombrowski and Rodger A. Payne, 'The Emerging Consensus for Preventive War', *Survival*, vol. 48, no. 2, 2006, p. 120.
[38] Dombrowski and Payne, 'The Emerging Consensus for Preventive War', p. 119.
[39] Fisk and Ramos, 'Actions Speak Louder', p. 176.
[40] Report of the High-Level Panel on Threats, Challenges, and Change, *A More Secure World: Our Shared Responsibility*, New York: United Nations, 2004, para. 191, emphasis added.

had weaponized drones. By May 2018 over two *dozen* countries had acquired them.[41] The US regularly uses these technologies for surgical strikes and targeted killings, but it is not the only one. Nigeria, for instance, deployed an armed UAV to bomb a logistics base allegedly used by Boko Haram in 2016.[42]

The reason this is germane to our discussion is that drone strikes are usually justified using a distinctly preventive logic. Targets are often selected on the basis of their 'patterns of life'—proximity to terrorists, possession of weapons, visitation of militant compounds—not necessarily on the basis of credible evidence that they are preparing an imminent attack. Such strikes are clearly preventive, not pre-emptive: the targets are people who might potentially commit violent acts at some point in the future, rather than people who are about to, or who are in the process of, carrying out an attack.[43] Indeed, many of those targeted by US drone strikes over the years have been low-level operatives who, according to Peter Bergen's testimony before Congress, 'do not have the capacity to plot effectively against the United States'.[44] When asked about such targeted killings in Yemen, a senior American intelligence official explained that the individuals selected were usually 'rising stars': 'They may not be big names now,' the official said, 'but these were the guys that would have been future leaders.'[45] In other words, these individuals are being singled out not so much because of who they are, but because of who they might one day become.

Of course the mere fact that a state acquires weaponized drones is not conclusive evidence that it intends to use them preventively in this way,

---

[41] Peter Bergen, David Sterman, Alyssa Sims, Albert Ford, and Christopher Mellon, 'The World of Drones', *New America*, 15 March 2017, section 3, available at: www.newamerica.org/in-depth/world-of-drones/3-who-has-what-countries-armed-drones/, last accessed November 2018.

[42] Clay Dillow, 'All of These Countries Now Have Armed Drones', *Fortune*, 12 February 2016, available at: http://fortune.com/2016/02/12/these-countries-have-armed-drones/, last accessed October 2018. Other countries have indicated an intention to do similar things with these technologies. A senior Indian politician was quoted telling a news agency that 'India cannot be denied the rights that the US has, including that of surgical strikes'. Fisk and Ramos, 'Actions Speak Louder', p. 174.

[43] Fisk and Ramos, 'Actions Speak Louder', pp. 169–72.

[44] Peter Bergen, 'Drone Wars: The Constitutional and Counterterrorism Implications of Targeted Killing', Testimony presented before the U.S. Senate Committee on the Judiciary, Subcommittee on the Constitution, Civil Rights and Human Rights, 23 April 2013, available at: www.judiciary.senate.gov/download/testimony-of-bergen-pdf, last accessed November 2018.

[45] Eric Schmitt, 'Embassies Open, but Yemen Stays on Terror Watch', *New York Times*, 11 August 2013.

or that it accepts preventive strikes as legitimate. But insofar as these technologies are ideally suited for such strikes, it is reasonable to infer from their acquisition a greater tolerance for preventive uses of force. As Fisk and Ramos say:

> While drones are not inherently designed for preventive self-defense, states' cost–benefit calculations regarding the options available for this purpose certainly lean towards drones as the weapon of choice, as they offer a trifecta of capabilities: precision, reconnaissance, and surveillance.[46]

Finally, it is worth highlighting that preventive logic has even found its way into the debate around humanitarian intervention and the responsibility to protect.

The standard altruistic justification for humanitarian intervention says that, if foreign nationals are being violently persecuted by their own government, we (the international community) have a right or even a moral duty to come to their rescue. This line of justification sometimes encounters what I, and others, have called an 'internal' objection.[47] This objection says that a purely altruistic intervention violates the rights of the people who pay for it: both the taxpayers of the intervening state, who finance it, and the soldiers who sacrifice or endanger their lives prosecuting it on the ground. The argument, roughly, is that citizens empower their government and entrust it with their resources, and soldiers risk their lives for the government, so that it might promote national interests, *not* so that it might defend the rights of foreigners. Therefore, any purely altruistic intervention breaches the terms of the social contract. At the time of Operation Restore Hope in Somalia, Samuel Huntington was famously quoted opining that 'it is morally unjustifiable and politically indefensible that members of the [US] armed forces should be killed to prevent Somalis from killing

---

[46] Fisk and Ramos, 'Actions Speak Louder', pp. 167–8.
[47] Ned Dobos, 'On Altruistic War and National Responsibility: Justifying Humanitarian Intervention to Soldiers and Taxpayers', *Ethical Theory and Moral Practice*, vol. 13, no. 1, 2010, pp. 19–31; Ned Dobos, *Insurrection and Intervention: The Two Faces of Sovereignty*, Cambridge: Cambridge University Press, 2012, chapter 5; Allen Buchanan, 'The Internal Legitimacy of Humanitarian Intervention', *Journal of Political Philosophy*, vol. 7, no. 1, 1999, pp. 71–87.

one another'.[48] On this view, in order for a humanitarian intervention to be consistent with the intervening state's responsibilities to its own people, the intervention must have some coinciding national security or national interest rationale.

Following the September 11 attacks, politicians started playing up this very rationale for the humanitarian operations being conducted by their states. They started alluding to the fact that failed states like Afghanistan—characterized by poverty and widespread human rights abuses—are a breeding ground for terrorists. This increasingly became part of the justification offered for humanitarian missions: we need to intervene not only to protect foreign nationals from their abusive governments, but also to ensure that those foreign nationals do not become radicalized and turn into our enemies in the future.[49] In 2013, long after he left office, former British Prime Minister Tony Blair made a case for intervention into Syria that relied on this very reasoning. 'We have collectively to understand the consequences of wringing our hands instead of putting them to work', Blair said. 'People wince at the thought of intervention. But contemplate the future consequence of inaction [in Syria] and shudder [...] a breeding ground of extremism infinitely more dangerous than Afghanistan in the 1990s'.[50] This is an unmistakably preventive rationale for humanitarian intervention. It suggests that putting a stop to atrocities beyond our borders is justified because it will keep us safer in the long term, not by thwarting our enemies before they acquire the means to attack us, but by preventing people from becoming our enemies in the first place.

Taken together, all this strongly suggests that a new norm regarding preventive military action has entered into the second phase of its evolution.

According to Martha Finnemore and Kathryn Sikkink, there are three distinct stages in the 'life cycle' of an international norm.[51] First, a 'norm

[48] Quoted in Nicholas J. Wheeler, *Saving Strangers: Humanitarian Intervention in International Society*, Oxford: Oxford University Press 2000, p. 31.

[49] Nicholas J. Wheeler, 'Humanitarian Intervention after September 11, 2001', in Anthony F. Lang Jr. (ed.), *Just Intervention*, Washington, DC: Georgetown University Press, 2003, p. 193.

[50] Melanie Hall, 'Tony Blair: Military Intervention in Syria Vital to Prevent "Breeding Ground for Extremism"', *The Telegraph*, 27 August 2013, available at: https://www.telegraph.co.uk/news/uknews/10267283/Tony-Blair-military-intervention-in-Syria-vital-to-prevent-breeding-ground-for-extremism.html, last accessed June 2018.

[51] Martha Finnemore and Kathryn Sikkink, 'International Norm Dynamics and Political Change', *International Organization*, vol. 52, no. 4, 1998, pp. 997–17.

entrepreneur' introduces it into the discourse, where it contests the prevailing order. This is what the Bush administration achieved with its National Security Strategy and the preventive strike on Iraq: it reopened a debate that the international community had long considered to be closed. If a norm withstands this initial period of contestation, the next stage of its life cycle is to 'cascade' or diffuse—that is, to spread to other players in the international arena and win their assent or endorsement. We are now seeing preliminary signs of this.[52] If the process continues unabated, the restrictive norm that prohibited preventive attacks in the twentieth century may come to be supplanted by a more permissive one. We cannot know for certain what the effect of this will be, but we can say that it would lift one powerful constraint on the preventive use of force that has helped keep the international system from degenerating into a Pre-emptive Strike Game writ large. Plausibly, if 'defensive aggression' becomes legitimized, we should expect to see more of it.[53]

Conclusion

In *Leviathan* Thomas Hobbes identifies three main causes of war. The first is 'competition', or what contemporary International Relations scholars sometimes call 'greed'. This covers wars waged to acquire land or resources—*'other men's persons, wives, children and cattle'*. The second cause of war is 'diffidence', by which Hobbes appears to mean mistrust and insecurity. The third cause is 'glory', or a desire for respect and recognition. Hobbes explains: 'The first [cause] maketh men invade for gain; the second for safety; and the third for reputation.'[54]

A state armed with a large military is probably less likely to become a victim of 'competitive' or opportunistic aggression, since it has the means to thwart and punish attempts on its territory or resources. To that

---

[52] Fisk and Ramos thus suggest that preventive military force is 'becoming part of the normative fabric of the international system'. Fisk and Ramos, 'Introduction: The Preventive Force Continuum', p. 15.

[53] David Luban, 'Preventive War', *Philosophy and Public Affairs*, vol. 32, no. 3, Summer 2004, pp. 227–8.

[54] Thomas Hobbes, *Leviathan*, CB Macpherson (ed.), London: Penguin Classics, 1985, chapter 13, p. 185.

extent, armed forces can be said to deter competitive attacks. When it comes to aggression motivated by diffidence, however, the opposite is true. A state does not decrease its risk of suffering such attacks by militarizing. On the contrary, insofar as a country's armed forces are usually the main source of its adversaries' insecurities, the armed forces are more likely to provoke than to forestall aggression based on diffidence. If a state wants to reduce its chances of coming under a fear-based defensive attack, the best thing it can do is deactivate or destroy its red button so to say, and abolish the military.

What this reveals is that a military's contribution to the security of its parent society is not unequivocally positive. There is a trade-off involved. It might be likened to open carrying a firearm into a gathering where some people are homicidal bandits, and others are paranoid schizophrenics. Both groups pose a threat, but they have different triggering conditions. The visibility of your firearm might rule you out as a target for the first group, but it simultaneously makes you a target for the second group; the more they fear you, the more likely they are to attack you. Openly displaying the means to use lethal force against these individuals increases their safety concerns, and with it the probability of their resorting to violence first. International society is like this gathering; some states are 'greedy' while others are 'vulnerable'. By keeping a military we might deter the former, but we also risk provoking the latter. Thankfully, international norms against the use of preventive force have limited the instances of fear-induced defensive aggression over the last century. That is why the abrasion of these norms today is especially worrying.

4

Cognitive Bias and the Misuse of Military Power

Introduction

The last two chapters focussed on the risks that a political community takes just by having a military establishment attached to it: the military might attack instead of protecting us, or it might provoke a foreign power to attack us, instead of deterring it. There is another danger, however, which is that our military will be *overused,* meaning that its deployment will not be confined to the prosecution of 'just wars' and interventions. As mentioned in the introduction to this book, this is one of the enduring worries of Japan's anti-militarists. They do not deny that circumstances might arise where the JSDF could wage a just war. They simply do not trust the JSDF to wage *only* these.

In what follows I argue that all militaries are prone to overuse, not just those with particular histories, cultures, and international entanglements. My contention is that some unjust wars are bound to be mistakenly perceived as just by our political decision makers, not because of the unique pressures they face, or because they are morally deranged, or because they are ignorant of the facts, but simply because they carry the same unconscious biases as the rest of us. Each section introduces a different bias and illustrates how it could lead a morally motivated decision maker to a faulty conclusion. If I am right about this, then the risk of a military being overused is not limited to societies whose political elites are hawkish warmongers, self-serving careerists, or whatever. We can fully expect that even 'decent' governments, genuinely committed to never waging unjust wars, will wage them sometimes. The risk of military misuse, then, is more intractable than is often supposed. It cannot be

Ethics, Security, and The War-Machine: The True Cost of the Military. Ned Dobos, Oxford University Press (2020).
© Ned Dobos.
DOI: 10.1093/oso/9780198860518.001.0001

managed simply by ensuring that war-making potential does not fall into the 'wrong hands'.

Before proceeding I should lay bare a few assumptions. I will be assuming that a predictably futile war is an unjust war. This is where there is no reasonable prospect of success, such that the horrors of war are unleashed to no end. I will also be assuming that an unnecessary war is an unjust war. This is where recourse to war is taken before feasible non-violent alternatives have been exhausted. Finally, I will be assuming that an otherwise just war can be rendered disproportional, and therefore unjust, by the expectation of excessive civilian casualties.

Admittedly, all of these assumptions are contested. There are different schools of thought within the Western just war tradition (traditionalist, revisionist)[1]; then there are non-Western variants of just war thinking (Islamic, Confucian); and some philosophers eschew the just war framework entirely in favour of a simpler approach to the moral evaluation of armed conflict (i.e. utilitarianism).[2] Given this, it is hardly surprising that unanimous agreement on any one point relating to the ethics of war is so rare. Having said that, I expect most readers will share my minimalist assumptions about futile, unnecessary, and disproportional wars being unjust.

Overconfidence and Reasonable Prospects of Success

While history provides us with some examples of states going to war fully cognizant that the odds were against them, it provides a great many more examples of states going to war confident of a victory that would either never come, or come at a far greater cost than anticipated.

Alfred Vagst notes that 'with only a few exceptions, the wars of the century from 1815 to 1914 were undertaken with each side believing that

---

[1] For an overview see Seth Lazar, 'Just War Theory: Traditionalists vs. Revisionists', *Annual Review of Political Science*, vol. 20, 2017, pp. 37–54; and James Pattison, 'The Case for the Non-ideal Morality of War: Beyond Revisionism versus Traditionalism in Just War Theory', *Political Theory*, vol. 46, no. 2, 2018, pp. 242–68.

[2] William H. Shaw, 'Utilitarianism and Recourse to War', *Utilitas*, vol. 23, no. 4, 2011, pp. 380–41.

it would win'.[3] This includes the First World War. Historian Geoffrey Blainey observes that all parties to it were certain that success would come quickly and easily. 'While German generals predicted that within six weeks of the outbreak of war their vanguard would be near Paris, many French generals predicted that their soldiers would be at or across the Rhine.'[4] The Russians were equally confident; so much so that they saw nothing imprudent about spreading their forces thin to enable an attack on Germany and Austria simultaneously.[5] Over in the UK, Viscount Esher commented that British high-society 'mostly look upon the war as a sort of picnic'. This rubbed off on the Viscount himself it seems: on 5 August 1914 he declared that 'unless the Kaiser possessed the talents of Napoleon, he is done a month hence when Russia advances'.[6] That same month, as German troops left for battle, the Kaiser assured them: 'you will be home before the leaves have fallen from the trees', while one of his generals stated matter-of-factly: 'In two weeks we shall defeat France, then we shall turn round, defeat Russia and then we shall march to the Balkans and establish order there.'[7]

Fast-forward to the most recent war in Iraq and again we find inflated assessments of the prospect of success. The London *Times* described US Secretary of Defence Donald Rumsfeld as having 'Teflon-like irrepressible confidence'.[8] Rumsfeld's assistant Ken Adelman predicted that the war would be 'a cakewalk' for the US and its allies.[9] After this proved false, Adelman scratched his head in *Vanity Fair*: 'I just presumed that what I considered to be the most competent National Security team since Truman was indeed going to be competent.'[10] In *The New Yorker* Adelman wondered 'How could this happen to someone [Rumsfeld] so good, so competent?'[11] Former chairman of the Joint Chiefs of Staff, General John Shalikashvili, admitted that the planning for post-war Iraq was based on 'the most rosy predictions', including that the US would be

[3] Quoted in Dominic Johnson, *Overconfidence and War: The Havoc and Glory of Positive Illusions*, Cambridge, MA: Harvard University Press, 2004, p. 3.
[4] Quoted in Johnson, *Overconfidence and War*, p. 67.
[5] Johnson, *Overconfidence and War*, p. 68.
[6] Johnson, *Overconfidence and War*, pp. 69–70.
[7] Johnson, *Overconfidence and War*, pp. 71–2.
[8] Johnson, *Overconfidence and War*, p. 203.
[9] Ken Adelman, 'Cakewalk in Iraq', *The Washington Post*, 13 February 2002, p. A27.
[10] David Rose, 'Neo Culpa', *Vanity Fair*, 5 December 2006.
[11] Jeffrey Goldberg, 'The End of the Affair', *The New Yorker*, 20 November 2006.

welcomed by the Iraqi people, that any resistance would peter out quickly, and that former Iraqi soldiers would willingly provide security.[12]

There are many possible explanations for these overoptimistic forecasts: faulty intelligence, trust in divine providence, wilful ignorance, mental disorder, etc. But there is another plausible explanation, more charitable to the parties involved, which is that even decent, well-adjusted people tend to be more confident than is objectively justified. Dominic Johnson summarizes the findings of experimental psychology:

> People consistently overrate various individual qualities such as their health, leadership ability, professional competence, sporting ability, and ethics. People tend to see themselves as better than others with respect to intelligence, attractiveness, fairness, or skill ... People tend to think they are more likely than others to have gifted children, get a good first job, and do well on future tasks, and that they will be happier, more confident, more hardworking, and less lonely in the future than their peers.[13]

Some of the statistics are striking. Ninety-four per cent of college professors believe they do 'above-average work'. Only 2 per cent of people believe that they have 'below average' leadership abilities. Twenty-five per cent of people place themselves in the top 1 per cent in terms of their ability to get along with others. We also underestimate the likelihood of bad things happenings to us—everything from car accidents, to crime, illness, earthquakes, depression, and unwanted pregnancy.[14]

Far from signalling a defective mind, Johnson suggests that overconfidence signals an adaptive one. The bias towards excessive optimism, Johnson argues, 'conferred significant advantages in our ancestral environment and therefore was selected for in our evolution'.[15] The story goes roughly like this: Our overconfident ancestors were more likely to actively pursue advantages than our under-confident ones; they would seize opportunities that the others tended to forego. Sometimes this would yield losses, but sometimes it would yield gains, and in the long

---

[12] Johnson, *Overconfidence and War*, p. 209.
[13] Johnson, *Overconfidence and War*, pp. 18–9.
[14] Johnson, *Overconfidence and War*, pp. 19–20.
[15] Johnson, *Overconfidence and War*, p. 5.

run the gains tended to outweigh the losses. The result is that over-optimistic types fared better in our evolutionary history—they had a greater chance of survival and reproduction. This is why overconfidence is so ubiquitous today according to Johnson, even though it might not serve the inhabitants of the modern world in the same way that it served past people. As Steve Yetiv puts it, overconfidence is 'a psychological holdover—a cognitive appendix—from an earlier period in human history'.[16]

Some researchers suggest that overconfidence tends to be inflamed further by the experience of political office. Lord David Owen and Jonathan Davidson call it 'hubris syndrome'. There are certain traits said to be common among people who seek high leadership positions. When these traits are combined with the exercise of political authority, according to Owen and Davidson, it can produce a personality change that brings with it an extreme self-assurance, and one that is particularly resilient to disconfirming experiences and feedback.[17] Owen and Davidson identify signs of hubris syndrome in numerous US and UK heads of government over the last century. They do not go so far as to say that politicians *invariably* come down with it, but the suggestion is that political power tends to make people—who are already prone to overconfidence—even more confident.

In light of all this, Johnson's grim forecast is hardly far-fetched: 'by virtue of human psychology', he writes, 'we should *fully expect a bias towards overconfidence by all sides in conflicts today*, whether they are superpowers, small states, freedom fighters, or terrorists' (emphasis added).[18] In other words, we should not be surprised to find all war-makers sincerely judging their own side to have a reasonable prospect of success, whether or not they actually do.

The fact that all parties to a conflict will usually regard their own cause as 'just' makes matters worse in this connection, if we take into account recent findings in experimental philosophy.

---

[16] Steve A. Yetiv, *National Security Through a Cockeyed Lens: How Cognitive Bias Impacts US Foreign Policy*, Baltimore, MD: Johns Hopkins University Press, 2013, p. 51.

[17] David Owen and Jonathan Davidson, 'Hubris Syndrome: An Acquired Personality Disorder? A Study of US Presidents and UK Prime Ministers over the last 100 Years', *Brain: a Journal of Neurology*, vol. 132, no. 5, 2009, pp. 1396–406.

[18] Johnson, *Overconfidence and War*, p. 15.

Our non-moral judgements influence our moral judgements. Hence if I make the (non-moral) judgement that A harmed B intentionally rather than accidentally, this will influence my (moral) judgement about how bad a person A is, or how wrong his conduct was. This is both obvious and completely appropriate. But it turns out that the relationship is not entirely unidirectional. Experiments have revealed that our moral judgements also influence our non-moral judgements: those who judge that A's infliction of harm on B is wrong (moral) are more likely to then judge that the harm was intended rather than accidental (non-moral). This curious phenomenon is called the 'Knobe effect', after its discoverer. It challenges the assumption of a one-way flow of judgement, and shows that sometimes our moral assessments of what is right/wrong, fair/ unfair, decent/indecent etc. can have a bearing on our beliefs about the non-moral 'facts'.[19]

One of the most recent experiments in this space is of particular relevance to the present discussion. Participants were randomly sorted into two groups and given the following scenario: A ship is caught in a storm and the captain realizes it will flood and sink unless he makes the ship lighter. The first group is told that the only way for the captain to lighten the vessel is to throw some cargo overboard. The second group is told that the only way for the captain to lighten the vessel is to throw some passengers overboard. All participants are then asked to rate their level of agreement with the statement 'it is feasible for the captain to save the ship' on a 7-point Likert scale. The results showed that participants from the first group tended to agree that saving the ship was feasible, while those from the second group tended to disagree. According to the authors of the study, this indicates that our normative judgements encroach on our ascriptions of feasibility. The only difference between the two conditions is the moral valence of the action required to save the ship: jettisoning cargo is relatively innocuous, while throwing people overboard is manslaughter. Therefore it is reasonable to suppose that the difference in the participants' non-moral feasibility ascriptions was

[19] Joshua Knobe and Shaun Nichols, 'Experimental Philosophy', *The Stanford Encyclopedia of Philosophy*, Winter 2017 Edition, Edward N. Zalta (ed.), available at: https://plato.stanford. edu/archives/win2017/entries/experimental-philosophy/.

due to their contrasting moral appraisals if the actions required to save the vessel.[20]

Experiments like this suggest that if I judge a particular plan or policy or endeavour to be morally right or admirable, I am more likely to believe that it will 'work' than I would if I had the opposite moral appraisal of the plan. The implication is obvious enough: If a war-maker believes that his cause is 'just'—as almost all war-makers do—this is liable to inflate his expectation of success. The moral judgement that there is a 'just cause' for war can distort the non-moral appraisal of how likely the war is to deliver on its objectives. If this is right, then in the context of war-making we can expect the psychological disposition towards overconfidence to be further compounded by the Knobe effect. States will exaggerate their prospects of success insofar as they are convinced that just cause is on their side.

To be clear, I am not suggesting that our politicians can never be expected to recognize when going to war would be futile. I am only saying that they will likely err in this judgement sometimes, given the unconscious bias towards overconfidence, and the forces that exacerbate it. This is enough to make my point though. A political community cannot rest assured that its political decision makers will never wage futile (and therefore unjust) wars, even if they rightly believe that those same decision makers are sincerely committed to never waging futile wars.

The Law of the Hammer and Last Resort

The Just War principle of last resort states that peaceful solutions must be exhausted before recourse to war is taken, otherwise war is unjust in virtue of being unnecessary. Two interpretations of this requirement are available. The 'chronological' version says that all non-violent alterna-tives must actually be tried and fail before military force can legitimately be used. The 'systematic' interpretation is less demanding. It requires only that all alternatives be seriously *considered*. If a judgement is

---

[20] Nicholas Southwood and Matthew Lindauer, 'Feasibility and the Problem of Normative Encroachment', unpublished manuscript.

THE LAW OF THE HAMMER AND LAST RESORT   87

reached, in good faith, that no such alternative is likely to be effective, then going to war can be a 'last resort' even where it is the first thing we actually try.[21]

Most commentators endorse the latter formulation of the principle, or something like it. George Weigel, for instance, writes:

> In the just war tradition, 'last resort' is not an arithmetic concept. One can always imagine 'one more' non-military tactic that could be tried, one more negotiating effort that could be launched, one more confer- ence that could be called—in a sequence that is, by definition, infinite in duration. No, what the tradition means by 'last resort' is that reasonable people can reasonably conclude that all reasonable efforts at a non-military solution have been tried, have failed, *and in all probability will continue to fail.*[22]

The final clause relieves agents of the duty to try something non-violent if they reasonably believe that it will probably be ineffective. According to Richard Regan, this is also the dominant legal interpretation. The UN Charter empowers the Security Council to authorize military force to preserve international peace and security, but only where this is 'neces- sary' (i.e. where it is a last resort). Regan explains that for this condition to be met, 'the council need only conclude that [...] non-military measures are unlikely to maintain or restore international peace and security'.[23]

Even against this less demanding standard, by most accounts the US- led war against Iraq in 2003 was not a last resort. Indeed, this was one of the main conclusions of the Chilcot inquiry. But US Secretary of Defense at the time, Donald Rumsfeld, did not see it that way. In a press conference held the day the war began, Rumsfeld told reporters:

---

[21] Nicholas Parkin, 'Non-Violent Resistance and Last Resort', *Journal of Military Ethics*, vol. 15, no. 4, 2016, p. 260.
[22] George Weigel, 'From Last Resort to Endgame: Morality, the Gulf War, and the Peace Process', in David E. Decosse (ed.), *But Was It Just? Reflections on the Morality of the Persian Gulf War*, New York: Doubleday, 1991, p. 24, emphasis added.
[23] Laurie Calhoun, *War and Delusion: a Critical Examination*, New York: Palgrave Macmillan, 2013. pp. 31–2.

Let me close by saying that war is the last choice; let there be no doubt. The American people can take comfort in knowing that their country has done everything humanly possible to avoid war and to secure Iraq's peaceful disarmament.[24]

Perhaps Rumsfeld didn't really believe what he was saying. But there is another possibility.

In a now famous experiment, psychologist Abraham Luchins divided subjects into two groups and supplied each with three different sized water jars. The groups were put through a series of tests wherein the challenge was to figure out how to produce specified measures of water using only the materials provided. The experimental group started out with five practice problems, each of them requiring a similar method for their solution (i.e. fill up jar B, then pour out enough to fill jar A once and jar C twice). The group was then presented with a series of critical test problems, some of which could be solved with a much simpler method. The control group, meanwhile, skipped the practice problems and went straight to these critical tests. What Luchins found was that the experimental group tended to overlook the simpler solutions introduced at the critical test phase, while the control group readily availed itself of these solutions. The experimental group's exposure to the practice problems seemed to cultivate a rigid, mechanized state of mind, whereby the 'tried and true' method was the only one salient to them even after other, better solutions presented themselves.[25]

This came to be known as the Einstellung Effect. It is the tendency to fixate on one particular kind of solution to a problem due to one's exposure to, or familiarity with, that solution. This is not the place for a full exposition of the causes and consequences of this effect, but it has been described as a kind of heuristic: a shortcut the mind takes to solve problems as efficiently as possible. After a finite number of encounters with a problem, our brains create a rule for dealing with such problems in future, generating a predisposition to apply a particular method, even where it may not be the best one, or even a good one.

---

[24] Pentagon Briefing, 20 March 2003, CNN Transcripts, available at: http://edition.cnn.com/TRANSCRIPTS/0303/20/se.08.html, last accessed 28 July 2017.
[25] Abraham S. Luchins, 'Mechanization in Problem Solving: The Effect of Einstellung', *Psychological Monographs*, vol. 54, no. 6, 1942, pp. i–95.

A related concept is the so-called 'law of the instrument' (also known as 'the law of the hammer' or 'Maslow's hammer'), captured by Abraham Kaplan's quip: 'give a small boy a hammer, and he will find that everything he encounters needs pounding'. Kaplan saw this law at work in many different arenas, including intellectual pursuits. In *The Conduct of Inquiry* he wrote: 'It comes as no particular surprise to discover that a scientist formulates problems in a way which requires for their solution just those techniques in which he himself is especially skilled'.[26] Billionaire investor Warren Buffet made a similar comment about the use of certain mathematical models in the study of financial markets: 'Once these [mathematical] skills are acquired, it seems sinful not to use them, even if the usage has no utility or negative utility'.[27] Some have even suggested that the law of the hammer is behind the excessive use of lethal weapons by police in the US, where many departments have become 'militarized'—that is, provided with equipment initially intended for the armed forces. John Kleinig puts it like this:

> Equipment purchased 'just in case...' suddenly finds a use in situations that do not readily justify it. The old police adage about 'coming on strong' finds a way to 'bring out the big guns'. It is tempting to use what one has, even if, if one did not have it, one would not need it. The point is not whether one can envisage a situation in which it would be legitimate to use such equipment [...] but whether, in having the equipment, one will look for ways to use it.[28]

While the Einstellung Effect describes a tendency to rely on tools that we have used before, the law of the instrument is a tendency to use things just because we possess them, and have invested time, energy, or resources in their acquisition. But the commonality between these biases is more important to us than the differences: both impair the agent's ability to make a clear-eyed, impartial assessment of what is feasible and

---

[26] Abraham Kaplan, *The Conduct of Inquiry: Methodology for Behavioral Science*, San Francisco, CA: Chandler Publishing, 1964, p. 28.
[27] Quoted in Charles R. Morris, *The Sages*, New York: PublicAffairs, 2009, pp. 68–9.
[28] John Kleinig, 'What's All the Fuss with Police Militarization?', *The Critique*, 17 March 2015.

likely to work. Their effect is to distort the appraisal of competing solutions to a problem, unbeknownst to the appraiser.

Returning now to Rumsfeld. Maybe he didn't sincerely believe that war against Iraq was a last resort. Or maybe he had been hit by Maslow's Hammer, and did sincerely believe it. States invest vast amounts of money in their war-making machinery, enough to dwarf other expenditures in many cases. Further, for some states military force has historically been the 'tried and true' method for solving an array of problems. Against these background conditions it may be wishful to expect that statespersons will be capable of an unbiased appraisal of the viability of non-military options, which of course is needed for an unbiased appraisal of the necessity of resorting to military ones. Again, we should be careful not to overstate things here. My claim is not that the law of the hammer will distort every judgement on the necessity of war. My claim is only that we cannot rule it out; this bias can, and probably will, produce a false positive regarding the necessity of war from time to time. If even this weaker premise is true, however, a political decision maker that is sincere about never taking us to war unnecessarily, might yet take us to war unnecessarily. We should not assume that only a bloodthirsty or psychopathic leader would start a war without exhausting all the alternatives first.

Illusions of Control and Accidental Civilian Casualties

Sometimes individuals can control what happens through the exercise of their agency—these are 'skill-situations'. Sometimes what happens is largely a matter of luck—these are 'chance situations'. Paradigmatic skill situations, like sporting contests, are characterized by the presence of competitors, the opportunity to practise, and to make choices. These 'skill cues' communicate to those present that how they perform can substantially influence the outcome. But some such cues can also appear in situations that are more heavily chance-determined. When this happens, we are liable to overestimate our ability to exert control over events. We fail to recognize just how helpless we really are, because we unconsciously confuse the chance situation we are in for a skill situation.[29] Hence, for example, an individual allowed to choose her own lottery ticket will fancy herself more likely to win than an individual given a ticket at random. Since making choices is something we normally do in skill situations, a 'skill orientation' is induced in the first player, leading her to behave as though the numbers she selects are more likely than other numbers to be randomly drawn in a lottery.[30]

Psychologists call this the 'illusion of control'. The effect has been replicated in many different contexts, and it turns out the illusion is more pronounced in some circumstances than in others. Where agents are emotionally invested in the achievement of a certain outcome, as war-makers presumably are, they are more likely to exaggerate their ability to maintain control over the sequence of events that will determine whether the outcome obtains.[31] The illusion is also stronger in adversarial or competitive situations, which clearly includes violent conflict.[32] And agents that have been familiarized with a task, say through a war-games simulation, show a more severe illusion of control vis-à-vis the real thing.[33] Furthermore, neither expertise nor sober reflection/rumination reliably dispel the illusion. Sometimes they make things worse.[34]

It is not difficult to imagine how this might play out in the context of war-making. Suppose the leaders of state A are considering war against neighbouring state B, in response to B's unlawful annexation of some territory along the border. Analysts and advisers warn the leadership of A that this war risks large numbers of civilian casualties, since the border regions are densely populated. But they also talk about training, planning, tactics, and strategies, thus making salient to the leadership a range

[29]   Ellen J. Langer, 'The Illusion of Control', *Journal of Personality and Social Psychology*, vol. 32. no. 2, 1975, pp. 311–28.

[30]   Langer, 'The Illusion of Control', pp. 315–17.

[31]   Suzanne C. Thompson, 'Illusions of Control: How We Overestimate Our Personal Influence', *Current Directions in Psychological Science, Association for Psychological Science*, vol. 8, no. 6, 1999, p. 187.

[32]   Mark Fenton-O'Creevy, Nigel Nicholson, Emma Soane, and Paul Willman, 'Trading on Illusions: Unrealistic Perceptions of Control and Trading Performance', *Journal of Occupational and Organizational Psychology*, vol. 76, no. 1, 2003, pp. 53–68.

[33]   Paul K. Presson and Victor A. Benassi, 'Illusion of Control: A Meta-Analytic Review', *Journal of Social Behavior & Personality*, vol. 11, no. 3, 1996, pp. 493–510.

[34]   Daniel Kahneman and Jonathan Renshon, 'Hawkish Biases', in Trevor Thrall and Jane Kramer (eds.), *American Foreign Policy and the Politics of Fear: Threat Inflation Since 9/11*, New York: Routledge, 2009, pp. 79–96.

of 'skill cues'. This activates the illusion of control, and the leaders grow unduly confident of their ability to rein in the predicted civilian casualties, by introducing various precautions, stringent policies on targeting decisions, closer oversight, and so on. As a result, they come to the view that the war can be prosecuted without causing a disproportional amount of harm to civilians. The reality, however, is that once soldiers are deployed, the capacity of the leaders to limit civilian casualties is decidedly limited. I should explain this briefly.

There are at least three kinds of civilian killing that take place in modern war: *intentional, incidental,* and *accidental.* Targeting decisions made precisely for the purpose of harming people that are known to be non-combatants are cases of *intentional* civilian victimization. Martin Shaw draws a finer distinction within this category. 'Degenerate' warfare involves deliberately harming civilian populations as an extension of the war against their state.[35] An example might be striking centres of economic activity, and the employees therein, so as to compromise their state's ability to finance its war effort. Another example would be killing civilians in order to weaken the morale of the politicians and soldiers prosecuting war on their behalf, á la the allies in Dresden. 'Genocidal' warfare, by contrast, involves 'war against a civilian population as such'.[36] Here civilian victimization is not a means to the end of defeating the state; it is an end in itself. Many of the conflicts of the 1990s were characterized by this kind of violence, including the 1994 massacre in Rwanda and ethnic cleansing in the former Yugoslavia.[37]

Incidental civilian killing (also known as 'double-effect killing' and 'collateral' killing) includes cases where civilian casualties are a foreseen but unintended consequence of a strike that is directed at a legitimate military target.[38] The strike is carried out not *because of,* but *despite* the expectation that civilians will be harmed—the military target is judged valuable enough to make the anticipated collateral damage worth it.

---

[35] Martin Shaw, 'Risk-Transfer Militarism, Small Massacres, and the Historic Legitimacy of War', *International Relations*, vol. 16, 2002, p. 353.

[36] Shaw, 'Risk-Transfer Militarism', p. 353.

[37] This led Mary Kaldor to describe atrocities against non-combatants as an 'essential component' of what she then called the 'new wars'. Mary Kaldor, *New and Old Wars: Organized Violence in a Global Era*, 3rd Edition, Stanford, CA: Stanford University Press, 2012.

[38] Neta C. Crawford, *Accountability for Killing*, New York: Oxford University Press, p. 76.

Accidental civilian killings are neither intended nor foreseen. The paradigm cases are those where a combatant uses lethal force unaware that civilians are in the area. But we might also include here scenarios where a combatant knowingly kills a civilian that she mistakenly believes (or reasonably suspects) is actually a combatant. The combatant intentionally kills *someone*, but she does not intentionally kill *a civilian*. In this (admittedly loose) sense the innocent person has been killed 'accidentally'.

Urban warfare produces accidental civilian casualties because there are so many uncertainties. It is often difficult to know the whereabouts of all civilians on the battlefield so as to ensure that violence is not directed at them. In addition to this 'location uncertainty', as Marcus Schulzke calls it, there is also a pervasive 'identity uncertainty': it is difficult to reliably distinguish threats from bystanders.[39] Several factors combine to create these uncertainties. For one, the enemy these days often wears civilian attire rather than camouflage, thus removing the visual indicators that would otherwise be relied upon to identify legitimate targets. And even when combatants wear uniforms or openly carry weapons, both combatants and non-combatants are often concealed in vehicles and behind structures, making it difficult to tell which persons are threatening and which aren't, and their proximity to one another.

Picture the following scenario: A soldier stationed at a military checkpoint sees a car fast approaching. The car has ignored signs by the side of the road written in the native language instructing the driver to stop. The soldier signals the car to stop, but it does not. The soldier fires a warning shot, but the car only speeds up. The same checkpoint has previously been targeted by suicide bombers driving cars full of explosives. They, too, failed to stop when instructed and went on to kill troops stationed at the checkpoint. Eventually the soldier shoots through the windshield and kills the driver, only to discover that he was an illiterate civilian that could not read the signs, misinterpreted the warnings and panicked. Situations like this were apparently all too common in Afghanistan and Iraq.[40]

---

[39] Marcus Schulzke, 'The Unintended Consequences of War: Self-Defense and Violence Against Civilians in Ground Combat Operations', *International Studies Perspectives*, vol. 1, 2016, pp. 1–8.
[40] Schulzke, 'The Unintended Consequences of War'.

What can a state that wages a war possibly do to prevent these kinds of accidents from happening after it has deployed its troops? It cannot change the fact that enemy combatants and non-combatants are intermingled in urban warzones. And it cannot completely remove the uncertainties that limit the ability of its soldiers to tell one from the other. Perhaps the state can train its soldiers to hold their fire in all cases except those where they are completely certain that no civilians will be harmed? I seriously doubt that any state could succeed in this even if it tried. Some soldiers—probably most—will use force if they believe that their survival depends on it. The human drive to self-preserve is strong enough to assure us of that. This comes through strongly when soldiers recount their wartime experiences. A British army corporal in Afghanistan who regularly came under attack from Taliban fighters hiding in civilian buildings—and who regularly returned fire—responded as follows when asked if he was concerned about civilian casualties: 'Not in the moment, only afterwards. When you're engaged everything happens too fast and you're just thinking about surviving. You only really think about it after and you just hope that any civilians made it through OK.'[41] Firing back when under fire is as much an impulse as it is a decision, and so I doubt that any state could successfully condition its soldiers to unfailingly hold their fire as long as any uncertainty remains.

As far as I can see, the only other way for a state to eliminate the kinds of 'accidents' described above would be to either remove its soldiers from the battlefield entirely, so that the impulse to self-preserve never kicks in, or to arm its soldiers with non-lethal weapons, so that when accidents do happen the civilians impacted are not killed at least. One day all this might come to pass. Soldiers might never need to use force out of self-preservation because they will do all their fighting by remote control; and non-lethal weapons might become so effective that they do everything bombs and bullets do today without the killing and maiming. This, however, would not be war as we know it. War as we know it involves sending human beings into life-threatening situations, clouded by uncertainties, with lethal force as their primary means of protection. As long as this is the case, there will be accidental civilian casualties.

---

[41]   Quoted in Schulzke, 'The Unintended Consequences of War', p. 13.

So while feasible measures could be taken to mitigate or even eliminate the first two kinds of civilian harm, war-makers are much more limited in their ability to prevent *accidental* civilian killings. Careful recruitment, proper training, and accountability will help ensure that most soldiers refrain from *intentional* civilian victimization, and *incidental* civilian deaths could be avoided by calling off or delaying strikes where collateral damage is foreseen, even where that means foregoing a valuable military target. But in urban settings where civilians are present, we can prevent our soldiers killing them by accident only by removing our soldiers from the battlefield, or by confiscating their lethal weapons. If neither of these things happens, civilians will be killed, even if nobody kills them intentionally or incidentally.

This goes some way towards explaining Neta Crawford's findings in her masterful book *Accountability for Killing*. Crawford tells us that:

> The US military increasingly emphasized civilian protection during the wars in Afghanistan and Iraq at rhetorical, doctrinal, and operational levels. Minimizing collateral damage went from being one concern among several, to an imperative that was institutionalized to a degree that it had never been before.[42]

As one example of this institutionalization, the US military began applying collateral damage mitigation practices to its air strikes. The result was that more than 99 per cent of these air strikes were carried out without causing *any* collateral harm at all.[43] And yet, on Crawford's own estimate, the wars in Afghanistan and Iraq produced *twenty-two thousand civilian casualties* between 2001 and 2012, many of them accidental.[44]

What I am suggesting is that a significant proportion of the civilian killings that occur in modern war are an ineliminable feature of it, not just a contingent one caused by bad institutional design, bad targeting decisions, or bad apples. While avoiding *intentional* and *incidental* civilian harms may be a matter of 'skill'—squarely within our control—avoiding *accidental* civilian killing is closer to a 'chance-situation' for the

---

[42] Crawford, *Accountability for Killing*, p. 156.
[43] Crawford, *Accountability for Killing*, p. 157.
[44] Crawford, *Accountability for Killing*, p. 76.

authorities who decide on the war. Leaders under the illusion of control might fail to appreciate this, and thus be unduly confident in their ability to wage a war that does not cause a disproportional amount of civilian harm.

Attribution Error and Proportionality

Before waging war, a morally motivated decision maker will consider the likely harms to civilians, and factor these into her assessment of the war's proportionality. But she might be inclined to apply a *discount* to these harms—to weigh them less heavily in the proportionality calculus—to the extent that she regards the civilians in question to be less than fully 'innocent'. This is not always inappropriate. If a civilian contributes to, or is somehow complicit in, her government's unjust aggression against a neighbouring state, then arguably harms that are expected to befall that civilian in the course of a defensive war against her government should not count for as much in the proportionality equation as harms that befall her completely uninvolved, completely blameless compatriots. There are certain civilians who—while not legitimate targets of attack—are nevertheless responsible enough to justify discounting their interests in the proportionality assessment.

There is a danger here, however. The danger is that war-makers will be inclined to *over-blame* civilians on the other side, and consequently to apply *too heavy* a discount to their interests when calculating proportionality. This danger exists not because of any particular psychological feature that is unique to political decision makers. It exists because of a widespread unconscious bias known as 'attribution error'.

When we see a person behaving badly, we might jump to an 'internal' explanation or an 'external' one. An internal explanation identifies some objectionable desire, attitude or disposition as the source of the bad behaviour: malicious intent, hatred, greed, indifference or whatever. On the other hand if we think that situational pressures forced the person to act as they did, we are offering an 'external' explanation for their behaviour. Attribution bias is the tendency people have 'to exaggerate the importance of dispositional [internal] over situational [external] factors when they explain undesirable behavior of others and the corresponding tendency to emphasize situational rather than dispositional factors when they explain their own behavior'.[45] When others behave badly we are prone to judge that it is because they are bad people, while our own equally bad behaviour is put down to difficult circumstances.

One explanation for the attribution bias appeals to the concept of 'perceptual salience', summarized here by Turner and Miles:

> People being observed are the most salient aspect of the situation [to the observer], as they are actually performing the action—they and their behaviour appear to go together, so an internal attribution is made. In contrast, when making self-attributions, we are focussed outwards and the situation is salient, and thus we attribute causality for our behaviour to external factors.[46]

This suggests that we are prone to attribute others' bad behaviour to their desires or character traits simply because we are invariably located outside of their minds. Over and above this, however, when it comes to the behaviour of 'out-group' members, social psychologists suggest there is also a motivational basis for internally attributing aggressive or otherwise objectionable conduct.

We tend to process information in a way that is conducive to maintaining and enhancing our self-esteem. Hence when a student earns a good grade she will normally attribute it to her own intelligence, talent, or hard work, and consequently feel good about her*self*. By contrast when a student receives a bad grade blame is often directed outwards: 'I wasn't given enough time' or 'the task wasn't clear' or 'the teacher dislikes me/disagrees with my argument'. These kinds of asymmetries in the interpretation of events are geared towards ego-protection. This same unconscious drive apparently leads us to make attributions that favour groups to which we belong, over 'others'.[47]

---

[45] Janice Gross Stein, 'Building Politics into Psychology: The Misperception of Threat', *Political Psychology*, vol. 9, no. 2, June 1988, p. 255.

[46] Rhiannon N. Turner and Miles Hewstone, 'Attribution Biases', in John M. Levine and Michael A. Hogg (eds.), *Encyclopedia of Group Processes and Intergroup Relations*, Los Angeles, CA: Sage, 2010, p. 43.

[47] Turner and Hewstone, 'Attribution Biases'.

To illustrate, one study asked both (non-German) Jews and (non-Jewish) Germans why they thought Germans mistreated Jewish people during the Second World War. The Jews were much more likely than the German participants to attribute the mistreatment to the internal characteristics of the wrongdoers, such as 'German aggression', rather than to situational pressures. Another study asked Dutch participants to make internal or external attributions for (1) Dutch mistreatment of Indonesians during colonization, and (2) German mistreatment of the Dutch during the Second World War. Again, the participants were more likely to make internal attributions for the bad behaviour of the out-group—the Germans—than about members of their own political community. When outsiders do bad things our default presumption is that they are bad people, while the equally abhorrent conduct of insiders is interpreted more charitably as being caused by the circumstances in which they find themselves. This bias is motivated; it makes us feel better about the groups to which we belong, and about ourselves by extension.[48]

Consider how this might distort appraisals of *ad bellum* proportionality. Let us return for a moment to our hypothetical from the previous section: the leaders of state A are considering war against neighbouring state B, in response to B's unlawful annexation of territory along the border. Analysts have warned the leadership of A that this war will likely cause civilian casualties. To determine how much weight to assign these casualties in the proportionality calculus, the leaders of A will need to consider how responsible/culpable the civilians of B are. This is where attribution bias is liable to warp the moral accounting.

If the citizens of B have remained passive in the face of their government's aggression, that might be because their government controls communication networks, prohibits assembly, and brutally represses any hint of dissent. In this case, the inaction of B's civilian population is largely due to situational or 'external' factors. To the extent that the leaders of A (and their advisers) are gripped by attribution bias, however, they will be inclined to attribute the inaction of B's civilians to 'internal' factors: the people support their government, endorse its aggressive ambitions, stand to benefit from the annexation, or don't really care, and so on. If proportionality is calculated using *these* assumptions, the

---

[48]   Turner and Hewstone, 'Attribution Biases'.

result will be to *over-blame* the citizens of B for their government's actions, and consequently, when making proportionality judgments, to *under-weight* any harms that they are expected suffer.

Attribution bias might also cause the leadership of A to exaggerate the extent to which the soldiers of B are fighting for 'internal' reasons, and thus to over-blame them as well. One might suggest that this has no bearing on proportionality; that since the soldiers of B are actively engaged in hostilities and therefore morally liable to attack, any harms that are expected to befall them do not need to be counted against proportionality by the decision makers of A. This is probably still the dominant view among just war thinkers, but it is worth noting that there are some prominent dissenting voices.

Henry Shue is the best example. He notes that just as markets do not necessarily reward the industrious with wealth and punish the lazy with destitution, wars do not have a mechanism to ensure that harms are distributed strictly according to deserts. Shue is worth quoting at length in this connection:

> On the one hand, the individuals who fight in wars—on both sides— suffer an exceptionally wide spectrum of harms... On the other hand, individual fighters bear equally great varieties of types and degrees of responsibility for fighting... Much of the horror of war consists in the intersection of the cruel diversity of fates with the wide variation in responsibility: the randomness with which the radically different fates are distributed across the radically different degrees of responsibility... The least morally responsible may return home quadriplegic and emotionally shattered, while the most responsible survive unscathed and covered in medals.[49]

It is because of this randomness that Shue insists harms inflicted on enemy soldiers cannot be completely excluded from proportionality assessments, even if these soldiers are participating in an unjust war and even if they are legitimate targets of attack.

---

[49] Henry Shue, *Fighting Hurt: Rule and Exception in Torture and War*, Oxford: Oxford University Press, 2016, pp. 390–1.

If a soldier is fully culpable for his participation in an unjust war—if he signed up enthusiastically and aware of all the relevant facts and moral considerations—*then* perhaps we could say that the expected death or wounding of this soldier should be entirely discounted from the proportionality assessment of the just side. In other words, the just side could legitimately refuse to count harms expected to befall this soldier as relevant moral costs that count against its going to war. The reality, however, is that unjust warriors seldom are fully culpable for their participation. Their moral blameworthiness is often mitigated by various factors. While some unjust warriors may be uncoerced and perfectly informed, Shue notes that 'others are conscripted by law or by poverty or otherwise coerced into participating in a conflict they know almost nothing about'.[50] When one of these less-than-fully culpable soldiers is killed or severely injured fighting in an unjust war, Shue says, this person is harmed beyond what is appropriate to his individual moral responsibility; he suffers more than he deserves. On Shue's view, his excess harm needs to count for something in the proportionality calculus. An enemy combatant might be a legitimate target of attack because he is involved in hostilities, but even so, if we can expect that a war against his state would cause him considerably more harm than he is individually liable to, then this is a morally relevant cost of our war that counts against its proportionality.

I think Shue is right, but I will not try to defend his position here. I will only highlight what it means for the present inquiry. Shue is saying that the suffering of enemy soldiers, not just the suffering of enemy civilians, should count for something in the proportionality calculations applied by our leaders when considering whether to take recourse to war. And he is saying that the weight given to a soldier's suffering in proportionality should be a function of our assessment of his/her blameworthiness or culpability. This is all well and good. But I am saying that, due to attribution bias, our leaders will have a tendency to *over-blame* enemy soldiers for their involvement, and thus to weight their suffering less heavily than they would were it not for the influence of said bias. The result is a proportionality calculation in which the suffering of both

[50] Shue, *Fighting Hurt*, p. 392.

civilians *and* soldiers counts for less than it should, increasing the likelihood of a faulty verdict on the proportionality of the war.

Before we conclude, it is worth adding that attribution bias can be incredibly robust. In another famous experiment, researchers asked participants to read essays that were either favourable to, or critical of, Cuban leader Fidel Castro. It was made clear to the participants that the essayists had *no choice* whether to take a pro-Castro or anti-Castro stance; the experiment designers had assigned each essayist a position to argue for. After reading the essays the participants were asked to guess whether the writer was a supporter or a detractor of Castro. Overwhelmingly, participants tended to believe that the position taken in the essay reflected the attitudes and beliefs of the writer, even though they were explicitly told that the orientation of the essay was not chosen by the writer.[51] This suggests the tendency to attribute the behaviour of others to their personal dispositions can withstand clear evidence to the contrary. If that is so, providing our political decision makers with more information/education about enemy civilians and combatants and the pressures they face is unlikely to correct the distorting effects of attribution error on their proportionality judgements. They will probably continue to over-blame enemy civilians, and combatants, and to therefore under-count their suffering in proportional assessments.

Conclusion

In *Contingent Pacifism*, Larry May admits that war can in theory be justified, but argues that all modern wars should be presumed unjust given 'the kind of wars that are likely to be fought *and the kind of people*

---

[51] See Kahneman and Renshon, 'Hawkish Biases'. Also worth adding is that certain contextual features have been shown to exacerbate attribution bias. Two in particular are germane to our discussion. First, in contexts where group membership is highlighted or made salient, intergroup attribution biases tend to be more pronounced (Turner and Hewstone, 'Attribution Biases', p. 44). Second, the biases are more acutely engaged when we feel threatened. Richard Werner, 'Just War Theory: Going to War and Collective Self-Deception', in Fritz Allhoff, Nicholas G. Evans, and Adam Henschke (eds.), *Routledge Handbook of Ethics and War: Just War Theory in the 21st Century*, New York and London: Routledge, 2013, p. 39. Since both of these conditions ordinarily obtain in the context of international armed conflict, we have all the more reason to expect that the *ad bellum* judgements of war-makers will be distorted by attribution bias.

likely to fight them' (emphasis added).[52] May does not elaborate much on the 'kind of people' he has in mind. Laurie Calhoun is more direct. For her, modern wars should be presumed unjust because political decision makers are the kinds of people that have no desire to act justly; they are 'closet realists' who use just war language when it suits them but who, behind it all, care only about power.[53] 'The realist dagger, wherever it may hide', writes Calhoun, 'lies cloaked in moral rhetoric.'[54] For radical Marxists, the 'kind of person' that wages unjust, imperialistic wars is the greedy capitalist, or his political puppet.[55] This notion that immoral wars happen only because military resources fall into the hands of certain kinds of people has been a recurring trope throughout history. A good example can be found among the propaganda videos shown to US soldiers after the Second World War. One of them justified the de-militarization of Japan on the grounds that 'the Japanese brain' had been programmed to be aggressive and expansionist, and therefore could not be trusted to make responsible use of an army and navy.[56]

These views might strike the reader as exceedingly cynical. But in a way they are not cynical *enough*. The trouble with them—aside from their reliance on simplistic and sometimes offensive generalizations—is their implication that the risk of military misuse/overuse only arises when war-making capacity falls into the 'wrong hands'. They tell us

---

[52] Larry May, *Contingent Pacifism: Revisiting Just War Theory*, Cambridge: Cambridge University Press, 2015, p. 233.

[53] Calhoun, *War and Delusion*, p. 114.   [54] Calhoun, *War and Delusion*, p. 112.

[55] The standard line is that, in capitalist countries, politicians are puppets of the exploiting class, committed to maximizing their share of economic resources at everybody else's expense. Therefore the citizens of these societies should fully expect that their militaries will be deployed in unjust wars from time to time—whenever this serves the private interest of the wealthy elites. Naomi Klein's *The Shock Doctrine: The Rise of Disaster Capitalism*, New York: Picador, 2008, and Stephen Pelletier's *America's Oil Wars*, Westport, CT: Praeger, 2004 go in this direction, though neither takes it quite this far. While this critique is often expressed in Marxist language, it isn't always. Engelbrecht and Hanighen made essentially the same point in different terms. H.C. Engelbrecht and F.C. Hanighen, *Merchants of Death: A Study of the International Armaments Industry*, New York: Dodd, Mead and Co., 1934. For an excellent account of the ways in which private economic and political interests motivate and perpetuate armed conflict, see David Keen, *Useful Enemies: When Waging Wars is More Important than Winning Them*, New Haven, CT: Yale University Press, 2012. 'A declared war against a "demon" enemy turns out to be an "excellent" context in which a wide variety of violent, profitable, and politically advantageous strategies can be pursued with a great deal of impunity' (Keen, *Useful Enemies*, p. 236). See also William D. Hartung, 'The New Business of War: Small Arms and the Proliferation of Conflict', *Ethics and International Affairs*, vol. 15, no. 1, 2001, pp. 79–96.

[56] Theodor S. Geisel, 'Our Job in Japan (1945): US Occupation Propaganda', available at: https://www.youtube.com/watch?v=5kor4TorC3A, last accessed January 2020.

that states cannot be relied upon to wage only just wars because states-persons are not sufficiently morally motivated, being too preoccupied with realpolitik, or economic imperialism, or whatever. I am not defending statespersons against these charges. But if the implication is that militaries would not be overused/misused if only our political decision makers *were* sufficiently morally motivated, this I submit is still unduly optimistic. The material presented in this chapter gives us reason to expect that even purely motivated and morally well-adjusted decision makers, who understand the concepts of just war theory and are genuinely committed to following its precepts, can be expected to misuse the militaries put at their disposal. Ordinary decent people are among the 'kinds of people' that are prone to wage unjust wars. The only way to completely eliminate the risk of our military being misused/overused would be to abolish the military.

5

Martial Values in Civilian Life

The following passage concludes Samuel Huntington's *The Soldier and the State*, first published in the 1950s:

> West Point is a gray island in a many colored sea, a bit of Sparta in the midst of Babylon. Yet is it possible to deny that the military values—loyalty, duty, restraint, dedication—are the ones America most needs today? That the disciplined order of West Point has more to offer than the garish individualism of Main Street? Historically, the virtues of West Point have been America's vices, and the vices of the military, America's virtues. Yet today America can learn more from West Point than West Point from America [...] If the civilians permit the soldiers to adhere to the military standard, the nations themselves may eventually find redemption and security in making that standard their own.[1]

The sentiment this passage expresses endures to the present day. A survey of American military officers at the turn of the century revealed a strong belief among them that 'society would be better off if it adopted military mores'.[2] Richard Kohn makes the observation that 'there is a widespread attitude among officers that civilian society has become corrupt, even degenerate, while the military has remained a repository of virtue, perhaps its one remaining bastion, in an increasingly unravelling social fabric, of the traditional values that make the country strong'.[3]

---

[1] Samuel P. Huntington, *The Soldier and the State: The Theory and Politics of Civil-Military Relations*, Cambridge, MA: Harvard University Press, 1959, p. 466.

[2] Peter D. Feaver and Richard H. Kohn, 'The Gap: Soldiers, Civilians, and their Mutual Misunderstanding', in Eugene R. Wittkopf and James M. McCormick (eds.), *The Domestic Sources of American Foreign Policy*, 4th Edition, Lanham, MD: Rowman and Littlefield, 2004, p. 87.

[3] Richard H. Kohn, 'The Erosion of Civilian Control of the Military in the United States Today', *Naval War College Review*, vol. 55, no. 3, 2002, p. 29.

Ethics, Security, and The War-Machine: The True Cost of the Military. Ned Dobos, Oxford University Press (2020).
© Ned Dobos.
DOI: 10.1093/oso/9780198860518.001.0001

There is something to be said for this. Arguably, things would be improved if only more of us lived our lives according to the military creed of 'service before self', or at least showed greater restraint in the pursuit of our private interests. 'Leave no man behind' is another particularly admirable maxim associated with the armed forces. It is a commitment to never abandoning one's fellows, even if they should become immobilized and therefore incapable of contributing any further to the collective effort. If the treatment of our elderly is anything to go by, this value has little purchase in the civilian world nowadays, with a growing number of seniors becoming so isolated that it is damaging their physical and mental health. Once they no longer contribute to the workforce and finish rearing their children to adulthood, these people get left behind. Perhaps if civilians embraced the same values as their military counterparts this would not happen nearly as often as it presently does.

Having said that, the values that Huntington lists approvingly— loyalty, duty, restraint, dedication—are only the select few that tend to get reproduced in the promotional literature of national armed forces: call them the *advertised military values*. This list is incomplete though. Military institutions also value things like toughness, stoicism, forcefulness, and hierarchical authority.[4] Professional militaries 'eroticize and institutionalize' these values, as John Hopton puts it, in order to ensure that they can effectively deploy organized violence on behalf of the state.[5] Let us call these the *suppressed martial values*. They are not necessarily objectionable in and of themselves, but unlike the advertised military values, they are prone to cause damage when they spill over into civilian society.

This is hardly a novel claim. Feminist scholars in particular have been imparting it for decades, and so I will begin by briefly recounting some of their insights. I then take a sample of three civilian domains—law enforcement, business, and education—and draw attention to some of the adverse consequences that their cultural 'militarization' appears to have had in the US in particular. This analysis suggests that when the

---

[4] Marek Thee, 'Militarism and Militarization in Contemporary International Relations', *Security Dialogue*, vol. 8, no. 4, 1977, pp. 296–309.
[5] See John Hopton, 'The State and Military Masculinity', in Paul R. Higate (ed.), *Military Masculinities: Identity and the State*, Westport, CT: Praeger, 2003, p. 115.

values, ideals, and assumptions of the armed forces encroach into, and take root in, civilian institutions, the proper functioning (or *telos*) of those institutions can be compromised. In the second half of the chapter I turn to consider whether, and the extent to which, this diffusion of martial values can be avoided in a society that maintains a standing army. I take as my starting point a recent essay by Marcus Schulzke, in which a useful distinction is drawn between 'necessary' and 'surplus' militarization.[6] What might appear at first blush to be surplus (avoidable), I will argue, reappears as necessary (unavoidable) once we appreciate how modern militaries reproduce themselves. If this is right, then as long as a permanent military establishment is present, our ability to resist the spread of its values into civilian life is more limited than we might think.

Militarization

When we talk of the 'militarization' of a society, this might mean one of three things: (1) the military establishment is getting bigger; (2) the state is increasingly displaying militaristic behaviour (the threat or use of force); or (3) the values, assumptions, and even language associated with the military are spreading beyond it into civilian society—what has been referred to as the military's normative 'penetration' into the civilian world.[7] This third form of militarization is what I will be focussing on for the most part. Ordinarily, the extent of it will depend on the size of the military establishment, and the frequency of its use, but even small and seldom deployed militaries can penetrate. Why (if at all) should this concern us? Feminist scholars offer one very powerful reason, and this is a good place to begin our discussion.

Start with the observation that the suppressed martial values—forcefulness, domination, emotional toughness—stand in direct contrast to the values that we usually associate with femininity—gentleness, cooperation, emotional sensitivity, and the like. (This is what George

---

[6] Marcus Schulzke, 'Necessary and Surplus Militarisation: Rethinking Civil Military Interactions and their Consequences', *European Journal of International Security*, vol. 3, no. 1, February 2018, pp. 94–112.

[7] See Tord Høivik and Solveig Aas, 'Demilitarization in Costa Rica: A Farewell to Arms?', *Journal of Peace Research*, vol. XVIII, no. 4, 1981, p. 333.

Gilder was getting at when he declared that, 'to create a solidaristic group of male killers, you kill the woman in them').[8] Given this binary opposition between martial values and feminine values, exalting the former strongly implies something about the latter. Indeed, admiration for martial values entails a certain disdain for femininity, its contradiction. This would not be particularly worrying, were it not for the fact that contempt for the abstraction 'femininity' naturally mutates into contempt for its representatives in the external world: women.[9] Hence Betty Reardon memorably described misogyny as 'the mother's milk of militarism'.[10] When martial values are embraced in civilian society, the argument goes, negative attitudes towards women usually follow, and after that, abusive behaviours towards them.

In 2012, the Oscar-nominated documentary film *The Invisible War* exposed the high rates of sexual assault within the US armed forces, and the disturbing institutional responses to it. Research published since the film's release has produced some troubling statistics: Up to 80 per cent of military women in the US have experienced sexual harassment, and 25 per cent have been sexually assaulted.[11] The wives and girlfriends of military men are also more likely to be assaulted, compared to women in the civilian population. According to one recent study, 23 per cent of US military wives report being battered, compared to 3 per cent of civilian wives.[12] There is no denying that a host of factors, including the high rates of psychological and emotional trauma among military personnel, contribute to these disparities. But what Reardon and others suggest is that the martial values celebrated by the armed forces are at least partly responsible.

[8] George Gilder, *Men and Marriage*, Gretna, LA: Pelican, 1986, p. 183.
[9] Marcia Kovitz, 'The Roots of Military Masculinity', in Paul R. Higate (ed.), *Military Masculinities: Identity and the State*, Westport, CT: Praeger, 2003, p. 6.
[10] Betty A. Reardon, *Sexism and the War System*, New York: Syracuse University Press, 1996, p. 52.
[11] Barbara J. Meade, Margaret K. Glenn and Oliver Wirth, 'Mission Critical: Getting Vets with PTSD Back to Work', *Medscape*, 29 March 2013.
[12] Deborah Harrison, 'Violence in the Military Community', in Paul R. Higate (ed.), *Military Masculinities: Identity and the State*, Westport, CT: Praeger, 2003, p. 79. See also Rhonda Hammer, 'Militarism and Family Terrorism: A Critical Feminist Perspective', *The Review of Education, Pedagogy, and Cultural Studies*, vol. 25, 2003, pp. 231–56. Veterans are responsible for nearly 21 per cent of domestic violence incidence in the United States, according to Stacy Bennerman, 'High Risk of Military Domestic Violence on the Home Front', *San Francisco Chronicle* (online), 7 April 2014, available at: https://www.sfgate.com/opinion/article/High-risk-of-military-domestic-violence-on-the-5377562.php.

If there is any truth to this, then we should expect to find that a civilian population in which the suppressed martial values are widely affirmed will also be characterized by the mistreatment of women. And that is exactly what we do find according to some scholars. An early example is the work of C.K. Ogden and Mary Florence. The more heavily militarized a society is, the authors argue, the worse its female members tend to fare, offering various historical examples to illustrate.[13] They observe that in the most pacifistic communities (like the Toda of Southern India, and those Eskimo tribes where warfare is apparently a foreign concept,) women stand on a more or less equal footing with men. These cases are compared to warrior societies, where women are usually subordinated. Ancient Greece is put forward as the paradigm: 'The Greek of history . . . is the most warlike of men, and his women suffer accordingly'.[13a] This leads Ogden and Florence to their conclusion that 'militarism has been *the* curse of women, as women, from the first dawn of social life'.[14]

One of the most recent contributions to this body of work, Tom Digby's *Love and War*, carries this motif further. Digby identifies two usual features of societies where martial values have become prevalent outside of the defence establishment: there is typically a *faith in force* to solve problems (accompanied by a glorification of people who display forceful behaviour), and a *presumption of adversariality* (often accompanied by a belief in 'zero-sumness'—that gain can only come at the expense of others).[15] Men that think in these terms are not only more likely to dominate and exploit the women in their lives, according to Digby, they are also more likely to be emotionally dysfunctional. If human relations are seen as inherently adversarial, a man 'must constantly be on guard against himself as a potential leaker of his fears to others', lest his weaknesses be exploited by an enemy.[16] The result is emotional self-denial and isolation.[17] Thus 'cultural militarism', as Digby

---

[13]   C.K. Ogden and Mary Florence, 'Militarism Versus Feminism', in Margaret Kamester and Jo Vellacott (eds.), *Militarism Versus Feminism: Writings on Women and War*, London: Virago Press 1987. Originally published by Allen and Unwin in 1915.

[13a]   Ogden and Florence, 'Militarism Versus Feminism', p. 92.

[14]   Ogden and Florence, 'Militarism Versus Feminism', p. 56.

[15]   Tom Digby, *Love and War: How Militarism Shapes Sexuality and Romance*, New York: Columbia University Press, 2014, p. 9.

[16]   Digby, *Love and War*, p. 71.

[17]   'The pursuit of the ideal of warrior masculinity radically individualizes a man'. Digby, *Love and War*, p. 72.

calls it, is harmful to women, *and* to men, *and* to the relationships between them. It is what entraps us in the 'war of sexes'.

The emphasis here is on the cultural infrastructure needed to support war-building, and the damage it does to the private lives of civilians. But it is worth adding that the functioning of civilian *institutions* can also be impaired by the influence of the suppressed martial values. In what follows I consider the cases of policing, business, and schooling.

Of Law Enforcement

Police militarization has gained considerable public attention of late, particularly in the United States after the so-called 'Battle of Ferguson' in 2014. This phenomenon can be broken down into component parts: *material, operational,* and *cultural.*[18]

Material militarization happens when police start using weapons and equipment that were designed for soldiers in combat. In the US, the Pentagon's 1033 weapons transfer program allows the Department of Defense to donate surplus equipment to domestic law enforcement agencies. The number of agencies on the receiving end of such transfers, and their net value, has been growing steadily. Between 2006 and 2014, police departments and other law enforcement agencies across the US received $1.5 billion worth of military equipment free of charge, including: around 80,000 assault rifles, 200 grenade launchers, 6000 MRAP (Mine Resistant Ambush Protected) vehicles, armoured personnel carriers, over $3.5 million worth of camouflage gear and other 'deception equipment', and 11,959 bayonets![19] In Montgomery County, Texas, the local police possess a weapons-capable drone. Tampa police have tanks. Keene, a small town in New Hampshire, has a Bearcat (Ballistic Engineered Armoured Response Counter Attack Truck), equipped with gun ports, a rotating roof-hatch, a battering ram, a tear-gas deployment nozzle, a remotely controlled weapons station, and a shell that protects

---

[18] Here, I am following Peter B. Kraska, 'Militarization and Policing—its Relevance to 21st Century Police', *Policing*, vol. 1, no. 4, 2007, pp. 501–13.

[19] Ryan Welch and Jack Mewhirter, 'Does Police Equipment Lead Police Officers to be More Violent? We Did the Research', *Washington Post*, 30 June 2017.

it against chemical, biological, and radiological explosives.[20] When asked to explain why Keene needs a Bearcat, the local police chief said it would be used to patrol the town's 'Pumpkin Festival and other dangerous situations'.[21]

Operational militarization occurs when police adopt tactics that were once the preserve of military units in war zones. The most obvious case in point is the deployment of heavily armed PPUs (Paramilitary Police Units) to conduct raids on domestic soil. The first SWAT teams in the US were established with the help of the Marines, and the acronym was originally meant to stand for 'Special Weapons Attack Teams'. This was changed to 'Special Weapons and Tactics' precisely to avoid the military connotation.[22] While SWAT teams were being deployed around 3000 times per year in the 1980s across the US, by 2015 that number had risen to over 50,000. In the 1980s, around 20 per cent of police departments in small cities had SWAT teams. By 2007, 80 per cent had one. Originally these units were formed to enter barricaded buildings and to deal with violent civil unrest, hostage situations, shoot-outs, and the like. Today they are used more liberally: for routine patrols in high crime areas, to execute drug-related search warrants, to break up illegal poker games, and to raid bars suspected of serving under-age drinkers. On one occasion a SWAT team in Florida was deployed to apprehend a suspected cockfighting promoter. A police tank burst into the man's yard, killing more than 100 of his birds as well as his dog.[23]

Finally, there is *cultural* militarization, which involves the adoption of a particular mindset. It happens when police start to think of themselves as combatants fighting a domestic enemy, rather than as public servants. A shift in priorities predictably follows: pacifying and defeating the enemy becomes more important than protecting and serving the public. Or at least, the mission of protecting and serving the public is *reduced to*

---

[20] Jeff Sparrow, 'What Will Happen When Australian Police Have Military Weapons?', *Crikey*, 15 August 2014. See also Jake Bleiberg, 'Here's How Police in Canada are Becoming More Militarized', *Vice News*, 22 January 2016; and Kevin Walby and Brendan Roziere, 'Rise of the SWAT Team: Routine Police Work in Canada is Now Militarized', *The Conversation*, 25 January 2018, available at: http://theconversation.com/rise-of-the-swat-team-routine-police-work-in-canada-is-now-militarized-90073.
[21] 'Why America's Police are Becoming So Militarized', *Business Insider*, 24 March 2014.
[22] Eliav Lieblich and Adam Shinar, 'The Case Against Police Militarization', *Michigan Journal of Race and Law*, vol. 23, no. 1–2, 2018, p. 115.
[23] Lieblich and Shinar, 'The Case Against Police Militarization'.

the mission of defeating the enemy. The 'service orientation' of police thus becomes supplanted by a conflict or combat orientation.[24] It is reasonable to suppose that cultural militarization in the US is partly a result of the steady stream of ex-servicemen and women joining the police after discharge from the military—the so-called 'vet-to-cop' pipe-line. Some of these veterans are bound to carry the combat orientation with them from one profession to the next. More on this shortly.[25]

Why is this a problem? There are broadly two kinds of answers to this question. The first says that the militarization of law enforcement has bad consequences: it results in police doing more harm than is necessary, and/or it undermines their effectiveness.

Empirical research does reveal a correlation between material militar-ization and police violence. One study tracked the relationship between transfers of military equipment to law enforcement agencies under the 1033 program, and fatalities from officer-involved shootings. The find-ings are as follows:

[R]eceiving no military equipment corresponds with 0.287 expected civilian killings in a given county for a given year, whereas receiving the maximum amount corresponds with 0.656 killings. In other words, moving from the minimum to the maximum expenditure values, on average, increases civilian deaths by roughly 129%.[26]

This means that more than twice as many civilians are likely to be killed by police in a county after its material militarization than before, con-trolling for confounding variables such as county wealth, household income, racial makeup, drug use, and the amount of violent crime. Researchers have also found—with the help of the Puppycide Database Project—that law enforcement agencies with more military equipment kill more neighbourhood pets.[27]

[24] Daryl Meeks, 'Police Militarization in Urban Areas: The Obscure War Against the Underclass', *The Black Scholar*, vol. 35, no. 4, Winter 2006, p. 36.

[25] Simone Weichselbaum and Beth Schwartzapfel, 'When Warriors Put On the Badge', *The Marshall Project*, 30 March 2017, available at: https://www.themarshallproject.org/2017/03/30/when-warriors-put-on-the-badge, last accessed February 2018.

[26] Casey Delehanty, Jack Mewhirter, Ryan Welch, and Jason Wilks, 'Militarization and Police Violence: The Case of the 1033 Program', *Research and Politics*, vol. 4, no. 2, 2017, p. 3.

[27] Welch and Mewhirter, 'Does Police Equipment Lead Police Officers to be More Violent?'.

There is also mounting evidence to suggest that police with military backgrounds are especially likely to resort to violence. In one survey 32 per cent of them admitted to firing their weapons while on duty, compared to 24 per cent of non-veteran officers. This coheres with some of the other data gathered. For instance, in Albuquerque, officers with military experience accounted for a disproportional number of fatal shootings between 2000 and 2014. In Boston and Miami, police with military backgrounds have in the past generated more complaints of excessive force, on average, than those without military experience. The US Justice Department, and the International Association of Chiefs of Police, seem to be cognizant of this trend. In 2009, they jointly produced guidelines for police departments recruiting military veterans.[28] The document contained the following warning:

> Sustained operations under combat circumstances may cause return-ing officers to mistakenly blur the lines between military combat situations and civilian crime situations, resulting in inappropriate decisions and actions—particularly in the use of less lethal or lethal force.[29]

The other unfortunate consequence of militarization is that it can make police less effective at their jobs, not more.

Culturally militarized police treat segments of the community as an enemy to be pacified. Not surprisingly, this alters people's attitudes towards law enforcement. The language used by protestors during the unrest in Ferguson is a good illustration: when confronted by police in battle dress and combat helmets, some described it as an 'occupation'.[30] They saw the police as oppressors to be feared, rather than as public servants there to help. These perceptions make ordinary bread-and-butter police work much more difficult. People who fear and resent the police are unlikely to report things to them, cooperate with them, and so on. They may even become inclined to actively obstruct or even sabotage police investigations and operations. This makes it substantially harder

---

[28] Weichselbaum and Schwartzapfel, 'When Warriors Put On the Badge'.
[29] Quoted in Weichselbaum and Schwartzapfel, 'When Warriors Put On the Badge'.
[30] See Peter Cassidy, 'Operation Ghetto Storm: The Rise in Paramilitary Policing', *Covert Action Quarterly*, vol. 62, 1997.

for police to do their jobs. Hence the *telos* of one institution is undermined by the cultural influence of another; the militarization of police undermines their effectiveness *as* police. In the words of Neill Franklin, Executive Director of the Law Enforcement Action Partnership,

> militarization has eroded public trust in the police, the effectiveness of law enforcement overall, and ultimately, public safety . . . [O]ur 'crime reduction' strategy of deploying SWAT teams is paradoxically creating an environment in which it's harder for police to solve crimes and protect people.[31]

These concerns are about what police militarization predictably leads to, rather than concerns about police militarization per se. But there is an *in principle* objection worth acknowledging as well.

Very occasionally—usually after a natural disaster or during major civil unrest—a liberal democratic state will deploy its army on home soil. That this happens so rarely and reluctantly may be due to concerns about soldiers using excessive force against citizens, or their lack of appropriate training, or the financial costs associated with their mobilization. But there is possibly another, deeper reason.[32]

When the police use coercive force, it is against members of their own political community. Police therefore operate *within* the social contract. The military, by contrast, is the state's instrument of external coercion: its function is to protect the social contract from outsiders. This confers upon the military a certain *symbolic* power. Its orientation towards particular others symbolically includes or excludes those others from the political collective; it makes them either insiders or outsiders. This explains why deploying the military at home is problematic and usually reserved for national emergencies. If the defining function of the military is to defend the state against outside threats or 'others', then deploying the military domestically temporarily transforms the citizenry into the

---

[31] Neill Franklin, 'Retired Police Major: Police Militarization Endangers Public Safety', *American Civil Liberties Union*, 1 September 2017, available at: https://www.aclu.org/blog/criminal-law-reform/reforming-police-practices/retired-police-major-police-militarization, last accessed January 2018.

[32] For a full elaboration of the following point see Lieblich and Shinar, 'The Case Against Police Militarization'.

'other' against which the state needs defending. In other words, it symbolically excludes the citizens from the state.

Once we understand this, we can see why police militarization may be cause for concern independently of its downstream consequences. When law enforcers adopt the appearances and behaviours that epitomize the military in a given culture, the expressive power of the military is transmitted to the police. That power is to symbolically exclude the targets of coercion from the political community, to convey that they occupy a space outside of the social contract or body politic. But the exclusion is not temporary this time, as when military forces are deployed for a short period during riots. It lasts until such time that the police become un-militarized once more, and thus shed the symbolic power (or baggage) of the military. The exclusion of the policed from the state, in other words, is *normalized* where the police are militarized. This is not the kind of relationship that ought to exist between the state and its citizens in a liberal democracy. Indeed, it is precisely the kind of relationship we find in totalitarian countries, where the entire state apparatus is set up to shield the regime from domestic forces that would challenge its power.[33]

Of Business

Sun Tzu's *The Art of War* has become a surprise hit among business elites. Some MBA programs now even include the ancient military guide in their syllabi. This has spurred something of a cottage industry: Donald Krause published *The Art of War for Executives* in the 1990s, at around the same time that Dennis Laurie wrote *From Battlefield to Boardroom*. More recently Partha Bose produced a text applying insights from history's best-known military practitioner, Alexander the Great, to the world of business strategy. And it is not only publishers that have capitalized.[34] 'Business war-gaming' is now a thing, where players make moves and countermoves in a simulated commercial setting. The

[33] Lieblich and Shinar, 'The Case Against Police Militarization', p. 135.
[34] Peter Stokes, 'The "Militarizing" of Organization and Management Studies: Reconnoitring the Tensions—Problems and Possibilities for Reshaping the Terrain?', *Critical Perspectives of International Business*, vol. 31, no. 1, February 2007, p. 15.

competitor is the 'enemy', the goal is 'victory', and the simulated market is the 'battlespace'. Some of the games are administered by consulting firms that have ties to military establishments. Sometimes players even dress up in military fatigues, apparently.[35] In light of this it is little wonder that managerial commentary and practice have become saturated in military metaphors. As Fineman and Gabriel point out, 'the very vocabulary of business has been invaded by military terminology—strategy (the art of generalship), tactics, raids, targets, penetration, out-flanking, ambushes, predators, sieges, flak, piracy'. Such language has become a normal part of the management lexicon.[36]

One effect this can have is to alter the mental model that managers operate on: their preconceptions and assumptions about how things work in business. This raises a few concerns.

Blaine McCormick argues that the adoption of a militarized mental model by corporate executives is liable to damage the long-term interests of the companies that they preside over. He highlights a crucial point of difference between war and commerce, to wit: the former is usually a one-off, win-lose encounter, while the latter typically involves continuing interaction over an indefinite period of time. Because of this, tactics that can be rational in war—like deception—are more often than not imprudent in a business setting: it is unwise to needlessly sour relations with competitors insofar as we can expect them to have an ongoing influence over our prosperity. Furthermore, McCormick warns, if business is seen as relevantly analogous to war, then the competition is the enemy; the enemy should be assumed to harbour hostile intentions; the objective is to vanquish this enemy; and there is no way to 'win' other than to destroy the adversary's ability to fight. The result of this preoccupation with defeating the adversary, McCormick suggests, is that it can make executives blind to 'integrative' or 'win-win' strategies that often create more value than 'distributive' or zero-sum approaches (those in which gains comes *at the expense of* other market actors). McCormick's advice to

---

[35] Mark Chussil, 'The War Game Metaphor', available at: http://whatifyourstrategy.com/2010/08/18/the-war-game-metaphor/.

[36] Stephen Fineman and Yiannis Gabriel, *Experiencing Organizations*, London: Sage, 1996, p. 73.

business leaders is thus to discard *The Art of War* in favour of Robert Axelrod's *The Evolution of Cooperation*.[37]

If McCormick is right, then the militarization of business is bad *for business*: it impedes the objective of wealth creation, which is the purpose that justifies the existence of commercial enterprises in the first place. But I think there is another less obvious danger associated with the militarization of business, namely, it invites business practitioners to help themselves to the ethical standards that govern warfare.

We see this happening when business leaders and analysts use expressions like 'collateral damage' in reference to the negative externalities generated by commercial activities.[38] The allusion here is to the Doctrine of Double Effect (DDE), which has had a prominent place in the Just War tradition since the Middle Ages. The doctrine states, roughly, that it is sometimes permissible to knowingly cause some evil, as long as that evil is a merely foreseen side effect of an action that is aimed at a morally good outcome, and as long as the evil is proportional to the good aimed at.

DDE is paradigmatically applied to the following kinds of scenarios. Suppose our country is attacked by a neighbouring state seeking to annex our territory and take control of our political institutions. In the neighbouring state there is a massive munitions factory, where bombs and armaments for the aggressive war effort are produced. If we destroy the factory with a missile, the enemy will be crippled, and the aggression rebuffed. However there are civilian offices and residences in close proximity to the factory, occupied by innocent bystanders who have nothing to do with their state's aggression. The missile that destroys the factory will inevitably kill some of them, suppose. We do not want this to occur, but it cannot be helped if the factory is to be destroyed. According to the DDE it would be permissible for us to launch the missile since the harm to the civilian bystanders is an unintended side effect of the strike and the positive value of the strike is substantial enough to make this collateral damage proportional.

---

[37] Blaine McCormick, 'Make Money, Not War: A Brief Critique of Sun Tzu's the Art of War', *Journal of Business Ethics*, vol. 29, no. 3, 2001, pp. 285–6.
[38] See, for example, some of the recent musings of business consultant Ichak Kalderon Adizes, 'The Destructive Nature of Entrepreneurship', *Huffington Post*, 27 April 2017.

Talk of collateral damage in business settings insinuates that businesspeople are also entitled to avail themselves of the DDE, so as to justify decisions and actions with foreseen harmful side effects or externalities. But this is problematic.

DDE is by no means universally accepted, even among just war theorists.[39] Many reject it, and for many different reasons, but we need not rehearse these here.[40] Let us concede, for the sake of discussion, that DDE can be legitimately applied in scenarios like the one sketched above, such that it is permissible for us to bomb the munitions factory even though civilian casualties are a foreseen side effect. There are two features of this scenario, and others where DDE has intuitive appeal, which are morally significant. First, in this scenario the good to be achieved by bombing the factory is in fact the prevention of a serious harm—foreign occupation, oppression, etc. In other words, the objective of firing the missile is not to create more value than what existed *ex ante*, but simply to preserve/restore the status quo. Second, the agent responsible for firing the missile—the government of the attacked country—stands in a special relationship to the beneficiaries of the strike, which it does not share with the victims. The victims are foreign nationals, distant

---

[39] See, for instance, Uwe Steinhoff, 'The Secret to the Success of the Doctrine of Double Effect (and Related Principles): Biased Framing, Inadequate Methodology, and Clever Distractions', *Journal of Ethics*, vol. 22, no. 3–4, 2018, pp. 235–63.

[40] One argument for why intentional harms are morally worse than merely foreseen harms appeals to the idea that the former are somehow more disrespectful than the latter. The claim is that intentionally inflicting harm on a person, as a means to an end, turns that person into an instrument or prop for the achievement of the attacker's objectives. The attacker reduces his victim to 'material to be strategically shaped or framed' (W.S. Quinn, 'Actions, Intentions, and Consequences: The Doctrine of Double Effect', *Philosophy and Public Affairs*, vol. 18, no. 4, 1989, p. 348). This adds insult to the injury. The same charge cannot be brought against those who cause harm with mere foresight, as a side effect of pursuing their ends. They do not *use* their victims or impose on them a 'forced strategic subordination' (Quinn, 'Actions, Intentions, and Consequences, p. 351); rather they pursue their goals *despite* the harm that their actions are expected to cause their victims. While there is still some disrespect inherent in this, it is apparently not of the same degree, since in this case the attacker does not treat his victims as though they exist *for* his purposes. Quinn writes that those who intentionally harm their victims, but not those who harm with mere foresight, manifest 'a shocking failure of respect for the persons who are harmed; they treat their victims as they would treat laboratory animals'. (Quinn, 'Actions, Intentions, and Consequences, p. 348). Quinn argues that this aggravates the wrongdoing suffered by the victims of intentional attacks, as compared to the wrongdoing suffered by the victims of unintended harm. But is this really the case? Jonathan Bennett goes so far as to suggest that the opposite is true. One who intentionally harms as a means to an end treats his victims as an opportunity to be exploited, which is certainly disrespectful. But one who knowingly causes harm as a side effect of his endeavours 'is treating [his victims] as *nothing*; they play no part in his plan; he is not *even* treating them as means' (Jonathan Bennett, *The Act Itself*, Oxford: Clarendon Press, 1995, p. 218).

strangers, while the beneficiaries are its own citizens, to whom special obligations of protection are owed.[41]

When a business causes 'collateral damage', often neither of these conditions will obtain. Take a simple case: A manufacturing company can cut costs by altering its method of production. This will result in more profits accruing to shareholders. However, the new production method will also introduce stressors into the work environment that did not exist previously, and this will predictably result in some employees becoming unwell. In this scenario it is far from obvious that it would be morally permissible for the company to adopt the alternative production method, even though the harm to workers would be a 'merely foreseen' side effect. This, I think, is because the purpose of the change here is not to protect shareholders from some grave harm, but rather to enrich them: to maximize the economic value of their investment. Furthermore, while the shareholders may share a special relationship with the executives of the company, so too do the employees.[42] Both the beneficiaries of the decision, and its victims—the bearers of the 'collateral damage'—share a special relationship with the executives grounded in prior commitments and interactions, and special obligations of protection are accordingly owed to both.

If the features that make the application of DDE appropriate in war do not standardly obtain in business, then exporting DDE from war to business threatens to yield morally perverse—usually overly permissive—ethical verdicts. This highlights an overlooked danger associated with the adoption of a militarized mental model in business: the temptation to transmit the ethical standards that govern warfare, like those embedded in Just War Theory, to commerce. This is liable to make it easier for business leaders to rationalize unjustifiable conduct.

---

[41] For discussion of the ethical implications of this relationship in the context of war, see Seth Lazar, 'Associative Duties and the Ethics of Killing in War', *Journal of Practical Ethics*, vol. 1, no. 1, 2013, pp. 3–48.

[42] G.J. Rossouw emphasizes this difference between war and business in 'Business is Not Just War: Transferring the Principle of Double Effect from War to Business', *South African Journal of Philosophy*, vol. 23, no. 3, 2003, pp. 236–46.

Having said all this, it would be remiss to pretend that there are no silver linings or potential upsides here. Arguably, the military is where we are most likely to find so-called 'servant leadership'.[43] Its practitioners are the kinds of people who put the team, the flourishing of its members, and the achievement of its objectives, above their own interests. They are willing to share risks with their followers, and to make the very same sacrifices that they expect the people underneath them to make. This is more than we can say for the average banking executive. If the military's service conception of leadership was to take root in the corporate world, it would likely improve on the status quo there, by morally rehabilitating relationships between employers and employees. Thus a militarized mental model could have some *positive* effects on business enterprises; I do not mean to dismiss this possibility. I am only saying that there are also appreciable dangers that we need to be wary of.

Of Education

The militarization of policing and business would have come as no surprise to Ogden and Florence. Writing in the early 1900s, they observed that schools were being increasingly militarized, and predicted that this would eventually lead to the militarization of everything else. They feared that the military would penetrate deeper into civil society *via* its education system.[44]

What, exactly, is meant by the militarization of education? Ogden and Florence seem to have at least three things in mind. First, students spend a disproportional amount of time learning about military affairs and events, which receive ample attention not only in history classes, but also in politics, literature, international law, etc. In other words, the *content* of

---

[43] See Simon Sinek's 2014 TED talk, 'Why Good Leaders Make You Feel Safe', available at: https://www.ted.com/talks/simon_sinek_why_good_leaders_make_you_feel_safe/discussion#t-142346. See also Jeffrey W. Foley, 'Five Army-Tested Lessons of Servant Leadership', in Ken Blanchard and Renee Broadwell (eds.), *Service Leadership in Action: How You Can Achieve Great Relationships and Results*, Oakland, CA: Berrett-Koehler Publishers, 2018.

[44] 'The influence of militarism on education is a grievous legacy, with far reaching consequences. And its workings are all the more insidious because when all have been impregnated alike it is particularly hard to inaugurate a change'. Ogden and Florence, 'Militarism Versus Feminism', pp. 120–1.

what is taught has been militarized. Colman McCarthy makes the point especially well: 'Eighteen-year-olds come into college knowing more about the Marine Corps than the Peace Corps, more about the Bataan death march than Ghandi's salt march, more about organized hate than organized cooperation.'[45] The unfortunate result, according to Ogden and Florence, is that 'the average voter, the average municipal counsellor, even—we may surely add—the average member of parliament, still thinks of the past in terms of warriors and battles'.[46]

There is some empirical evidence for this over-weighting of military issues in school curricula. In a review of history textbooks used in the US at the elementary, middle-school, and high-school levels, Laura Finley found that an average of 89 pages were devoted to war and military engagements. By contrast fewer than five pages were devoted to non-violence, pacifism, and peace-movements.[47] There are plenty of references to America's military generals, but none to its Nobel Peace laureates.[48] This imbalance clearly implies something to students. As Riane Eisler reminds us, 'including certain kinds of information in the curriculum—and not including other kinds of information—effectively teaches children what is, and what is not, valuable'.[49]

Second, the way that lessons are delivered has been influenced by military norms—teaching *methods* have been militarized, not just contents. Brazilian philosopher Paulo Freire devoted the best part of his career to challenging what he referred to as the 'banking model' of education, so called because it reduces the learner to an empty account into which the educator makes deposits of knowledge.[50] On this model, education involves the transmission of information from the teacher to the student. This is essentially just a replica of the military drill, according to Ogden and Florence. 'Learning' involves students regurgitating information that they have been fed, in the same way that recruits repeat

---

[45] Colman McCarthy, *All of One Peace: Essays on Nonviolence*, New Brunswick, NJ: Rutgers University Press, p. 6.

[46] Ogden and Florence, 'Militarism Versus Feminism', p. 119.

[47] Laura L. Finley, 'Militarism Goes to School', *Essays in Education*, vol. 4, 2003, p. 11.

[48] Laura L. Finley, 'How Can I Teach Peace When the Book Only Covers War?', *The Online Journal of Peace and Conflict Resolution*, vol. 5, no. 1, Summer 2003.

[49] Riane Eisler, *Tomorrow's Children: A Blueprint for Partnership Education in the 21st Century*, Boulder, CO: Westview Press, 2000, p. 39.

[50] Paulo Freire, 'The Banking Model of Education', reprinted in Eugene F. Provenzo, *Critical Issues in Education: an Anthology of Readings*, Thousand Oaks, CA: Sage, 2006, pp. 105–17.

after the drillmaster. In both contexts there is absolute deference to authority; it is all one way, rather than anything approaching a critical exchange or a dialogue. Finley admits that this method of training/teaching may be suitable in the military, given its need for quick reactions, but it also suppresses independent thought and produces rote conformity, both of which do not serve civilian students well in their careers, or their lives.[51]

Finally, there is the physical presence of (current and former) military personnel in schools, which we find more in some countries than in others. The purpose of this, according to Ogden and Florence, is to instil in the youth a deep respect for, and habit of obedience towards, 'the wearers of the King's uniform'.[52] The American organization NNOMY (the National Network Opposing the Militarization of Youth) has made a point of highlighting that one of the most senior positions in the US school system—that of superintendent—has several times been occupied by military veterans, including two former generals.[53] For organizations such as NNOMY, however, this is not nearly as worrying as the formal, institutional presence of the US Armed Forces in schools, by way of the Junior Officer Reserve Training Corps (JORTC) program—a federally funded initiative through which retired military personnel are embedded in high schools and, using military-provided materials, deliver 'character education' to participating students ('cadets').

Schools sometimes also mirror the military in their administrative structures. Finley notices the resemblance to the chain of command:

… students are beholden to teachers, teachers to building level principals and vice principals, building administration to the superintendent and central office administration, and everyone to the local school board… where each person in command has more authority over the next… Students have input in the school curriculum no more than grunts in the trenches get a vote where and when to attack the enemy.[54]

[51] Finley, 'Militarism Goes to School', p. 7.
[52] Ogden and Florence, 'Militarism Versus Feminism', p. 123.
[53] Rebecca Perez, 'School to Prison Pipeline: Military Influence in Schools', available at: http://nnomy.org/index.php/en/content_page/396-military-presence-in-our-schools/554-school-to-prison-pipeline-military-influence-in-schools.html, last accessed February 2018.
[54] Finley, 'Militarism Goes to School', p. 4.

There are several other important resemblances. Both soldiers and students wear uniforms with insignia, to allow easy recognition of in- and out-groups.[55] Both are subject to a strictly controlled timetable, deviation from which normally requires express permission from a higher authority. Both students and soldiers are put through physical fitness programs. Both undergo standardized testing. Students are encouraged to compete for accolades such as valedictorian/dux, while soldiers compete for decorations.[56] The military has traditionally relied on negative reinforcement to discipline soldiers, and public schools have often done the same with their pupils.

So, the militarization of content gives students the impression that war and warriors are very important to national life. The militarization of methods habituates students into absolute deference to epistemic author- ities. The presence of military personnel in schools instils in students a familiarity with, and respect for, the armed forces. And on top of this, the aspects of schooling that Finley highlights serve to normalize military structures, processes, and ways of relating, until students come to see these as natural and unproblematic. School boards and teachers seldom *intend* to produce any of these effects, to be sure. They are best thought of as features of the so-called 'hidden curriculum'—lessons that students learn at school, but that are not necessarily intended by anyone. In other words, these lessons are the *side effects* of schooling, rather than its aims. But they are effects nevertheless.

Finley and others are to be commended for drawing attention to the various ways in which education has been militarized, but they largely assume that this development is undesirable, rather than explicating clear reasons to believe so. When they do turn to ethical critique, it usually centres on the link between militarized education and eventual military service.

The claim is that the militarization of schools amounts to back-door recruitment. The stated objective of programs like JROTC may not be to enlist students into the armed forces, but they do try to cultivate favourable dispositions towards the military, and to give students a taste for its culture. The predictable result is that a large proportion of cadets that complete the JROTC program do go on to enter a branch of

---

[55] Finley, 'Militarism Goes to School', p. 9.   [56] Finley, 'Militarism Goes to School', p. 5.

the US armed forces—around 45 per cent in fact.[57] This led the American Civil Liberties Union to complain, in May 2008, that JROTC violates the UN Convention on the Rights of the Child, which prohibits enticing children to participate in armed conflict.[58] The normative force of this objection, however, depends on an undeclared assumption that military service is an unfortunate, or at least a non-ideal, life choice. If we happen to think that military service is a good thing for young people, then we are unlikely to be particularly concerned by the prospect that militarized schools encourage kids to sign up for the armed forces down the track.

There is, however, a different argument against the militarization of schools that everyone should be able to appreciate, regardless of their views on military service. That objection, put plainly, is that a militarized education is a bad education, or worse than it could be. Just as it does to policing and business, militarization impedes the *telos* of education—it prevents schools from achieving the ends that they are intended to achieve, and that justify their existence in the first place.

There are many competing accounts of the proper ends of education. To avoid getting derailed into this literature let us focus on three specific aims that, most anyone would agree, schools should aspire towards. We usually expect students to gain some *knowledge* through schooling—i.e. to learn about history, and science, and economics and so on. But we also expect that schooling will help turn students into logical, critical thinkers, able to distinguish truth from fiction, able to reason independently, and able to make sound judgements. In other words, we expect students to gain some *wisdom* through schooling, for want of a better term. Third, we might expect students to acquire some useful skills at school, in particular those for which there is social demand. Call this the *preparatory* aim of schooling. People will disagree over which of these aims should take priority, or how to strike the right balance between them, but I think most readers will be willing to accept that, ideally, students should leave school with more knowledge and wisdom than they had before entering, and better prepared for their future endeavours.

---

[57] Catherine Lutz and Leslie Bartlett, *Making Soldiers in the Public Schools: An Analysis of the Army JROTC Curriculum*, Collingdale, PA: Diane Publishing, 1995, p. 5, available at: web.archive.org/web/20050507003139/http:/www.afsc.org/youthmil/militarism-in-schools/msitps.pdf.

[58] American Civil Liberties Union, *Soldiers of Misfortune: Abusive US Military Recruitment and Failure to Protect Child Soldiers*, 2008.

The militarization of education can obstruct these ends. A report on the aforementioned JROTC program is instructive in this connection. Authored by Catherine Lutz and Leslie Bartlett, the report contains the following key findings about the program:

(1) JROTC 'promotes authoritarian values instead of democratic ones; and ... uses rote learning methods and drill in lieu of critical thinking and problem-solving skills'.[59]

(2) The JROTC curriculum is 'distorted by the omission of certain facts and/or perspectives ... History is described as a linear series of accomplishments by soldiers, while the progress engendered by regular citizens is marginalized'.[60]

(3) JROTC 'consigns most of student time in the program to learning skills ... drill, and protocol, that have little relevance except in the military'.[61]

The authors are effectively saying that the JROTC program does a substandard job of producing wisdom (1), and knowledge (2), and that it also falls short in terms of giving graduates transferrable skills to meet social needs (3). Admittedly, this report addresses itself to the JROTC program specifically, but the features of the program that are identified as the source of dysfunction we might expect to find, to some degree, in all militarized educational settings. To the extent that the findings generalize at all, we have some reason to believe that the military's penetration into schools can be deleterious to them *as schools*.

Necessary vs. Surplus Militarization

If the spread of martial values into civilian society is likely to have unwanted effects, is there any way to prevent it from happening? Is 'penetration' a necessary consequence of having a military establishment, or a contingent one that can be reined in? The answer lies somewhere

---

[59] Lutz and Bartlett, *Making Soldiers in the Public Schools*, p. 3.
[60] Lutz and Bartlett, *Making Soldiers in the Public Schools*, p. 16.
[61] Lutz and Bartlett, *Making Soldiers in the Public Schools*, p. 3.

in between, according to a recent essay by Marcus Schulzke. He acknowledges that civilian society and its institutions can become excessively militarized—Schulzke calls this 'surplus militarization'. But he also appreciates that some degree of militarization is probably unavoidable as long as a permanent military establishment is present. This is 'necessary' militarization: it cannot be helped, at least not without prohibitive risks or costs.

Schulzke's argument is that militarization is a by-product of contact between soldiers and civilians, and that some degree of contact is imperative to ensure that: (1) the military obtains the information it needs to do its job; (2) the civilian population has the information it needs to critically evaluate military spending and deployments; (3) the civilian authorities maintain meaningful control over the military; and (4) military personnel feel part of the broader community, rather than detached from (and potentially resentful of) it. Any militarization that occurs as a result of the contact needed to achieve these ends is 'necessary' militarization, according to Schulzke. It cannot be prevented without isolating the military from civilian society to such an extent as to make it ineffective, unresponsive, or even dangerous. Anything beyond the minimum needed to achieve these ends is surplus. Schulzke cites things like recruitment drives in schools, and the valorization of soldiers at sporting events, as examples of the latter.

Schulzke is correct in saying that some militarization is unavoidable, but I think he radically understates his case. In particular, he overlooks the fact that militaries probably need to widely propagate their values simply to reproduce themselves. Once we appreciate this point, more and more of what appears at first blush to be 'surplus' militarization starts to look indispensable to the project of maintaining functional armed forces.

In order for a state to keep up its war-making capacity, it must be able to continuously replenish its armed forces with new recruits. These recruits must be willing to fight despite their fears, and to persist in fighting despite trauma and fatigue. Various means have been used through history to ensure that they are. Alcohol is one of them. The British army traditionally offered a daily 'rum ration' to soldiers, which was doubled before particularly dangerous offensives. This 'served to suppress soldiers' fears, reward their efforts, overcome their social inhibitions regarding aggressive violence, and help them numb the pain of combat', Joshua Goldstein explains.[62] The downside is that alcohol can also make soldiers clumsy, reckless, and even defiant. It is therefore not an ideal solution to the 'fear problem' as Goldstein calls it. Religion is another tool that has been used to keep soldiers fighting. In particular, notions of martyrdom, and the promise of rewards in the afterlife, have been used to temper the fear of death and encourage self-sacrifice. As with alcohol, though, religion has limitations in this regard. Belief in the afterlife might make soldiers more willing to die, but often it also makes them less willing to kill. And as General Patton said in 1944, wars are won by 'making the *other* poor dumb bastard die for *his* country', not by dying for one's own.[63]

According to Goldstein, gender constructs are now the instrument of choice for building and maintaining war-making capacity; political units use them to condition young men into thinking and behaving as the military needs them to, without the downsides that often accompany alcohol, religion, and other 'non-gendered' solutions to the fear problem.

It works like this. From an early age boys are taught to believe that a 'real man' is defined precisely by the suppressed martial values—he is tough, dominant, emotionless etc. In other words, we are conditioned to see these qualities as constitutive of masculinity, and therefore to believe that we are deficient *as men* if we lack them. (It is telling that the name 'Staff Sergeant Max Fightmaster' has become a slang term for 'someone who is unbelievably manly', according to Urban Dictionary).[64] This has two effects. First, it ensures that there is an abundant supply of potential recruits in the population who possess just those values and attitudes that are most conducive to competent military service. Second, it turns military service into the ultimate test, and expression, of manhood, and attracts young me to it. Cynthia Enloe elaborates:

> Acquisition of military manpower involves both getting recruits and keeping recruits. Military officials and their civilian allies never have

[62] Joshua S. Goldstein, *War and Gender: How Gender Shapes the War System and Vice Versa*, Cambridge: Cambridge University Press, 2001, p. 257.

[63] Goldstein, *War and Gender*, p. 258.

[64] https://www.urbandictionary.com/define.php?term=Staff%20Sergeant%20Max%20Fightmaster.

been able to solve this problem once and for all. It has never been enough to tap the supposedly intrinsic domineering or violent qualities in men in order to fill the ranks with soldiers numerous enough, politically reliable enough and technically skilled enough to satisfy the military elite. Acquisition of manpower has required an elaborate gender ideology and social structure, not just smooth-talking recruiters and strong-armed press-gangs...It has required that male soldiers feel they cannot test their 'manliness' unless they serve in the military...Ignore gender—the social constructions of 'femininity' and 'masculinity' and the relations between them—and it becomes impossible adequately to explain how military forces have managed to capture and control so much of society's imagination and resources.[65]

Of course, without direct access to the subconscious minds of recruits, we cannot know for sure what role gender constructs, and the internal pressures they generate, ultimately play in enticing people into the armed forces and inspiring them to fight valiantly when hostilities erupt. But it is worth pointing out that Goldstein's narrative helps us make sense of some otherwise curious phenomena.

Take, for instance, the stubborn opposition to women in combat roles, which somehow manages to persist despite the various rationales for it falling apart under close scrutiny. (Even when acceptance comes, it is often grudging). Norman Dixon suggests that this opposition gives us a clue into what, deep down, motivates those members of the military who form the opposition. His book *On the Psychology of Military Incompetence* speculates that a proportion of the young men who volunteer for professional military service make this career choice because they have 'unconscious doubts about [their] own masculinity and sexual adequacy'.[66] In other words, they fight to prove their manhood. But if it turns out that women can also fight, then doing it is no longer proof of manhood. Hence women must be kept out, lest one's real reason for joining is undercut.

[65] Cynthia Enloe, *Does Khaki Become You? The Militarisation of Women's Lives*, London: Pluto Press, 1983, pp. 211–12.
[66] Norman Dixon, *On The Psychology of Military Incompetence*, London: Jonathan Cape, 2976, p. 141.

Such individuals will be attracted to organizations which set upon them the seal of masculinity. By being admitted to a society of men bent upon the most primitive manifestations of maleness—violence and aggression—the individual achieves the reassurance he requires. But to maintain this reassurance he will in turn have to contribute, by word and deed, to the elaborate defences against effeminacy of the citadel which he has entered.[67]

For our purposes the important insight is just this. If militaries are to be effective, they need to recruit enough people, and these people need to share, or at least be receptive to, the suppressed martial values. In order to ensure that there is a big enough pool of such people to recruit from, said values must be propagated among the general population. Nowadays this is achieved, according to the likes of Goldstein and Enloe, by the construction of gender narratives that teach us that the qualities of a good warrior also just happen to be the qualities of a quintessential man. Thus it is no coincidence that the suppressed martial values appear in civilian society as the very values that define masculinity. Our military establishments could not persist in their current form without this. Martial values must be spread widely so that men will continue to enlist, and to behave in ways that are conducive to successful war-making while enlisted.[68]

What Schulzke fails to appreciate, I think, is the extent of the civil–military intercourse needed to achieve all of this. If professional militaries limited their interactions with the civilian population to the minimum needed for information exchange, operational effectiveness, and civilian oversight, it is doubtful that a critical mass of men in society would embrace the suppressed martial values as their own. To make that happen, there *must* be some valorization of soldiers at football games, some glorification of war in movies, some toy machineguns produced for

---

[67] Enloe, *Does Khaki Become You?*, p. 211.
[68] See also Kovitz, 'The Roots of Military Masculinity'. Contrary to the idea of innate male aggression, Kovitz argues that combativeness must be 'deliberately induced or constructed' (p. 5). Her proof is that men will try anything and everything to avoid involvement in armed conflict—desertion, self-mutilation, feigning illness, insanity, sexual deviance, hiring surrogates, going AWOL or even committing suicide. Masculine values, Kovitz argues, are propagated by military institutions in a deliberate attempt to reprogram men to be more useful to the military establishment.

boys to play with, some quasi-military institutions (like the scouts) to give them a taste for its culture, and so on. In other words, much of what Schulzke labels 'surplus militarization' is only surplus if we look solely at what militaries need to be effective and well-regulated *right now*, without any regard to what they need to replenish themselves into the future. Once we correct this myopia, what may have appeared surplus reappears as necessary. For militaries to persist in anything like their current form, there needs to be much more militarization of their parent societies than Schulzke lets on.[69]

Conclusion

I began this chapter by drawing a distinction between *advertised* and *suppressed* military values. Maybe it would be a good thing if more civilians embraced the former, but this should not blind us to the ways in which the latter can have pernicious effects when they spread beyond the armed forces, and that is what I have been concentrating on. Thus nothing I have said should be misconstrued as suggesting that militaries are pure poison in their moral and cultural influence. My point is just that there are respects in which military mores can cause damage when they penetrate into civilian society and its institutions. Importantly though, I have suggested that some such diffusion of martial values is largely unavoidable in a society with a permanent military establishment (at least one that requires a steady inflow of recruits with the appropriate

---

[69] It is worth adding that the diffusion of martial values can also help maintain the morale of the civilian population during wartime: the same values that keep our soldiers fighting, keep up our support *for* the fight. Militaries in Western democracies have learned how politically important civilian morale is to their operations (and how inconvenient civilian *de*moralization can become). Thus it is unsurprising that considerable investments have been made in figuring out how to manipulate it. The work of Jackie Orr provides an impressively detailed overview of the historical efforts of the US defence establishment in particular to 'bring the public psychology into conformity with the requirements of national security policy'. Promoting the uptake of martial value in the civilian population has for a long time been part of this project. If steps were taken to prevent this kind of thing from happening, it would probably not jeopardize the existence of the armed forces (this is 'surplus' not 'necessary' militarization). But as long as militaries recognize the importance of civilian morale to the operations, it gives them an additional incentive to penetrate. See Jackie Orr, 'The Militarization of Inner Space', *Critical Sociology*, vol. 30, no. 2, 2004, pp. 452–81, quoted at p. 464.

dispositions). The reality for most political communities, then, is that they will have to tolerate some of the baneful effects of cultural militarization as long as they want to have professional armed forces at the ready. This is unlikely to ever be a decisive consideration in its own right, but if we want to think seriously about whether a military is worth having, it is surely something that needs to be taken into account.

Conclusion

Although best known for his contributions to mathematical psychology, Anatol Rapoport became an outspoken military abolitionist during the Vietnam War era. In the foreword to *Understanding War* he writes:

> [T]he identification of national security with military potential, the belief in the effectiveness of 'deterrence', the belief that dismantling military institutions must lead to economic slump and unemployment, the belief that military establishments perform a useful social function by 'defending' the societies on which they feed, and so on. All these beliefs qualify as superstitions by the usual definition of a superstition as a stubbornly held belief for which no evidence exists.[1]

For every advantage that professional militaries are commonly said to confer on their parent societies, Rapoport was quick to register his scepticism. This book has done no such thing. The preceding chapters are silent on the benefits of militarization, neither affirming nor disputing them. Instead, I have focussed on the various risks and costs that a political community bears by having a permanent military establishment attached to it. Whatever we gain by having professional armed forces on standby—and I do not deny that there are benefits—I have tried to show that this arrangement costs us a lot more than money.

Needless to say things might always change. In *Army of None* Paul Scharre envisages a future in which our wars are fought largely by autonomous weapons systems.[2] Should this ever come to pass it would

---

[1] Anatol Rapoport, Foreword to John McMurty, *Understanding War: A Philosophical Inquiry*, Downsview: Samuel Stevens and Company, University of Toronto Press, 1989, pp. vi–vii.
[2] Paul Scharre, *Army of None: Autonomous Weapons and the Future of War*, New York: W.W. Norton and Co, 2018.

Ethics, Security, and The War-Machine: The True Cost of the Military. Ned Dobos, Oxford University Press (2020).
© Ned Dobos.
DOI: 10.1093/oso/9780198860518.001.0001

probably rein in some of the dangers and costs that our militaries presently generate (while introducing others, no doubt). But my analysis has been confined to military organizations as we know them, not military organizations as they might be. As long as our armed forces rely on a steady inflow of (human) recruits, with values conducive to competent military service, who are then separated off from civilian society, and trained to use organized violence on behalf of the state, under conditions of international uncertainty, militarized societies will invariably sustain some combination of the risks and costs discussed in this book.

As I made clear at the outset, this does not bring us to the conclusion that military abolition is a moral and/or prudential imperative for every state, or indeed for any state. Whether the costs of militarization are worth bearing can only be determined on a case-by-case basis. No valid generalization can be made about whether military organizations are justified in existing based on the material presented here. But perhaps a somewhat weaker conclusion can be drawn.

I have shown that militaries are very costly institutions, not just financially, but morally and socially. Even in peacetime the war-machine can be harmful to the individuals in it, and to its parent society, and dangerous to everybody else. This being the case, we might reasonably insist that the existence of a military is justified only if it significantly increases the security of its civilian population (i.e. reduces the likelihood of its members becoming victims of lethal violence or comparably serious harms). But in light of Chapters 2 and 3, it is not clear that we *can* confidently presume that, as a rule, militaries have this effect. They mitigate some of the dangers we face, no doubt, but they seem to introduce and exacerbate others. This does not get us to the strong conclusion that militaries are not justified in existing. But perhaps it is enough to shift the burden of argument onto the proponents of standing armies. The weaker conclusion is that there is a moral presumption against militaries that needs to be overturned, rather than a presumption in favour of their continued existence.

At the very least I hope to have convinced the reader that whether a military is worth having ought always to be treated as an open question. Currently we think of it as a foregone conclusion. Citizens and politicians no longer seriously interrogate whether their national militaries are justified; we simply assume that they must be. There are a number of possible explanations for this.

The first I have already flagged: we assume that the *ad bellum* question (can war-making be justified?) settles the *ante bellum* question (is war-building justified?). If pacifism is mistaken, and going to war can be morally permissible sometimes, as most of us believe, then we infer that it must be permissible to prepare for war by creating and maintaining an institution that specializes in it. On this reasoning, the justice of war-building depends entirely on the justice of war-making; they stand or fall together. I hope to have exposed this fallacy for what it is. But a faulty inference from *ad bellum* to *ante bellum* is not the only possible explanation for why we no longer give much thought to whether or not our militaries are justified in existing.

In *A Treatise of Human Nature*, David Hume hypothesizes that we have a tendency to unreflectively assign positive moral properties to existing states: we assume that what *is, ought to be*.[3] Goodness is inferred from mere existence. Empirical research confirms Hume's suspicion. A study published in the *Journal of Personality and Social Psychology* finds that: 'In all matters there seems to be a general proclivity among people to ascribe worth, value, and goodness to extant states of the world.' The authors label this proclivity 'existence bias'.[4] Essentially, if something exists, we begin with the assumption that it is justified in existing—this becomes our cognitive default. 'People have an immediate favourable response to what is established';[5] they 'imbue the *status quo* with an unearned quality of goodness, in the absence of deliberative thought, actual experience or reason to do so'.[6]

Contiguous with the existence bias is the so-called longevity bias. Simply put, the longer something has existed, the more likely we are to unreflectively attribute positive qualities to it. In one experiment participants were asked to read descriptions of the 'advanced interrogation' techniques being used against suspected terrorists by the US government.

---

[3] David Hume, *A Treatise of Human Nature*, New York: Prometheus, 1992/1739.

[4] Scott Eidelman, Christian S. Crandall, and Jennifer Pattershall, 'The Existence Bias', *Journal of Personality and Social Psychology*, vol. 97, no. 5, 2009, p. 765.

[5] Scott Eidelman and Christian S. Crandall, 'The Intuitive Traditionalist: How Biases for Existence and Longevity Promote the Status Quo', *Advances in Experimental Social Psychology*, vol. 50, 2014, p. 58.

[6] Eidelman and Crandall, 'The Intuitive Traditionalist', p. 61.

Those who were told that these techniques are decades old were more likely to approve of them than those who were told that they are recent innovations. Long-standing states of the world are presumed to be better.[7] This, of course, does not mean that we are incapable of dispassionate inquiry into whether existing arrangements are, in fact, justified. But it might explain why we often fail to inquire in the first place, especially where the existing arrangements have long histories and time-honoured traditions behind them.

The fact that so many of us (myself included) have vested interests in military establishments might also contribute to our reluctance to openly interrogate whether they should be kept or discarded.[8] US President Dwight Eisenhower coined the term 'military–industrial complex' in his farewell address, drawing attention to the deep interconnections between the American defence establishment and various other social, political, and commercial institutions, the result of which is that the latter become increasingly dependent on, and influenced by, the former.[9] Nick Turse breaks 'the complex' down into its component parts. He writes of the 'military–corporate–conference complex'; the 'military–petroleum complex', the 'military–academic complex', and so on.[10] His point is to show that very few US civilians are not materially connected to the country's defence establishment in one way or another.[11] Americans are not unique in this; dependence on the war-machine is a reality for many civilians the world over.

It is understandable, in light of this, that politicians, scholars, and ordinary citizens seldom reflect on whether their national militaries ought to be retained or dismantled. But while these factors might help

[7] Eidelman and Crandall, 'The Intuitive Traditionalist', pp. 54–5; Scott Eidelman and Christian Crandall, 'Bias in Favour of the Status Quo', *Social and Personality Psychology Compass*, vol. 6, no. 3, 2012, p. 274.

[8] Alex C. Michalos is probably right when he suggests that 'people whose livelihoods depend on militarization will be relatively uncritical of militarization'. Alex C. Michalos, 'Militarism and the Quality of Life', *Annals of the New York Academy of Sciences*, vol. 577, no. 1, December 1989, p. 225.

[9] For a glimpse into how the complex works, see William D. Hartung, 'Eisenhower's Warning: The Military Industrial Complex Forty Years Later', *World Policy Journal*, vol. 18, no. 1, Spring 2001, pp. 39–44.

[10] See also William D. Hartung and Michelle Ciarrocca, 'The Military-Industrial-Think Tank Complex: Corporate Think Tanks and the Doctrine of Aggressive Militarism', *Multinational Monitor*, vol. 24, no. 1/2, 2003, pp. 17–20.

[11] Nick Turse, *The Complex: How the Military Invades our Everyday Lives*, New York: Metropolitan Books, 2008.

explain why we fail to entertain the prospect of military abolition, they do not *justify* it. Given the significant costs that a society incurs, and the risks that it takes, simply by virtue of maintaining a war-machine, the question of whether even to have one is at least as important as the question of when and where to use it.

In order to answer this *ante bellum* question, we need to appreciate all of the costs and risks that come with militaries, not just their functions and advantages. The purpose of this book has been to give readers a better sense of some of these costs. The few that I have singled out for attention are not meant to be exhaustive. I have not even touched on the environmental and ecological consequences of militarization.[12] Nor have I dealt with its economic consequences in any detail. (If advocates of the so-called 'depletionist' thesis are correct, 'military spending undercuts economic performance by drawing skilled personnel out of the civilian sector, diverting capital into unproductive military activities, and encouraging wasteful management practices both inside and outside the military–industrial complex').[13] I have concentrated instead on the moral and cultural costs of the military, and the ways in which it detracts from our security, if only because these things are so often overlooked.

The first chapter explored some of the morally damaging effects of war-building. I argued that insofar as combat training aims to desensitize people to violence, it corrodes virtue, and is therefore morally injurious by design. The second and third chapters challenged the assumption that militaries make an unequivocally positive contribution to the security of the civilian populations that they are charged with protecting. Militarization introduces the risk of a coup into our lives (Chapter 2), and also exposes us to fear-induced defensive aggression from the outside (Chapter 3). Thus, while going without a military is risky, so too is

[12] See Kenneth A. Gould, 'The Ecological Costs of Militarization', *Peace Review*, vol. 19, no. 3, 2007, pp. 331–4; G. Hooks and Chad L. Smith, 'The Treadmill of Destruction: National Sacrifice Areas and Native Americans', *American Sociological Review*, vol. 69, no. 4, 2004, pp. 558–75; and Mark Woods, 'The Nature of War and Peace: Just War Thinking, Environmental Ethics, and Environmental Justice', in Michael W. Brough, John W. Lango, and Harry van der Linden (eds.), *Rethinking the Just War Tradition*, New York: SUNY Press, 2007, pp. 17–34.
[13] Subba Muthuchidambaram, 'From Swords to Plowshares: An Evaluation of the US Legislative Attempts on Economic Conversion and Human Resource Planning', *Business Ethics Quarterly*, vol. 2, no. 1, 1992, p. 7. See also Trish Kelly and Meenakshi Rishi, 'An Empirical Study of the Spin-Off Effects of Military Spending', *Defence and Peace Economics*, vol. 14, no. 1, 2003, pp. 1–7.

having a military: there is a trade-off involved. In Chapter 4 I argued that militaries are liable to be misused even when entrusted to morally motivated, suitably informed, and politically accountable decision makers. Preventing the misuse of military capabilities is not simply a matter of ensuring that they do not fall into the 'wrong hands', as some have suggested. Chapter 5 looked at the ways in which a permanent military establishment can deform the civilian institutions of the parent society it attaches to, even when no military operations are being conducted. This happens when some of the martial values cultivated by professional armed forces spill over into civilian society.

These costs and risks are not borne equally by all militarized states. Some are more coup-prone than others. Some military conditioning regimes may be more morally damaging than others. Some military establishments 'penetrate' deeper into civilian society. Some are more likely than others to provoke what they try to deter. Having said that, I take these considerations to be generalizable to some degree, rather than idiosyncratic to any particular country or region. Reflecting on these costs and risks will not necessarily yield the conclusion that military abolition is the right course of action for every, or any, political community to take. But it will prevent our commitment to militarization from ever becoming a 'dead dogma'. Once we appreciate the true cost of the military, we are bound to see that there are powerful considerations against 'war-building'—or in favour of demilitarization—regardless of what one happens to believe about the prospects for just 'war-making' under current conditions.

Epilogue

Towards 'Post-Military' Defence?

Introduction

Militaries are exceedingly costly, not to mention dangerous, institutions. Are these costs and risks worth bearing? The answer is always going to depend on a number of factors, one of them being the availability of alternative arrangements for national defence. If there is no viable alternative, this does not *guarantee* that a military is justified in existing (since the costs of militarization might sometimes be prohibitive even in the absence of alternatives; some polities might be better off having *nothing at all* than having professional armed forces on standby). But if there really are no other options, this will certainly make it easier for governments to justify imposing on their people the costs of maintaining a military. If there is an alternative, on the other hand, then justifying the costs of a military will be more difficult, especially if that alternative turns out to be substantially less costly.

Gene Sharp—founder of the Albert Einstein Institution and three-time Nobel Peace Prize nominee—spent his career advocating for what he called a 'post-military' civilian defence system (henceforth CDS).[1] It would perform the core functions currently entrusted to armed forces, including national defence against external aggression, but it would rely on non-violent means and methods—the very same that citizens might employ to depose a local dictator. Sharp envisaged a world in which the

---

[1] Gene Sharp, *Civilian-Based Defense: A Post-Military Weapons System*, Princeton, NJ: Princeton University Press, 1990.

Ethics, Security, and The War-Machine: The True Cost of the Military. Ned Dobos, Oxford University Press (2020). © Ned Dobos.
DOI: 10.1093/oso/9780198860518.001.0001

energies and resources currently spent on militaries would be redirected into these radically different-looking defence institutions. He called this process 'trans-armament', as opposed to disarmament, to emphasize that it would not involve throwing our weapons down, but rather replacing them with other (in Sharp's estimation, better) ones.

This epilogue proceeds as follows. First, drawing on some of the empirical research in this space, I argue that a CDS should be treated as a genuine alternative to the military. By this I simply mean that it ought not be dismissed as an idealistic fantasy that could not possibly 'work' in the 'real world'. I then argue that, while a CDS might cause some problems of its own, it would largely avoid the more significant risks and costs that typically come with military establishments. In fact, a CDS might deliver positive moral *advantages* that a military does not, and cannot, produce. The upshot is that we do have a less costly alternative that is worth taking seriously. Of course, the cost of *transitioning* from military to post-military is another matter altogether, and I cannot get into that here.

One point of clarification before proceeding: I will not be arguing that a CDS could do all of various things that we currently rely on militaries to do. Nowadays, some states use their militaries to do what is essentially police work (e.g. to fight drug smuggling, illegal immigration) and even as a source of cheap labour for civil construction projects.[2] These activities are certainly beneficial, but they are not what militaries are for; they can (and arguably should) be left to other social institutions.[3] My argument in what follows is only that the core 'functional imperative' of the military—the purpose that *defines* it, namely defence of the polity against armed foreign aggression—could feasibly be served by a CDS.[4]

---

[2] Timothy Edmunds, 'What *Are* Armed Forces For? The Changing Nature of Military Roles in Europe', *International Affairs*, vol. 82, no. 6, November 2006, pp. 1059–75.

[3] Edmunds suggests that militaries are increasingly engaging in activities outside of this 'functional imperative' in order to 'legitimate their institutional existence and budgetary demands'. Edmunds, 'What *Are* Armed Forces For?' p. 1061.

[4] As Andrew Alexandra writes, 'The legitimate goals of the armed forces, which are at the heart of the institution of war, are deterrence of external violent usurpation of political authority and resistance to such usurpation if it is nevertheless attempted'. 'Pacifism: Designing a Moral Defence Force', in Jeroen Van Den Hoven, Seumas Miller, and Thomas Pogge (eds.), *Designing In Ethics*, Cambridge: Cambridge University Press, 2017, p. 159.

Civilian Defence Systems

There was renewed faith in 'people power' in the wake of the Arab Spring. It showed us that even the most intransigent tyrants can be deposed by ordinary citizens acting non-violently. But this faith remains narrowly circumscribed. We may be prepared to accept that citizens can remove their abusive governments through civil resistance, but foreign aggression is another matter entirely—we still insist that only soldiers with guns can defend us against *that*. Prior to his death in 2018, Gene Sharp led the way in questioning this widely held and deeply entrenched assumption.

The archetypal foreign aggressor comes to conquer and rule. His ambition is to annex territory, extract resources, gain control over the native people and their political institutions, and profit off their labour. Sharp's key insight is that in order for the aggressor to achieve these objectives, he needs the native population to behave in certain ways. To profit off their labour, he needs them to labour. To implement policies, he needs bureaucrats to administer them, and citizens to comply. There is a kind of *dependency relationship* between the aggressor and the population targeted;[5] he simply cannot get what he came for without some measure of cooperation from the public.[6] Sharp was adamant that ordinary citizens could leverage this dependency to expel most any aggressor without violence, or even threats thereof. This would usually involve some combination of *protest*, *non-cooperation*, and *non-violent intervention* or obstruction.[7]

Protest actions communicate disapproval and raise awareness of the resistance, so as to attract more participation and support. This includes everything from marches to petitions to street theatre. *Non-cooperation* involves withdrawing from the institutions put in place by the aggressor,

---

[5] Ralph Summy, 'Nonviolence and the Case of the Extremely Ruthless Opponent', *Global Change, Peace, and Security*, vol. 6, no. 1, 1994, pp. 1–29; Ralph Summy, "The Efficacy of Nonviolence: Examining the 'Worst Case Scenario', *Peace Research*, vol. 25, no. 2, May 1993, pp. 1–9.

[6] For his most thorough elaboration and defence of this claim, see Gene Sharp, *The Politics of Nonviolent Action*, Boston, MA: Porter Sargent Publishers, 1973 (3 volumes).

[7] Hardy Merriman, 'Theory and Dynamics of Nonviolent Action', in M.J. Stephan (ed.), *Civilian Jihad: Nonviolent Struggle, Democratization, and Governance in the Middle East*, New York: Palgrave Macmillan, 2009.

or withholding the goods that the aggressor needs to rule effectively and promote his interests. This comes in three forms. *Economic* non-cooperation involves consumer boycotts, labour strikes, voluntary unemployment, tax evasion, and the like. These tactics deprive the aggressor state of what it needs to achieve its economic ends. *Political* non-cooperation means withholding information from police, refusing to participate in government programs (like when the Druze in the Golan Heights refused to accept Israeli identification documents)[8], and general non-compliance with laws and regulations. *Social* non-cooperation involves the suspension of social activities (sports, festivals, etc.), ignoring/avoiding interactions with representatives of the aggressor state, ostracizing those who do cooperate with it, and so on. Finally, *non-violent intervention* involves actively obstructing the aggressor state's ability to function, through sit-ins, blockades (of buildings, streets, mines, etc.), as well as the sabotaging of equipment and infrastructure that the aggressor state relies on.[9]

Sharp's published work details nearly two hundred discreet methods of protest, non-cooperation, and obstruction for civilians to use against illegitimate/unwelcome authorities—both domestic and foreign—and in private correspondence before his death he apparently claimed to have discovered many more.[10] By shrewdly mobilizing some combination of these non-violent 'weapons', Sharp argues, communities can render themselves 'politically indigestible' to foreign conquerors. If enough people behave obstructively and refuse to cooperate for long enough, the occupation bears no fruit—at least not enough to make it worthwhile. The occupying regime thus succumbs to 'political starvation' and must retreat.[11] Jack Salmon summarizes the strategy like this:

---

[8] R. Scott Kennedy, 'Noncooperation in the Golan Heights: A Case of Nonviolent Resistance', in M.J. Stephan (ed.), *Civilian Jihad: Nonviolent Struggle, Democratization, and Governance in the Middle East*, New York: Palgrave Macmillan, 2009, pp. 119–30.

[9] The creation of parallel 'counter-state' institutions has also been characterized as a form of non-violent intervention, but it might be more accurate to include it under 'non-cooperation'. While the creation of these institutions might involve acts of commission rather than omission, the aim is ultimately to facilitate withdrawal or divestment from the institutions of the aggressor state, to make it easier for members of the resisting group to do this without sustaining prohibitive personal costs. No direct interference with the functioning of the existing institutions need be involved.

[10] Summy, 'Nonviolence and the Case of the Extremely Ruthless Opponent', p. 11.

[11] Sharp, *Civilian-Based Defense*, p. 23.

...non-violent resistance defeats an attacker not by inflicting direct damage in retaliation but through political economics, by creating a negative cost–benefit equation. Government consumes resources in order to administer, police, and direct a society. If a 'conquered' society refuses to supply those resources [...] they must be supplied by the conqueror from his own resources. There develops a resource sink condition to the disadvantage of the conqueror: no longer is there profit in conquest, but there are expenses.[12]

At this point one might reasonably ask: what if the aggressor uses force to compel cooperation? Can he not use violence to knead the local population into 'political digestibility'? Of course he can. But this will not only consume more resources, bringing the negative cost–benefit equation even closer; it is also liable to backfire in various ways. If the aggressor uses violence against passive resisters, two things are likely (though admittedly not guaranteed) to happen. First, locally and internationally, people will feel greater sympathy for the resisters, and for their cause by extension. This could mean that even more people feel inclined to join (or abet) the resistance movement, further increasing the costs of enforcement.[13] Second, some of the aggressor state's functionaries— those responsible for directly employing the violence—will start feeling guilty and ashamed about it. Some of them might defect outright. Others might simply become disposed to 'withhold effort' on the job, to borrow a term from human resource management. This might sound like wishful thinking, but it has happened time and again through history.

In 1919, Chinese students in the Shantung province staged a peaceful protest against Japanese control. Soldiers were ordered to arrest those involved, but according to a report in *The Independent*, when they found the protesters kneeling in the street and crying, the soldiers took pity and let the students be.[14] A decade later in India two platoons of the Garhwal regiment refused orders to open fire on non-violent resisters in

[12] Jack D. Salmon, 'Can Non-violence Be Combined with Military Means for National Defense?', *Journal of Peace Research*, vol. 25, no. 1, 1988, pp. 70–1.

[13] Merriman, 'Theory and Dynamics of Nonviolent Action', p. 20; Lewis Lipsitz and Herbert M. Kritzer, 'Unconventional Approaches to Conflict Resolution: Erikson and Sharp on Nonviolence', *The Journal of Conflict Resolution*, vol. 19, no. 4, December 1975, p. 727.

[14] Quoted in Adam Roberts, 'Civilian Defense and the Inhibition of Violence', *Philosophy East and West*, vol. 19, no. 2, 1969, p. 187.

Peshawar.[15] During the 1956 Hungarian revolution, again there were reported cases of Russian soldiers refusing to shoot at unarmed resisters.[16] In 1979, Iran's army commanders ordered the troops back to the barracks and refused any further part in the repression of peaceful protesters. The Shah subsequently fled the country. In the Philippines, Ferdinand and Imelda Marcos ordered soldiers to open fire on thousands of protesters that were blocking their path, but the soldiers refused.[17] In both Serbia (2000) and Ukraine (2004), some members of the army and police took issue with their own side's behaviour, and consequently 'chose to carry out orders less efficiently'.[18] Sometimes they simply ignored orders to repress non-violent resisters, or feigned ignorance that the orders had been issued in the first place.

[15]   Roberts, 'Civilian Defense and the Inhibition of Violence'.

[16]   Roberts, 'Civilian Defense and the Inhibition of Violence', pp. 187–8.

[17]   Michael Randle, 'The Dynamics of Nonviolent Action', in Michael Randle (ed.), *Challenge to Nonviolence*, Bradford: University of Bradford, 2002, p. 80. Even Nazi soldiers sometimes refused instructions to victimize civilians. The German food policy in the East was to allow the population there 'the minimum for existence', and to withhold the rest for German consumption. But as prominent historian Geoffrey Megargee writes: 'For all the propaganda, and despite widespread faith in their cause, many German soldiers could not stand by and let women, children, and old people starve in front of their eyes without being affected, and without doing something about it. At the corps headquarters level, which actually had to deal with the civilians, the commands were pleading for food to give them, while some soldiers did what they could to alleviate the locals' suffering.' Geoffrey P. Megargee, *War of Annihilation: Combat and Genocide on the Eastern Front 1941*, Lanham, MD: Rowman and Littlefield, 2006, p. 120.

[18]   Merriman, 'Theory and Dynamics of Nonviolent Action', p. 28. Adam Roberts cites some of these examples as evidence of what he calls the 'mechanism of inhibition', which he thinks is key to the success of peaceful resistance. His claim is not that security forces will never be able to bring themselves to repress peaceful resisters with violence—that is patently false. The proposition is only that, normally, a soldier/police officer will find it more difficult to use violence against people who are obviously non-threatening; he/she will feel at least somewhat emotionally and morally inhibited when confronted by non-violent resisters. Roberts, 'Civilian Defense and the Inhibition of Violence', pp. 181–93. Even the Nazis might have been hindered by the mechanism of inhibition to some degree. Military historian B.H. Liddell Hart, who interrogated German generals after the Second World War, touched on this in his commentary on why the Nazis failed to deal effectively with the resistance in Holland, Norway, and Denmark: 'Their evidence also showed the effectiveness of non-violent resistance…Even clearer was their inability to cope with it. They were experts in violence, and had been trained to deal with opponents who used that method. But other forms of resistance baffled them—and all the more in proportion as the methods were subtle and concealed. It was a relief to them when resistance became violent and when non-violent forms were mixed with guerrilla action, thus making it easier to combine drastic repressive action against both at the same time.' Quoted in Summy, 'Nonviolence and the Case of the Extremely Ruthless Opponent', p. 20. This is remarkable. Nazi functionaries admitted that they felt *relieved* when resisters in northern Europe added violence to their hitherto entirely non-violent methods, perhaps because the introduction of violence switched off the mechanism of inhibition that had been engaged up to that point.

What this reveals is that non-violent resistance puts an aggressor in a kind of lose-lose situation. If he tolerates the non-cooperation and obstruction of the natives, it effectively means relinquishing control of the territory and its people. It probably also means losing the ability to extract resources, insofar as this depends on the participation of local labourers, farmers, technicians, transport workers, and the like. This would seem to defeat the very purpose of the aggression, leaving the occupier with little reason to remain. On the other hand, if the aggressor uses violence in an attempt to compel cooperation, this is both expensive and liable to backfire in the ways just described, and again the aggressor cedes power.[19] Hence Sharp describes non-violent resistance as 'political jiu jitsu'. If the attacker does not use force he cannot take down the defender. But if the attacker does use force, his own momentum is turned against him, he is thrown off balance, and again the defender is left standing.[20]

In calling for trans-armament towards civilian defence systems, what Sharp proposed was the creation of formal state institutions devoted to national defence using only the aforementioned non-violent means and methods. The state would actively recruit non-violent defenders, just as it currently recruits young men and women into the armed forces. The 'fighters' would undergo advanced preparation and training just as soldiers do. They would be supplied with all the resources they need to do their jobs effectively, just as soldiers are. Those injured or killed on the job would be cared for, compensated and commemorated. Private enterprises might compete for government tenders to develop equipment for the post-military forces, while researchers might investigate new strategies for them to use against different kinds of threats. In many ways the

---

[19] For more on the idea that unarmed resistance creates a lose-lose situation for the oppressor/aggressor, see Christopher J. Finlay, 'How Subversive Are Human Rights? Civil Subversion and the Ethics of Unarmed Resistance', in Michael L. Gross and Tamar Meisels (eds.), *Soft War: The Ethics of Unarmed Conflict*, Cambridge: Cambridge University Press, 2017. Michael Randle similarly argues that non-violent resistance presents the authorities with a dilemma: 'If they ignore the defiance, their authority has been successfully challenged. If they use draconian methods to suppress non-violent protest they may lose moral and political standing at home and abroad.' 'The Dynamics of Nonviolent Action', p. 86.

[20] See Brian Martin, 'From Political Jiu-Jitsu to the Backfire Dynamic: How Repression can Promote Mobilization', in Kurt Schock (ed.), *Civil Resistance: Comparative Perspectives on Nonviolent Struggle*, Minneapolis, MN: University of Minnesota Press, 2015, pp. 145–67.

civilian defence establishment might come to resemble the military; we might even get a post-military–industrial complex! But there would be one important difference: a CDS would not rely on killing and maiming to achieve its objectives.

Would this be a viable alternative to the military? Would a CDS be comparably effective at defending us against foreign aggressors? We cannot prove anything definitively, since there are no civilian defence systems in existence that have been tried and tested. But the data we have on non-violent resistance more generally gives us some reason to be optimistic.

An influential study by Erica Chenoweth and Maria Stephan finds that, between 1900 and 2006, non-violent resistance outperformed violent resistance by a ratio of almost 2:1. Major non-violent campaigns succeeded 53 per cent of the time, compared to only 26 per cent for violent ones.[21] And in cases where the target regime used violence in an attempt to suppress the resistance, non-violence fared even better comparatively: it was *six times likelier* to achieve full success than violent campaigns that also faced regime repression.[22] This bears out my earlier point that repression against non-violent resisters tends to backfire. It also explains why some of history's most astute practitioners of non-violence made it part of their strategy to provoke a violent response from the oppressor/invader.[23] The US civil rights movement under Martin Luther King Jr. is a good example. Controversially, King involved children in the movement, expecting reprisals against them, and expecting that this would 'awaken a sense of shame within the oppressor and challenge his false sense of superiority', which it did.[24]

What makes these statistics especially impressive is that, while vast resources are continuously invested in war-building, history's successful non-violent movements have, for the most part, been improvised,

---

[21] Maria J. Stephan and Erica Chenoweth, 'Why Civil Resistance Works: The Strategic Logic of Nonviolent Conflict', *International Security*, vol. 33, no. 1, Summer 2008, p. 8.

[22] Stephan and Chenoweth, 'Why Civil Resistance Works', p. 20.

[23] Mark A. Mattaini, 'Constructing Nonviolent Alternatives to Collective Violence: A Scientific Strategy', *Behavior and Social Issues*, vol. 12, 2003, p. 156.

[24] Quoted in Cheyney Ryan, 'Bearers of Hope: On the Paradox of Nonviolent Action', in Michael Gross and Tamar Meisels (eds.), *Soft War: The Ethics of Unarmed Conflict*, Cambridge: Cambridge University Press, 2017, p. 75. Ryan offers a thoughtful ethical appraisal of this tactic.

without advance preparation, funding, or central coordination. Sharp invites us to:

> imagine how successful wars would be if there were no prior organized armies, no training of soldiers, no development and amassing of weapons and ammunition, no studies of military strategy, no preparation of officers' corps, no arrangements for transportation and communication, and no emergency supplies of blood and provision for medical services.[25]

Plausibly, if even a fraction of the energies currently invested in the military were devoted to preparing for organized civil subversion—which is precisely what the creation of a CDS would involve—the latter would outperform the former by an even greater margin.

Non-violence has been used effectively against all kinds of regimes, including some of history's most ruthless. Its success has not been limited to 'relatively benign' states, as former Australian Defence Minister Kim Beazley once insinuated.[26] In *Unarmed Against Hitler*, Jacques Semelin documents how Norway's civil subversives got the best of Vidkun Quisling, Germany's puppet in Norway, following the invasion of 1940. Representatives of the clergy, sporting associations, railroad workers, teachers, and other professionals all defied the conquering regime and its local agent. Quisling was particularly frustrated by the teachers. He had ordered them to introduce a curriculum that promoted fascist ideas and values—this was part of Hitler's plan to establish a 'New Order' in Europe built upon Nazi ideology. The teachers refused. Many were arrested and sent to concentration camps, but months later when it became apparent that the teachers were not about to relent, Hitler intervened and called the whole thing off. Quisling complained: 'The teachers are responsible for the fact that we have not yet made peace with Germany. You teachers have destroyed everything for me.'[27]

---

[25] Sharp, *Civilian-Based Defense*, p. 9.
[26] Summy, 'Nonviolence and the Case of the Extremely Ruthless Opponent', pp. 5–6.
[27] Quoted in Summy, 'Nonviolence and the Case of the Extremely Ruthless Opponent', p. 19.

There are plenty more examples from the twentieth century alone. Of all the groups involved in resisting British rule in the Indian subcontinent, the Khudai Khidmatgar (Servants of God, also called the 'Red Shirts') are particularly interesting.[28] Formed in 1929 and led by Ghaffar Khan, its members underwent demanding physical training and education, performed military-style drills, were organized into military-style units (company, brigade), held military-style ranks and titles (captain, lieutenant), and lived by military-style discipline and daily routines. But the Red Shirts were not military. They were a peaceful resistance movement committed to non-violent struggle against British occupation in the North West Frontier of India (now in Pakistan). Recruits pledged to 'always live up to the principle of non-violence' upon enlistment, and those who broke the pledge were expelled for extended periods, or even excommunicated entirely. Instead of physical force, this 'non-violent army'—which swelled to over 100,000 members at one point—was trained to use a range of peaceful resistance methods to pressure the British into withdrawal, including picketing government offices, boycotting courts, schools, and police services, tax evasion, non-cooperation with state authorities, and the social exclusion of locals that worked for or with the British.

At around the same time, the British Empire was also facing non-violent resistance closer to home, in Ireland. Here the leader of the movement was Arthur Griffith, founder of Sinn Fein. His civil subversion strategy included a negative component—what he called 'abstentionism'—as well as a positive one. Abstentionism consisted of a systematic divestment from the institutions of English rule. Locals were urged to not only disengage from British party politics, but also to refrain from taking legal disputes to British courts; to evade British taxes; to refuse jobs in the British civil service or education system; to boycott the Royal Irish Constabulary police force, and so on. The positive part of the strategy involved the creation of parallel institutions, or a 'counter-state'. This included things like alternative courts that locals could bring their grievances to, and an Irish civil service to which those working in the

---

[28] Mohammad Raqib, 'The Muslim Pashtun Movement of the North-West Frontier of India, 1930–34', in M.J. Stephan (ed.), *Civilian Jihad: Nonviolent Struggle, Democratization, and Governance in the Middle East*, New York: Palgrave Macmillan, 2009.

British one could defect. This combination of strategies was intended 'to purloin the national administration from beneath the noses of the British authorities'.[29]

The German people adopted similar strategies to expel the French and Belgians, who had invaded in 1923 to secure the scheduled payment of reparations after the First World War. Citizens refused to obey orders issued by the occupiers, workers refused to mine coal and to operate the railroads for the occupiers, and shopkeepers refused to sell goods to members of the occupying forces. Poor people even refused to eat at soup kitchens that had been organized by the occupiers to feed the hungry. When the resisters were put on trial, masses of demonstrators picketed the courtrooms. There were also more active forms of sabotage. For instance railroad equipment was dismantled and essential parts hidden away, so that the occupiers could not make use of it even if they brought their own manpower. By June 1925 the French and Belgians decided it was no longer worth the trouble and withdrew.[30]

Of course, non-violence is going to fail sometimes.[31] But this is true of violence as well, and the historical record gives us no reason to suppose that the latter generally has stronger prospects of success. This, I submit, should be reason enough for us to treat Sharp's CDS as a genuine alternative to the military as an arrangement for national defence. Some readers, no doubt, will remain sceptical. They will insist that the only realistic way to deal with foreign aggression is armed force.[32] All I can say is that this shows more faith in violence than the available evidence can support.

---

[29] For a detailed discussion of this case, see Finlay, 'How Subversive Are Human Rights?'
[30] Sharp, *Civilian-Based Defense*, pp. 14–16.
[31] Perhaps especially in response to certain rare kinds of aggression. Most foreign aggressors come to conquer and rule, but some have extermination as their objective. This apparently was Hitler's intention for parts of the Soviet Union. He had impressed upon the German people the need to conquer additional *lebenstraum* (living space) in the east. It later became apparent that annihilation was to be the means of achieving this: the mainly Slavic inhabitants of the land were to be killed, forcibly starved, or expelled to make room for German occupants. It is not obvious how the intended victims could have obstructed the realization of this plan by withholding their cooperation, since the absence of these people from the social, political, and economic life of the region is precisely what Hitler was going for.
[32] In a 2005 interview, Sharp expressed frustration that non-violent defence is held to a higher standard of 'success' than violence is. 'Guerrilla warfare has huge civilian casualty rates [...]. The same is true in conventional war, of course. But then they say that if you get killed in nonviolent struggle, then nonviolent struggle has failed.' Quoted in Mark Engler, 'The Machiavelli of Nonviolence: Gene Sharp and the Battle against Corporate Rule', *Dissent*, Fall 2013.

Post-Military Pathologies and Advantages

So far I have argued only that a CDS should be treated as a genuine alternative to the military as an arrangement for national defence. But would *this* institution not also generate costs and risks for its parent society? It would be disingenuous to deny it. Brian Martin has identified several 'pathologies' that might accompany post-military defence establishments, and it is important that we acknowledge these.[33]

One potential danger is that trained non-violent defenders will occasionally misuse their 'weapons', just as soldiers do. These people would be taught how to organize targeted protests and boycotts, frustrate the designs of authorities, sabotage existing institutions, set up parallel institutions, enlist more people into their cause, and so on. It might later occur to some of them to use their knowledge and expertise for nefarious purposes. Martin offers the example of affluent citizens using non-violent obstruction to impede their state's ability to admit refugees into the country, but we can easily imagine countless other possibilities.

A second pathology of civilian-based defence is that it could lead to a 'benign neglect' of oppressed foreigners, according to Martin.[34] Militarized societies have capacity to project power beyond their borders, and occasionally they use it to defend foreign nationals against human rights abuses—so-called 'humanitarian intervention'. The concern is that a CDS would lack any such capacity, and would therefore be consigned to passivity in the face of atrocities abroad. This is a legitimate worry, but we should be careful not to overstate things. It is simply not true that a CDS would *necessarily* be devoid of expeditionary capabilities. NGOs like Peace Brigades International and Nonviolent Peaceforce already send 'civilian peacekeepers' into conflict zones, not to engage in hostilities, but to watch and witness, to relay information to the international media, to facilitate communication between warring parties where it has broken down, and even to act as voluntary human shields—to literally interpose their bodies between the perpetrators of violence and their

---

[33] Brian Martin, 'Possible Pathologies of Future Social Defence Systems', *Pacifica Review*, vol. 7, no. 1, 1995, pp. 61–8.
[34] Martin, 'Possible Pathologies of Future Social Defence Systems', p. 64.

intended victims.[35] A demilitarized state that is committed to preventing human rights abuses abroad has the option of establishing and resourcing a civilian peacekeeping arm of its own.

Another potential downside of trans-armament is that it would necessitate the re-introduction of something akin to conscription. If we suppose that civilian-based defence requires large numbers of participants—more than a modern military needs—and that some states will not be able to recruit enough volunteers, compulsory national service may be the only way to create a functional CDS. Of course, this only counts against trans-armament if we think that compulsory national service is a bad thing. Some would beg to differ, on the grounds that the burdens of national defence *should* be spread equitably across the population rather than concentrated on the shoulders of a few 'volunteers'. Still, insofar as this would curtail the liberties of citizens, it can be counted among the moral costs of a post-military defence system.

Having said all this, one of the major selling points of a CDS, according to Sharp, is that it does not carry the more significant dangers that come with standing armies.

In *Making Europe Unconquerable*, Sharp argues that a CDS, being as it is devoid of offensive capabilities, 'would eliminate the motive for a pre-emptive attack by neighbours fearful of being attacked themselves'.[36] In other words, a state equipped with a CDS instead of armed forces would not need to worry about provoking the kind of 'defensive aggression' we discussed in Chapter 3. Sharp also argues that trans-armament would reduce a society's coup-proneness. Militaries often attack the governments that they have been entrusted to defend. Sharp reckons that a CDS would be less likely to attempt any such 'internal usurpation', since its members are less likely to become alienated from their parent society.[37] And even if a CDS-led coup did transpire, the consequences would hardly compare to those typically associated with a military takeover. As argued in Chapter 2, we have reason to expect that a military regime

[35] For discussion of civilian peacekeeping, see James Pattison, 'Unarmed Bodyguards to the Rescue? The Ethics of Nonviolent Intervention', in Michael L. Gross and Tamar Meisels (eds.), *Soft War: The Ethics of Unarmed Conflict*, Cambridge: Cambridge University Press, 2017, pp. 134–51.
[36] Gene Sharp, *Making Europe Unconquerable: The Potential of Civilian-based Deterrence and Defense*, Cambridge, MA: Ballinger, 1985, p. 67.
[37] Andrew Alexandra makes a similar point in 'Pacifism: Designing a Moral Defence Force'.

that comes to power via a coup will abuse the rights of its citizens, in addition to undermining their political self-definition. A CDS would lack the means to do likewise. 'Due to their non-violent nature', Sharp writes, 'the weapons of civilian-based defense cannot generally be used for purposes of repression.'[38] It goes without saying that a CDS would also lack the means to unjustly invade other countries.

We can add that a CDS would not be as culturally damaging as a military, nor as morally injurious. In fact, trans-armament might deliver some positive cultural and moral advantages.

In order to produce effective warriors, militaries must instil certain values in their personnel. When these values 'penetrate' into civilian society, they can cause damage there. We discussed this at length in Chapter 5. The values that a CDS would need to cultivate, by contrast, would arguably *improve* the quality of our civilian institutions. Take, for example, our political institutions. Many democratic citizens participate in politics by voting from time to time, but not much else. Besides casting ballots periodically they are disengaged from the political system and play no role in directing it or the outcomes that it produces. This is less than ideal. The health of a democracy is enhanced when citizens are actively and regularly involved—publicly deliberating and debating policies, lobbying their representatives, relaying politically relevant information to the media, blogging, petitioning, organizing and fundraising to bring about social change, protesting, boycotting, and so on. The quality of a democracy is partly a function of how 'participatory' it is.

Citizens that are interested in public affairs are more likely to get involved in these non-electoral political activities than their apathetic compatriots. But political interest, or lack thereof, is not the whole story; there are likely various other determinants of non-electoral participation. For instance, those who believe that their participation might actually achieve something tangible are going to be more inclined to petition, protest, lobby etc. than cynical types convinced that whatever they do will be futile or purely symbolic. Perceptions of efficacy matter. Moreover, citizens that have past experience in civic engagement, even of an apolitical kind, may be more likely to get involved in non-electoral

---

[38] Sharp, *Civilian-Based Defense*, p. 145.

politics simply because they have some relevant practical know-how. Others might want to do something, but have no idea where to begin.

Now consider the kinds of training and education that those recruited into a CDS would undergo. Just as officer cadets in the armed forces are taught military history and strategy, trainees in a CDS might be schooled on the dynamics of non-violence, and familiarized with its various techniques of protest, non-cooperation, and obstructive intervention. They might receive history lessons on where and why non-violence worked and where and why it did not.[39] They might be put through simulations and practical exams in which the task is to achieve defined political outcomes without coercive force. They might have their own version of 'war-games', where the winner is the team that devises the optimal strategy for entrapping a fictional aggressor in a 'negative cost–benefit equation' in the least amount of time. They might be taught how to organize targeted protests and boycotts, rally support, enlist more people into their cause—everything they would need to do to frustrate the ability of a foreign aggressor to benefit from his aggression.

Those involved would come away changed in at least two ways. If they previously thought that non-electoral political action couldn't achieve anything tangible, they will have been disabused of this notion. And if they previously lacked the practical know-how necessary to effectively take such action themselves, they will have gained some valuable experience—and perhaps even a taste for it. I can only speculate, but I would venture to guess that these men and women would henceforth be *better democratic citizens*, in the sense that they would be more inclined to participate in politics beyond casting their votes in periodic elections. A post-military defence system, established to deal with a certain rare scenario, would double as a kind of participatory citizenship training.

Interestingly, Martin suggests that this is *precisely why* no government has established a CDS: states are threatened by empowered citizens that are able and willing to pressure (or punish) them outside of electoral mechanisms, and a CDS would have some such empowering effect. Martin writes:

---

[39] Mattaini, 'Constructing Nonviolent Alternatives to Collective Violence', p. 160.

Developing skills in nonviolent struggle contains the seeds of wider transformation. If people learn about their own agency to collectively challenge repression, then what is to stop them using their skills and commitment against other targets, such as neoliberalism? [...] Every capacity that can be used to deter or resist a foreign occupation can be used against employers and government. The radical potential of social defence suggests why it has been neglected. Governments do not want to empower their own citizens in ways that might be used against governments themselves.[40]

Whether or not we buy into the conspiracy theory, I think Martin is right to suggest that individuals prepared for non-violent defence against outsiders are, ipso facto, better equipped to be active citizens in their own communities.

Next, consider again the moral effects of military conditioning. One of its aims is to make trainees more comfortable with violence, so that they can commit acts of it in battle, repeatedly and without hesitation. To the extent that this conditioning succeeds, it is destructive of virtue, or so I argued in Chapter 1. Emotional indifference to violence and the suffering it causes is a morally degraded state for a person to be in. Since a CDS would not rely on violence, it would not need to desensitize its personnel to it, and to that extent post-military conditioning would not be morally injurious in the same way that military conditioning is. But I would take this one step further.

Even though violence is morally permissible sometimes, we surely want people to have peaceful *habits*, or to be peaceful in character. Circumstances under which violence is acceptable in domestic society are exceedingly rare, and so someone with a violent temperament is very likely to overuse it, or to commit violent acts more often than is justified. For this reason we are right to regard peacefulness—a general disinclination or aversion to violence—as a virtue. If this character trait were more prevalent, we would still have wrongful violence in society, no doubt, but probably much less of it.

---

[40] Brian Martin, 'Whatever Happened to Social Defence?', *Social Alternatives*, vol. 33, no. 4, 2014, pp. 57–8.

So what, if anything, can be done to cultivate peaceful dispositions in people? Aristotle argues that virtues are relevantly similar to skills, in that both can be developed through repeated, focussed effort. This explains why, despite his otherwise rigorous attention to the virtues, Aristotle nowhere offers an account of how they are formed. As Daniel Russell points out, Aristotle 'thinks that there is no special problem in understanding how virtues are acquired. On the contrary, [he] thinks of that process as a particular instance of something people do all the time: getting better at something through practice and training.'[41] If this is right, then we should be able to gain some useful insights into moral development from the wealth of contemporary research into how ordinary skills are developed.

What we know from that research is that the environment in which one practises is crucial to whether, and the extent to which, the practice translates into skill. Nobel Prize-winning behavioural economist Daniel Kahneman identifies two conditions that are particularly important. First, the environment must be structured so that acts produce effects in a predictably regular way. Second, the environment must provide feedback clearly enough for the learner to perceive and respond to these regularities in the course of his/her practice. Consider driving. Every time you press the accelerator the car will move, and you will feel it moving immediately. Every time you press the break the car will stop, and you will experience this immediately. There is both regularity, and unambiguous feedback. This makes learning to drive quicker and easier than it would otherwise be.[42] If Aristotle is right in thinking that the cultivation of virtues is relevantly similar to the acquisition of skills like driving, then there is clearly something we can do to facilitate our own moral development. We can create forums and environments in which people get to 'practise' or externally manifest the virtues, and receive clear and consistent feedback.

A post-military defence academy would effectively function as one such forum, and the chief virtue that it would produce is peacefulness. Recruits would be subjected to hostile situations and be expected to resist

[41] Daniel C. Russell, 'Aristotle on Cultivating Virtue', in Nancy E. Snow (ed.), *Cultivating Virtue: Perspectives from Philosophy, Theology, and Psychology*, Oxford: Oxford University Press, p. 18.
[42] Russell, 'Aristotle on Cultivating Virtue', pp. 36–8.

the temptation to lash out physically. Those who succeed would receive consistent positive reinforcement, while the rest would be negatively reinforced.[43] This would be repeated again and again, à la military drill training. A non-violent response to danger and provocation would thus be gradually internalized and become a habit. Consequently, the recruits would develop more peaceful dispositions; they would be less inclined to resort to violence under pressure than they were prior, simply on account of having been given the opportunity to practise non-violence under conditions conducive to skill acquisition.

Peacefulness is one virtue that a civilian defence system would help cultivate, but not necessarily the only one. In fact, the same virtues that we have traditionally relied on military service to instil might be promoted just as (or more) effectively under the post-military alternative.

The idea that war makes people virtuous has a long intellectual history. Roman poet Juvenal warned of 'the evils of long peace'. It 'hatches terrors worse than wars', apparently.[44] These sentiments were echoed by Hegel centuries later: 'Just as the blowing of the winds preserves the sea from the foulness which would be the result of prolonged calm, so also corruption in nations would be the product of prolonged, let alone "perpetual" peace.'[45] More recently, anthropologist Sir Arthur Keith wrote that 'nature keeps her orchard healthy by pruning; [and] war is her pruning hook'.[46] Not surprisingly, many of history's villains endorsed these teachings. During the First World War, German Field Marshall Hellmuth von Moltke declared that 'in war, man's noblest virtues come into play'.[47] Similarly Benito Mussolini wrote, in *The Doctrine of Fascism*, that 'war alone brings all human energies to their highest tension and sets a seal of nobility on peoples who have the virtue to face it'.[48]

---

[43] 'Nonviolence training often involves explicit rehearsal for refusing to reciprocate harmful actions under any circumstances.' Mattaini, 'Constructing Nonviolent Alternatives', p. 155.

[44] Quoted in Lawrence LeShan, *The Psychology of War: Comprehending its Mystique and its Madness*, Chicago, IL: The Noble Press Inc., 1992, p. 16.

[45] Georg Wilhelm Friedrich Hegel, *The Philosophy of Right*, T.M. Knox (trans.), Oxford: Clarendon Press of Oxford University Press, 1952, p. 210.

[46] Quoted in LeShan, *The Psychology of War*, p. 16.

[47] Quoted in LeShan, *The Psychology of War*, p. 16.

[48] Quoted in LeShan, *The Psychology of War*, p. 17.

Juvenal did not offer a precise account of the 'terrors' he thought associated with prolonged peace, but William James tried to. A world without war, James famously feared, would become a place with 'no scorn, no hardness, no valour anymore'.[49] James was no militarist, but he saw in armed conflict at least one redeeming feature: it produced the virtues of hardihood and self-sacrifice. In earlier chapters I called into question whether these things *are* actually virtues, but we need not revisit these points here. Let us grant that they are. Even so, there are two points worth emphasizing about James' position. First, he admits that war has negative effects on character as well as positive ones—it has a 'bestial side' and can therefore be morally and spiritually corrupting as well as ennobling. Second, the experience of war instils virtue not because of the killing and maiming, according to James, but because of the danger and daring. People become 'hard' and courageous not by inflicting violent death on others, but by enduring circumstances where their own injury or death for a greater good is a live possibility.[50]

Once we appreciate this second point, it becomes clear that war is not the *only* way to cultivate the virtues of hardihood and bravery. There are alternatives. The one that James proposed was a 'war against nature', wherein youth would be conscripted into various forms of gruelling and dangerous manual labour on behalf of the community. Like war, this would have the effect of knocking the 'childishness' out of young people, according to James, so that when they come back into society, they come back 'with healthier sympathies and soberer ideas'.[51] A post-military defence system might be an even better option though, (not least because we can hardly afford any more environmental degradation). Its personnel would face dangerous situations and put their lives at risk, just as soldiers do. They would take on these risks unarmed, which arguably demands even greater courage and bravery. Further, since they would not inflict violence on others, they would not risk becoming desensitized to the suffering of others. A CDS could cultivate the same virtues that war ostensibly does, without the moral injuries.

---

[49] William James, 'The Moral Equivalent of War', *Essays in Religion and Morality*, Cambridge, MA: Harvard University Press, 1982, p. 166.
[50] Jane Roland Martin, 'Martial Virtues or Capital Vices? William James' Moral Equivalent of War Revisited', *Journal of Thought*, vol. 22, no. 3, Fall 1987, pp. 33–4.
[51] James, 'The Moral Equivalent of War'.

Conclusion

It is hardly controversial to point out that militaries are very costly institutions. Compared to the obvious financial expense, however, the moral and social costs are often overlooked. The purpose of this book has been to shine a light on these, as well as to draw attention to the ways in which militaries actually detract from the security of their parent societies. The purpose of this epilogue has been to disabuse readers of the notion that polities have no choice other than to bear these costs if they want to maintain any institutional preparedness to resist foreign aggression. A civilian defence establishment, of the kind advocated by the likes of Gene Sharpe, is an alternative that is worth taking seriously. Trans-armament towards this option would no doubt generate some costs and risks of its own. But a CDS would mitigate the danger of coup events, it would not require the infliction of moral damage on its personnel, it could not provoke fear-based aggression from the outside, it could not be misused to wage unjust wars, and the spread of its values into civilian society would not be cause for concern. For these reasons Sharp's post-military alternative warrants much closer, and broader, attention than it currently receives.

Select Bibliography

Alexandra, Andrew, 'Pacifism: Designing a Moral Defence Force', in Jeroen van den Hoven, Seumas Miller, and Thomas Pogge (eds.), *Designing in Ethics*, Cambridge: Cambridge University Press, 2017.

American Civil Liberties Union, *Soldiers of Misfortune: Abusive US Military Recruitment and Failure to Protect Child Soldiers*, New York: ACLU, 2008.

Anders, Günther and Eatherly, Claude, *Burning Conscience: The Case of the Hiroshima Pilot, Claude Eatherly, Told in his Letters to Gunther Anders*, New York: Monthly Review Press, 1962.

Baker, Deane-Peter, 'Defending the Common Life: National Defence After Rodin', *Journal of Applied Philosophy*, vol. 23, no. 3, 2006, pp. 259–75.

Baker, Deane-Peter, 'Civil–Military Relations', in Deane-Peter Baker (ed.), *Key Concepts in Military Ethics*, Sydney: UNSW Press, 2015, p. 45.

Bazargan-Forward, Saba, 'Varieties of Contingent Pacifism in War', in Helen Frowe and Gerald Lang (eds.), *How We Fight*, Oxford: Oxford University Press, 2014, pp. 1–8.

Beinart, Peter, 'How America Shed the Taboo Against Preventive War', *The Atlantic*, 21 April 2017.

Belkin, Aaron and Schofer, Evan, 'Toward a Structural Understanding of Coup Risk', *Journal of Conflict Resolution*, vol. 47, no. 5, 2003, pp. 594–620.

Bell, Curtis, 'Coup d'État and Democracy', *Comparative Political Studies*, vol. 49, no. 9, 2016, pp. 1167–200.

Bell, Daniel, *Just War as Christian Discipleship*, Grand Rapids, MI: Brazos Press, 2009.

Berger, Thomas U., 'From Sword to Chrysanthemum: Japan's Culture of Anti-Militarism', *International Security*, vol. 17, no. 4, Spring 1993, pp. 119–50.

Böhm, Robert, Rusch, Hannes, and Gürerk, Özgür, 'What Makes People Go To War? Defensive Intentions Motivate Retaliatory and Preemptive Intergroup Aggression', *Evolution and Human Behavior*, vol. 37, 2016, pp. 29–34.

Boudreau, Tyler, 'The Morally Injured', *The Massachusetts Review*, vol. 52, no. 3/4, 2011, pp. 746–54.

Bourke, Joanna, *An Intimate History of Killing: Face-to-Face Killing in Twentieth Century Warfare*, London: Granta Books, 1999.

Brough, Michael W., 'Dehumanization of the Enemy and the Moral Equality of Soldiers', in Michael W. Brough, John W. Lango, and Harry van der Linden (eds.), *Rethinking the Just War Tradition*, New York: SUNY Press, 2007, pp. 149–67.

Buchanan, Allen, 'The Internal Legitimacy of Humanitarian Intervention', *Journal of Political Philosophy*, vol. 7, no. 1, 1999, pp. 71–87.

Calhoun, Laurie, *War and Delusion: A Critical Examination*, New York: Palgrave Macmillan, 2013.

Chinen, Mark A., 'Article Nine of Japan's Constitution: From Renunciation of Armed Forces "Forever" to the Third Largest Defense Budget in the World', *Michigan Journal of International Law*, vol. 27, 2005, pp. 55–114.

Coates, Anthony J., 'Culture, the Enemy and the Moral Restraint of War', in Richard Sorabji and David Rodin (eds.), *The Ethics of War: Shared Problems in Different Traditions*, Aldershot: Ashgate, 2006, pp. 208–21.

Coates, Anthony J., 'Humanitarian Intervention: A Conflict of Traditions', in Terry Nardin and Melissa S. Williams (eds.), *NOMOS XLVII: Humanitarian Intervention*, New York and London: New York University Press, 2006, pp. 58–83.

Collmer, Sabine, 'The Cultural Gap between the Military and the Parent Society: The German Case', in Giuseppe Caforio and Gerhard Kümmel (ed.), *Military Missions and their Implications Reconsidered: The Aftermath of September 11th* (Contributions to Conflict Management, Peace Economics and Development, Volume 2), Bingley: Emerald Group Publishing Limited, 2006.

Crawford, Neta C., *Accountability for Killing: Moral Responsibility for Collateral Damage in America's Post 9/11 Wars*, New York: Oxford University Press, 2013.

Dandeker, Christopher, 'On the Need to be Different: Military Uniqueness and Civil–Military Relations in Modern Society', *The RUSI Journal*, vol. 146, no. 3, 2001, pp. 4–9.

Davis, Grady Scott, *Warcraft and the Frugality of Virtue*, Moscow, ID: University of Idaho Press, 1992.

Debs, Eugene V., 'Standing Armies', *Locomotive Firemen's Magazine*, vol. 9, no. 8, August 1885, pp. 471–3.

Delehanty, Casey, Mewhirter, Jack, Welch, Ryan, and Wilks, Jason, 'Militarization and Police Violence: The Case of the 1033 Program', *Research and Politics*, vol. 4, no. 2, 2017, pp. 1–7.

Digby, Tom, *Love and War: How Militarism Shapes Sexuality and Romance*, New York: Columbia University Press, 2014.

Dixon, Norman, *On The Psychology of Military Incompetence*, London: Jonathan Cape, 1976.

Dobos, Ned, 'On Altruistic War and National Responsibility: Justifying Humanitarian Intervention to Soldiers and Taxpayers', *Ethical Theory and Moral Practice*, vol. 13, no. 1, 2010, pp. 19–31.

Dobos, Ned, *Insurrection and Intervention: The Two Faces of Sovereignty*, Cambridge: Cambridge University Press, 2012.

Dobos, Ned, 'Moral Trauma and Moral Degradation', in Tom Frame (ed.), *Moral Injury: Unseen Wounds in an Age of Barbarism*, Sydney: NewSouth Publishing, 2015.

Dobos, Ned, 'Punishing Non-Conscientious Disobedience: Is the Military a Rogue Employer?' *Philosophical Forum*, vol. XLVI, no.1, 2015, pp. 105–19.

Dombrowski, Peter and Payne, Rodger A., 'The Emerging Consensus for Preventive War', *Survival*, vol. 48, no. 2, 2006, pp. 115–36.

Dowd, Alan W., 'Shield and Sword: The Case for Military Deterrence', *Providence: A Journal of Christianity and American Foreign Policy*, Fall 2015.

Eberle, Christopher J., *Justice and the Just War Tradition: Human Worth, Moral Formation, and Armed Conflict*, New York and London: Routledge, 2016.

Edmunds, Timothy, 'What *Are* Armed Forces For? The Changing Nature of Military Roles in Europe', *International Affairs*, vol. 82, no. 6, November 2006, pp. 1059–75.

Eidelman, Scott, and Crandall, Christian S., 'Bias in Favour of the Status Quo', *Social and Personality Psychology Compass*, vol. 6, no. 3, 2012, pp. 270–81.

Eidelman, Scott and Crandall, Christian S., 'The Intuitive Traditionalist: How Biases for Existence and Longevity Promote the Status Quo', *Advances in Experimental Social Psychology*, vol. 50, 2014, pp. 53-104.

Eidelman, Scott, Crandall, Christian S., and Pattershall, Jennifer, 'The Existence Bias', *Journal of Personality and Social Psychology*, vol. 97, no. 5, 2009, pp. 765–75.

Engelbrecht, Helmut Carol and Hanighen, F.C., *Merchants of Death: A Study of the International Armaments Industry*, New York: Dodd, Mead and Co., 1934.

Enloe, Cynthia, *Does Khaki Become You? The Militarisation of Women's Lives*, London: Pluto Press, 1983.

Faden, Ruth R. and Beauchamp, Tom L., 'The Right to Risk Information and the Right to Refuse Workplace Hazards', in Tom Beauchamp, Norman Bowie, and Denis G. Arnold (eds.), *Ethical Theory and Business*, 8th International Edition, Harlow: Pearson, 2008, pp. 129–36.

Feaver, Peter D., 'Civil–Military Relations', *Annual Review of Political Science*, vol. 2, no. 1, 1999, pp. 211–41.

Feaver, Peter D. and Kohn, Richard H., 'The Gap: Soldiers, Civilians, and their Mutual Misunderstanding', in Eugene R. Wittkopf and James M. McCormick (eds.), *The Domestic Sources of American Foreign Policy*, 4th Edition, Lanham, MD: Rowman and Littlefield, 2004, pp. 85–95.

Fiala, Andrew, 'Pacifism', in Edward N. Zalta (ed.), *Stanford Encyclopedia of Philosophy*, Fall 2018 Edition, https://plato.stanford.edu/archives/fall2018/entries/pacifism/.

Fiala, Andrew, *Transformative Pacifism: Critical Theory and Practice*, London: Bloomsbury, 2018.

Finlay, Christopher J., 'How Subversive Are Human Rights?: Civil Subversion and the Ethics of Unarmed Resistance', in Michael L. Gross and Tamar Meisels (eds.), *Soft War: The Ethics of Unarmed Conflict*, Cambridge: Cambridge University Press, 2017, pp. 134–51.

Finlay, Christopher J., 'Just and Unjust Coups d'état? Zimbabwe and the Ethics of Military Takeover', *Stockholm Centre for the Ethics of War and Peace*, at http://stockholmcentre.org/just-and-unjust-coups-detat-zimbabwe-and-the-ethics-of-military-takeover/.

Finley, Laura L., 'Militarism Goes to School', *Essays in Education*, vol. 4, article 3, 2003, pp. 1–5.

Finley, Laura L., 'How Can I Teach Peace When the Book Only Covers War?', *The Online Journal of Peace and Conflict Resolution*, vol. 5, no. 1, Summer 2003, pp. 150–65.

Finnemore, Martha, and Sikkink, Kathryn, 'International Norm Dynamics and Political Change', *International Organization*, vol. 52, no. 4, 1998, pp. 887–917.

Fisk, Kerstin and Ramos, Jennifer M., 'Actions Speak Louder Than Words: Preventive Self-Defense as a Cascading Norm', *International Studies Perspectives*, vol. 15, no. 2, 2014, pp. 163–85.

Fisk, Kerstin and Ramos, Jennifer M. 'Introduction: The Preventive Force Continuum', in K. Fisk and J.M. Ramos (eds.), *Preventive Force: Drones, Targeted Killing, and the Transformation of Contemporary Warfare*, New York: New York University Press, 2016.

Forsling, Carl, 'Selfless Service and the Veteran Superiority Complex', *Task and Purpose*, 28 March 2019, available at: https://taskandpurpose.com/vet-superiority-complex.

French, Shannon E., and Jack, Anthony I., 'Dehumanizing the Enemy: The Intersection of Neuroethics and Military Ethics' in David Whetham and Bradley J. Strawser (eds.), *Responsibilities to Protect: Perspectives in Theory and Practice*, Leiden: Brill, 2015, pp. 165–95.

Garran, David, 'Soldiers, Slaves and the Liberal State', *Philosophy and Public Policy Quarterly*, vol. 27, no.1/2, Winter/Spring 2007, pp. 8–11.

Glaser, Charles L., 'The Security Dilemma Revisited', *World Politics*, vol. 50, no. 1, October 1997, pp. 171–201.

Glover, Jonathan, *Humanity: A Moral History of the 20th Century*, 2nd Edition, London and New Haven, CT: Yale University Press, 2012.

Goldstein, Joshua S., *War and Gender: How Gender Shapes the War System and Vice Versa*, Cambridge: Cambridge University Press, 2001.

Gould, Kenneth A., 'The Ecological Costs of Militarization', *Peace Review*, vol. 19, no. 3, 2007, pp. 331–4.

Grossman, David, *On Killing: The Psychological Cost of Learning to Kill in War and Society*, Boston, MA: Little Brown and Co, 1995.

Halevy, Nir, 'Preemptive Strikes: Fear, Hope, and Defensive Aggression', *Journal of Personality and Social Psychology*, vol. 112, no. 2, 2017, pp. 224–37.

Harrison, Deborah, 'Violence in the Military Community' in Paul R. Higate (ed.), *Military Masculinities: Identity and the State*, Westport, CT: Praeger, 2003.

Hartung, William D., 'Eisenhower's Warning: The Military Industrial Complex Forty Years Later', *World Policy Journal*, vol. 18, no. 1, Spring 2001, pp. 39–44.

Hartung, William D., 'The New Business of War: Small Arms and the Proliferation of Conflict', *Ethics and International Affairs*, vol. 15, no. 1, 2001, pp. 79–96.

Hartung, William D. and Ciarrocca, Michelle, 'The Military–Industrial–Think Tank Complex: Corporate Think Tanks and the Doctrine of Aggressive Militarism', *Multinational Monitor*, vol. 24, no. 1/2, 2003, pp. 17–20.

Hautzinger, Sarah J. and Scandlyn, Jean, *Beyond Post-Traumatic Stress: Homefront Struggles with the Wars on Terror*, London: Routledge, 2016.

Hechter, Michael, *Alien Rule*, New York: Cambridge University Press, 2013.

Heinecken, Lindy, Gueli, Richard, and Neethling, Ariane, 'Defence, Democracy and South Africa's Civil–Military Gap', *Scientia Militaria: South African Journal of Military Studies*, vol. 33, no. 1, 2005, p. 124.

Henry, Michael, Fishman, Jennifer, and Youngner, Stuart, 'Propranolol and the Prevention of Post-Traumatic Stress Disorder: Is it Wrong to Erase the "Sting" of Bad Memories', *The American Journal of Bioethics*, vol. 7, no. 9, 2007, pp. 12–20.

Hiroi, Taeko and Omori, Sawa, 'Causes and Triggers of Coups d'État: An Event History Analysis', *Politics and Policy*, vol. 41, no. 1, 2013, pp. 39-64.

Hobbes, Thomas, *Leviathan*, edited by C.B. Macpherson, London: Penguin Classics, 1985.

Høivik, Tord and Aas, Solveig, 'Demilitarization in Costa Rica: A Farewell to Arms?', *Journal of Peace Research*, vol. XVIII, no. 4, 1981, pp. 333–51.

Holsti, Ole R., 'A Widening Gap Between the US Military and Civilian Society? Some Evidence, 1976–96', *International Security*, vol. 23, no. 3, Winter 1998–1999, pp. 5–42.

Hopton, John, 'The State and Military Masculinity', in Paul R. Higate (ed.), *Military Masculinities: Identity and the State*, Westport, CT: Praeger, 2003.

Huntington, Samuel P., *The Soldier and the State: The Theory and Politics of Civil–Military Relations*, Cambridge, MA: Harvard University Press, 1957.

Izumikawa, Yasuhiro, 'Explaining Japanese Antimilitarism: Normative and Realist Constraints on Japan's Security Policy', *International Security*, vol. 35, no. 2, Fall 2010, pp. 123–60.

Jackson, Joshua J., Thoemmes, Felix, Jonkmann, Kathrin, Lüdtke, Oliver, and Trautwein, Ulrich, 'Military Training and Personality Trait Development: Does the Military Make the Man, or Does the Man Make the Military?', *Psychological Science*, vol. 23, 2012, pp. 270-7.

James, William, 'The Moral Equivalent of War', *Essays in Religion and Morality*, Cambridge, MA: Harvard University Press, 1982.

Jervis, Robert, *Perception and Misperception in International Politics*, Princeton, NJ: Princeton University Press, 1976.

Johnson, Dominic, *Overconfidence and War: The Havoc and Glory of Positive Illusions*, Cambridge, MA: Harvard University Press, 2004.

Kahneman, Daniel, and Renshon, Jonathan, 'Hawkish Biases', in Trevor Thrall and Jane Kramer (eds.), *American Foreign Policy and the Politics of Fear: Threat Inflation Since 9/11*, New York: Routledge, 2009, pp. 79–96.

Kant, Immanuel, *Perpetual Peace: A Philosophical Proposal*, Helen O'Brien (trans.), London: Sweet and Maxwell, 1927.

Kaplan, Abraham, *The Conduct of Inquiry: Methodology for Behavioral Science*, San Francisco, CA: Chandler Publishing, 1964.

Keen, David, *Useful Enemies: When Waging Wars is More Important than Winning Them*, New Haven, CT: Yale University Press, 2012.

Kegley Jr., Charles W. and Raymond, Gregory A., 'Preventive War and Permissive Normative Order', *International Studies Perspectives*, vol. 4, 2003, pp. 385–94.

Kelly, Trish and Rishi, Meenakshi, 'An Empirical Study of the Spin-Off Effects of Military Spending', *Defence and Peace Economics*, vol. 14, no. 1, 2003, pp. 1–7.

Klay, Phil, 'The Citizen-Soldier: Moral Risk and the Modern Military', *The Brookings Institution*, 24 May 2016, available at: http://csweb.brookings.edu/content/research/essays/2016/the-citizen-soldier.html, accessed July 2018.

Kleinig, John, 'What's All the Fuss with Police Militarization?', *The Critique*, 17 March 2015.

Kohn, Richard H., 'The Erosion of Civilian Control of the Military in the United States Today', *Naval War College Review* vol. 55, no. 3, Article 2, 2002, pp. 1–52.

Kovitz, Marcia, 'The Roots of Military Masculinity', in Paul R. Higate (ed.), *Military Masculinities: Identity and the State*, Westport, CT: Praeger, 2003.

Kraska, Peter B., 'Militarization and Policing—its Relevance to 21st Century Police', *Policing*, vol. 1, no. 4, 2007, pp. 501–13.

Kydd, Andrew, 'Sheep in Sheep's Clothing: Why Security Seekers Do Not Fight Each Other', *Security Studies*, vol. 7, no. 1, 1997, pp. 114–55.

Langer, Ellen J., 'The Illusion of Control', *Journal of Personality and Social Psychology*, vol. 32. no. 2, 1975, pp. 311–28.

Lazar, Seth, 'Just War Theory: Traditionalists vs. Revisionists', *Annual Review of Political Science*, vol. 20, 2017, pp. 37–54.

Lebow, Richard Ned, 'Deterrence: A Political and Psychological Critique', in Richard Ned Lebow (ed.), *Richard Ned Lebow: Key Texts in Political Psychology and International Relations Theory*, Basel: Springer, 2016.

Lebow, Richard Ned, and Stein, Janice Gross, 'Rational Deterrence Theory: I Think, Therefore I Deter', *World Politics*, vol. 41, no. 2, January 1989, pp. 209–24.

LeShan, Lawrence, *The Psychology of War: Comprehending its Mystique and its Madness*, Chicago, IL: The Noble Press Inc., 1992.

Levy, Jack S., 'Declining Power and the Preventive Motivation for War', *World Politics*, vol. 40, no. 1, October 1987, pp. 82–107.

Levy, Jack S., 'The Diversionary Theory of War: A Critique', in Manus I. Midlarsky (ed.), *Handbook of War Studies*, Boston, MA: Unwin Hyman, 1989, pp. 259–88.

Liebknecht, Karl, *Militarism and Anti-Militarism*, Grahame Lock (trans.), Cambridge: Rivers Press Limited, 1973.

Lieblich, Eliav and Shinar, Adam, 'The Case Against Police Militarization', *Michigan Journal of Race and Law*, vol. 23, no. 1–2, 2018, pp. 105–53.

Lobel, Jules, 'Preventive War and the Lessons of History', *University of Pittsburgh Law Review*, vol. 68, 2006, pp. 307–40.

Luban, David, 'Preventive War', *Philosophy and Public Affairs*, vol. 32, no. 3, Summer 2004, pp. 207–48.

Luchins, Abraham S., 'Mechanization in Problem Solving: The Effect of Einstellung', *Psychological Monographs*, vol. 54, no. 6, 1942, pp. i–95.

Luttwak, Edward, *Coup d'État: A Practical Handbook*, Revised Edition, Cambridge, MA: Harvard University Press, 2016.

Lutz, Catherine and Bartlett, Leslie, *Making Soldiers in the Public Schools: An Analysis of the Army JROTC Curriculum*, Darby, PA: Diane Publishing, 1995.

Machiavelli, Niccolo, *The Art of War*, Ellis Farneworth (trans.), Indianapolis, IN: Bobbs-Merrill, 1965.

Marinov, Nikolay and Goemans, Hein, 'Coups and Democracy', *British Journal of Political Science*, vol. 44, no. 4, 2013, pp. 799–825.

Marshall, Samuel Lyman Atwood, *Men Against Fire: The Problem of Battle Command in Future War*, Washington, DC: Infantry Journal Press, 1947.

Martin, Brian, 'Possible Pathologies of Future Social Defence Systems', *Pacifica Review*, vol. 7, no. 1, 1995, pp. 61–8.

Martin, Brian, 'Whatever Happened to Social Defence?', *Social Alternatives*, vol. 33, no. 4, 2014, pp. 55–60.

Martin, Brian, 'From Political Jiu-Jitsu to the Backfire Dynamic: How Repression can Promote Mobilization', in Kurt Schock (ed.), *Civil Resistance: Comparative Perspectives on Nonviolent Struggle*, Minneapolis, MN: University of Minnesota Press, 2015, pp. 145–67.

Martin, Jane Roland, 'Martial Virtues or Capital Vices? William James' Moral Equivalent of War Revisited', *Journal of Thought*, vol. 22, no. 3, Fall 1987, pp. 32–44.

May, Larry, *Contingent Pacifism: Revisiting Just War Theory*, Cambridge: Cambridge University Press, 2015.

McCarthy, Colman, *All of One Peace: Essays on Nonviolence*, New Brunswick, NJ: Rutgers University Press.

McCormick, Blaine, 'Make Money, Not War: A Brief Critique of Sun Tzu's the Art of War', *Journal of Business Ethics*, vol. 29, no. 3, 2001, pp. 285–6.

McMurty, John, *Understanding War: A Philosophical Inquiry*, Downsview: Samuel Stevens and Company, University of Toronto Press, 1989.

Mearsheimer, John, *The Tragedy of Great Power Politics*, New York: W.W. Norton, 2001.

Merriman, Hardy, 'Theory and Dynamics of Nonviolent Action', in Maria J. Stephan (ed.), *Civilian Jihad: Nonviolent Struggle, Democratization, and Governance in the Middle East*, New York: Palgrave Macmillan, 2009, pp. 17–29.

Michalos, Alex C., 'Militarism and the Quality of Life', *Annals of the New York Academy of Sciences*, vol. 577, no. 1, December 1989, pp. 216-30.

Mollendorf, Darrel, 'Jus Ex Bello', *The Journal of Political Philosophy*, vol. 16, no. 2, June 2008, pp. 123–36.

Møller, Bjørn, 'Common Security and Non-Offensive Defence as Guidelines for Defence Planning and Arms Control?', *International Journal of Peace Studies*, vol. 1, no. 2, July 1996, pp. 47–66.

Montgomery, Evan Braden, 'Breaking out of the Security Dilemma: Realism, Reassurance, and the Problem of Uncertainty', *International Security*, vol. 31, no. 2, Fall 2006, pp. 151–85.

Muthuchidambaram, Subba, 'From Swords to Plowshares: An Evaluation of the US Legislative Attempts on Economic Conversion and Human Resource Planning', *Business Ethics Quarterly*, vol. 2, no. 1, 1992, pp. 1–27.

Myers, Chris D., 'The Virtue of Cold Heartedness', *Philosophical Studies*, vol. 138, 2008, pp. 233–44.

O'Donovan, Oliver, *In Pursuit of a Christian View of War*, Bramcote, Notts: Grove Books, 1977.

Ogden, Charles Kay, and Florence, Mary, 'Militarism Versus Feminism', in Margaret Kamester and Jo Vellacott (eds.), *Militarism Versus Feminism: Writings on Women and War*, London: Virago Press 1987.

Orend, Brian, 'Justice After War', *Ethics and International Affairs*, vol. 16, no. 1, March 2002, pp. 43–56.

Orr, Jackie, 'The Militarization of Inner Space', *Critical Sociology*, vol. 30, no. 2, 2004, pp. 452–81.

Owen, David, and Davidson, Jonathan, 'Hubris Syndrome: An Acquired Personality Disorder? A Study of US Presidents and UK Prime Ministers over the last 100 Years', *Brain: A Journal of Neurology*, vol. 132, no. 5, 2009, pp. 1396–406.

Parkin, Nicholas, 'Non-Violent Resistance and Last Resort', *Journal of Military Ethics*, vol. 15, no. 4, 2016, pp. 259–74.

Pattison, James, *The Morality of Private War: The Challenge of Private Military and Security Companies*, Oxford: Oxford University Press, 2014.

Pattison, James, 'Unarmed Bodyguards to the Rescue? The Ethics of Nonviolent Intervention', in Michael L. Gross and Tamar Meisels (eds.), *Soft War: The Ethics of Unarmed Conflict*, Cambridge: Cambridge University Press, 2017, pp. 134–51.

Pattison, James, 'The Case for the Non-Ideal Morality of War: Beyond Revisionism versus Traditionalism in Just War Theory', *Political Theory*, vol. 46, no. 2, 2018, pp. 242–68.

Pilster, Ulrich and Bohmelt, Tobias, 'Do Democracies Engage Less in Coup Proofing? On the Relationship Between Regime Type and Civil–Military Relations', *Foreign Policy Analysis*, vol. 8, 2012, p. 355–72.

Powell, Jonathan, 'Determinants of the Attempting and Outcome of Coups d'état', *Journal of Conflict Resolution*, vol. 56, no. 6, 2012, pp. 1017–40.

Presson, Paul K., and Benassi, Victor A., 'Illusion of Control: A Meta-Analytic Review', *Journal of Social Behavior & Personality*, vol. 11, no. 3, 1996, pp. 493–510.

Pudner, Kalynne Hackney, 'What's So Bad about Self-Sacrifice?', *Proceedings of the American Catholic Philosophical Association*, vol. 81, 2007, pp. 241–50.

Rahbek-Clemmensen, Jon, Archer, Emerald M., Barr, John, Belkin, Aaron, Guerrero, Mario, Hall, Cameron, and Swain, Katie E.O., 'Conceptualizing the Civil–Military Gap: A Research Note', *Armed Forces and Society*, vol. 38, no. 4, 2012, pp. 669–78.

Randle, Michael, 'The Dynamics of Nonviolent Action', in Michael Randle (ed.), *Challenge to Nonviolence*, Bradford: Department of Peace Studies, University of Bradford, 2002.

Raqib, Mohammad, 'The Muslim Pashtun Movement of the North-West Frontier of India, 1930–34', in Maria J. Stephan (ed.), *Civilian Jihad: Nonviolent Struggle, Democratization, and Governance in the Middle East*, New York: Palgrave Macmillan, 2009.

Reardon, Betty A., *Sexism and the War System*, New York: Syracuse University Press, 1996.

Ricks, Thomas E., 'The Widening Gap between Military and Society', *The Atlantic*, July 1997.

Roberts, Adam, 'Civilian Defense and the Inhibition of Violence', *Philosophy East and West*, vol. 19, no. 2, 1969, pp. 181–93.

Roberts, Robert C., 'Aristotle on Virtues and Emotions', *Philosophical Studies*, vol. 56, 1989, pp. 293–306.

Rodin, David, 'The War Trap: Dilemmas of Jus Terminatio', *Ethics*, vol. 125, no. 3, 2015, pp. 674–95.

Rossouw, G.J., 'Business is Not Just War: Transferring the Principle of Double Effect from War to Business', *South African Journal of Philosophy*, vol. 23, no. 3, 2003, pp. 236–46.

Rousseau, Jean Jacques, *A Lasting Peace through the Federation of Europe*, C.E. Vaughan (trans.), London: Constable, 1917.

Russell, Daniel C., 'Aristotle on Cultivating Virtue', in Nancy E. Snow (ed.), *Cultivating Virtue: Perspectives from Philosophy, Theology, and Psychology*, Oxford: Oxford University Press, 2014, pp. 17–48.

Ryan, Cheyney, *The Chickenhawk Syndrome: War, Sacrifice, and Personal Responsibility*, Lanham, MD: Rowman and Littlefield, 2009.

Ryan, Cheyney, 'Pacifism, Just War, and Self-Defense', *Philosophia*, vol. 41, no. 4, 2013, pp. 977–1005.

Ryan, Cheyney, 'Pacifism', in Seth Lazar and Helen Frowe (eds.), *The Oxford Handbook of Ethics of War*, Oxford: Oxford University Press, 2016.

Ryan, Cheyney, 'Bearers of Hope: On the Paradox of Nonviolent Action', in Michael Gross and Tamar Meisels (eds.), *Soft War: The Ethics of Unarmed Conflict*, Cambridge: Cambridge University Press, 2017, pp. 166–83.

Salmon, Jack D., 'Can Non-Violence Be Combined with Military Means for National Defense?', *Journal of Peace Research*, vol. 25, no. 1, 1988, pp. 69–80.

Scharre, Paul, *Army of None: Autonomous Weapons and the Future of War*, New York: W.W. Norton and Co, 2018.

Schelling, Thomas C., *The Strategy of Conflict*, Cambridge, MA: Harvard University Press, 1960.

Schulzke, Marcus, 'The Unintended Consequences of War: Self-Defense and Violence Against Civilians in Ground Combat Operations', *International Studies Perspectives*, vol. 1, 2016, pp. 1–8.

Schulzke, Marcus, 'Necessary and Surplus Militarisation: Rethinking Civil Military Interactions and their Consequences', *European Journal of International Security*, vol. 3, no. 1, February 2018, pp. 94–112.

Scobell, Andrew, 'Is There A Civil–Military Gap in China's Peaceful Rise?', *Parameters*, vol. XXXIX, no. 2, Summer 2009, pp. 4–22.

Segal, Mady Wechsler, 'The Military and the Family as Greedy Institutions', *Armed Forces and Society*, vol. 13, no. 1, Fall 1986, pp. 9–38.

Sharp, Gene, *The Politics of Nonviolent Action*, Boston, MA: Porter Sargent Publishers, 1973.

Sharp, Gene, *Making Europe Unconquerable: The Potential of Civilian-Based Deterrence and Defense*, Cambridge, MA: Ballinger, 1985.

Sharp, Gene, *Civilian-Based Defense: A Post-Military Weapons System*, Princeton, NJ: Princeton University Press, 1990.

Shaw, William H., 'Utilitarianism and Recourse to War', *Utilitas*, vol. 23, no. 4, 2011, pp. 380–401.

Shields, Patricia M., 'Civil–Military Relations: Changing Frontiers', *Public Administration Review*, vol. 66, 2006, pp. 924–8.

Shue, Henry, *Fighting Hurt: Rule and Exception in Torture and War*, Oxford: Oxford University Press, 2016.

Shue, Henry, 'Last Resort and Proportionality', in Seth Lazar and Helen Frowe (eds.), *The Oxford Handbook of Ethics of War*, New York: Oxford University Press, 2018.

Simunovic, Dora, Mifune, Nobuhiro, and Yamagishi, Toshio, 'Pre-emptive Strike: An Experimental Study of Fear-Based Aggression', *Journal of Experimental Social Psychology*, vol. 49, no. 6, November 2013, pp. 1120–3.

Smith, David Livingstone, 'Dehumanization, Essentialism, and Moral Psychology', *Philosophy Compass*, vol. 9, no. 11, 2014.

Spiller, Roger J., 'S.L.A. Marshall and the Ratio of Fire', *The RUSI Journal*, Winter, 1988, pp. 63–71.

St. Augustine of Hippo, *City of God*, Henry Benson (trans.), New York: Penguin, 1972.

Stein, Janice Gross, 'Building Politics into Psychology: The Misperception of Threat', *Political Psychology*, vol. 9, no. 2, June 1988, pp. 245–71.

Stein, Janice Gross, 'Reassurance in International Conflict Management', *Political Science Quarterly*, vol. 106, no. 3, Autumn 1991, pp. 431–51.

Steinhoff, Uwe, 'The Secret to the Success of the Doctrine of Double Effect (and Related Principles): Biased Framing, Inadequate Methodology, and Clever Distractions', *Journal of Ethics*, vol. 22, no. 3–4, 2018, pp. 235–63.

Stephan, Maria J., and Chenoweth, Erica, 'Why Civil Resistance Works: The Strategic Logic of Nonviolent Conflict', *International Security*, vol. 33, no. 1, Summer 2008, pp. 7–44.

Stokes, Peter, 'The "Militarizing" of Organization and Management Studies: Reconnoitring the Tensions—Problems and Possibilities for Reshaping the Terrain?', *Critical Perspectives of International Business*, vol. 31, no. 1, February 2007, pp. 11–26.

Strachan, Hew, 'The Civil–Military "Gap" in Britain', *Journal of Strategic Studies*, vol. 26, no. 2., 2003, pp. 43–63.

Summy, Ralph, 'The Efficacy of Nonviolence: Examining the "Worst Case Scenario"', *Peace Research*, vol. 25, no. 2, May 1993, pp. 1–9.

Summy, Ralph, 'Nonviolence and the Case of the Extremely Ruthless Opponent', *Global Change, Peace, and Security*, vol. 6, no. 1, 1994, pp. 1–29.

Tamir, Yael, *Liberal Nationalism*, Princeton, NJ: Princeton University Press, 1993.

Tang, Shiping, 'Offence–Defence Theory: Towards a Definitive Understanding', *The Chinese Journal of International Politics*, vol. 3, no. 2, 2010, pp. 213–60.

Thee, Marek, 'Militarism and Militarization in Contemporary International Relations', *Security Dialogue*, vol. 8, no. 4, 1977, pp. 296–309.

Thompson, Suzanne C., 'Illusions of Control: How We Overestimate Our Personal Influence', *Current Directions in Psychological Science, Association for Psychological Science*, vol. 8, no. 6, 1999, pp. 187–90.

Turner, Rhiannon N. and Hewstone, Miles, 'Attribution Biases', in John M. Levine and Michael A. Hogg (eds.), *Encyclopedia of Group Processes and Intergroup Relations*, Los Angeles, CA: Sage, 2010.

Turse, Nick, *The Complex: How the Military Invades our Everyday Lives*, New York: Metropolitan Books, 2008.

United Nations, *A More Secure World: Our Shared Responsibility*, Report of the High-Level Panel on Threats, Challenges, and Change, New York: United Nations, 2004.

Vance, Laurence M., 'Brutus on the Evils of Standing Armies', LewRockwell.com, available at: https://www.lewrockwell.com/2004/02/laurence-m-vance/the-evil-of-standing-armies-2/, 7 February 2004, accessed November 2018.

Van Den Hoven, Jeroen, Miller, Seumas, and Pogge, Thomas (eds.), *Designing In Ethics*, Cambridge: Cambridge University Press, 2017.

Vennesson, Pascal, 'Civil–Military Relations in France: Is There a Gap?', *Journal of Strategic Studies*, vol. 26, no. 2, 2003, pp. 29–42.

Walzer, Michael, *Just and Unjust Wars: A Moral Argument with Historical Illustrations*, New York: Basic Books, 1977.

Walzer, Michael, 'The Moral Standing of States: A Response to Four Critics', *Philosophy and Public Affairs*, vol. 9, no. 3, 1980, pp. 209–29.

Werner, Richard, 'Just War Theory: Going to War and Collective Self-Deception', in Fritz Allhoff, Nicholas G. Evans, and Adam Henschke (eds.), *Routledge Handbook of Ethics and War: Just War Theory in the 21st Century*, New York and London: Routledge, 2013.

Wheeler, Nicholas J., 'Humanitarian Intervention after September 11, 2001', in Anthony F. Lang Jr. (ed.), *Just Intervention*, Washington, DC: Georgetown University Press, 2003, pp. 192–216.

Winslow, Donna, 'Canadian Society and its Army', *Canadian Military Journal*, Winter 2003–2004, p. 19, available at: http://www.journal.forces.gc.ca/vo4/no4/doc/military-socio-eng.pdf.

Wolfendale, Jessica, *Torture and the Military Profession*, Houndmills and New York: Palgrave Macmillan, 2007.

Wolfendale, Jessica, 'Performance-Enhancing Technologies and Moral Responsibility in the Military', *The American Journal of Bioethics*, vol. 8, no. 2, 2008, pp. 28–38.

Wood, David, 'The Grunts: Damned if they Kill, Damned if they Don't', *Huffington Post*, 18 March 2014.

Wood, David, 'A Warrior's Moral Dilemma', *Huffington Post*, 20 March 2014.

Wood, David, 'Healing: Can We Treat Moral Injury?', *Huffington Post*, 20 March 2014.

Woods, Mark, 'The Nature of War and Peace: Just War Thinking, Environmental Ethics, and Environmental Justice', in Michael W. Brough, John W. Lango, and Harry van der Linden (eds.), *Rethinking the Just War Tradition*, New York: SUNY Press, 2007, pp. 17–34.

Wrona, Richard M. Jr., 'A Dangerous Separation: The Schism between the American Society and Its Military', *World Affairs*, vol. 169, no. 1, Summer 2006, pp. 25–38.

Yetiv, Steve A., *National Security Through a Cockeyed Lens: How Cognitive Bias Impacts US Foreign Policy*, Baltimore, MD: Johns Hopkins University Press, 2013.

Index

For the benefit of digital users, indexed terms that span two pages (e.g., 52–53) may, on occasion, appear on only one of those pages.

Printed and bound by CPI Group (UK) Ltd, Croydon, CR0 4YY